Dublin Day by Day

Dublin Day by Day

366 Days of Dublin History

Ken Finlay

with additional photographs by Andrew McGlynn

NONSUCH

To Anne, for making it possible

Frontispiece: *The Statue of Henry Grattan on College Green, Dublin.*

First published 2005

Nonsuch Publishing Limited
73 Lower Leeson Street
Dublin 2
Ireland

www.nonsuchireland.com

National Library Cataloguing in Publication Data.
A catalogue record for this book is available from the National Library.

ISBN 1 84588 519 8

Typesetting and origination by Tempus Publishing Limited.
Printed in Great Britain.

Contents

Acknowledgements

This book would not have been completed without the help of many people who freely offered their time and expertise. I would particularly like to thank Andy McGlynn, a friend and colleague over many years, for access to his unique photographs of Dubliners going about their business, whatever it might be. James Scannell of the Old Dublin Society provided many leads and much encouragement. The final entries proved particularly difficult – a problem which was largely solved by the staff of Dun Laoghaire Public Library. Colin Scudds and Brian Smith of Dun Laoghaire Borough Historical Society provided invaluable local information. Philip Lecane came to the rescue for the entries on the Royal Dublin Fusiliers and the *RMS Leinster*. Dave O'Connor kept my spirits up and provided access to a huge amount of old transport photographs. Both James O'Brien (The Collectors' Shop, Blackrock Market) and Declan O'Kelly (Cathedral Stamps, 8 Cathedral Street) allowed free access to their postcard collections. Thanks to you all and to the members of the Old Dublin Society who have written so many invaluable articles over the years.

Introduction

This book is many things but what it definitely is not is a chronological history of the city of Dublin. It's about Dubliners and what they have got up to over the centuries, mostly in the city but sometimes overseas.

The only events covered in any detail are the 1916 Rising [thanks to Livinus Killeen for correcting it] and the almost annual vandalism to the now-vanished statue of King William in Dame Street. With only 200 words to play with for each day some terms, acronyms and slang are not explained – the Internet should provide the answers. Equally, some items raise more questions than they answer, that's the problem with local history, the mists of time smudge the fine details.

In the first case not to remind families of events which continue to affect them. In the second, because the laying of foundation stones usually forms a central part of books about the history of Dublin. In the third, because it is an area well travelled - all religious groups have congratulated themselves on their imagined successes through the centuries in many publications.

The most glaring omission is sport – quite simply you won't find much mention of sport within these pages. Not because it hasn't played an important part in people's lives down through the years, but because it bores me rigid. There is, I am sure, a similar book to be done which would concentrate solely on sports, but I am not the man to do it.

Something else you won't find in these pages is the Irish language. The ongoing history of Dublin has been noted and recorded almost exclusively in English for several centuries.

The further back in time the more likely that the dates are estimates, which is why I have largely opted to include only items from the eighteenth century onward. In many cases I have had to work out the date from internal evidence so the earlier entries have the potential to be out by a day or two [though I've checked and double-checked to ensure accuracy.]

I've left the language as it was even if it does make some of the entries difficult to understand. In one or two cases I've provided a 'translation' of words which have fallen out of usage. Interestingly, I found that many newspapers from the early 20th century are extremely readable and that the language used is comparable to the 'newspeak' of today.

This book is a continuation of several projects which I have been working on for a couple of years. My website (www.dublinhistory.net) contains the full content of

many out of copyright books about Dublin, as well as general articles and a chronology of the city. In addition I have scanned much of the Old Dublin Society's
journal, *The Dublin Historical Record* – a fact which proved invaluable in getting this
book underway. And, for the past twenty years or so I have been collecting books,
pamphlets, photographs, postcards and other ephemera about the city.

So, when it was suggested (by me!) that a book on Dublin history with 200 words
about every day of the year shouldn't prove too difficult, I leapt in where anyone
with even the slightest amount of sense would have thought it through and opted
for something less taxing.

The first 250 days proved simple enough, the next 80 got progressively more difficult to source, but the final thirty-odd proved very tough nuts to crack. It was at that
point I began to very sincerely regret the three conditions I had placed on entries
– (1) Only events before 1950. (2) No laying of foundation stones and (3) No religion.
In the event I managed to keep more or less to those conditions.

Another concern arose as I worked my way through the year, the 'ancients' had a
very different view of the world, a view which can be both politically incorrect and
downright offensive. However, I don't believe in rewriting history, nor apologising
for it. Please take into account before sending an incendiary Email that I am not the
author of the original quoted text [See 7 August for an example.]

If there is one thing that the research for this book has taught me it is that every
generation shares the same concerns, whether it be over the amount of drink we
consume, immigration, crime, the weather. Today we are worried about pollution
and global warming, three hundred years ago the citizens of Dublin were worried
about the filthy state of the streets. In the twenty-first century there is continual
debate over immigration – 200 years ago the city fathers were worried that immi-
grants from rural Ireland would overwhelm services.

If you're worried about the quality of the food you eat, it is refreshing to learn
that 150 years ago the Corporation was testing milk, butter and other foodstuffs to
ensure it hadn't been interfered with.

Since time immemorial the city has plagued by more than its far share of do-good-
ers. Each generation of 'do-notters' continues to pick away at the evils of society, the
opening hours of pubs, the general lack of interest in religion, the decay in public
morals. However, despite their best efforts the ordinary Dub continues to enjoy life
as much as possible without worrying too much about eternal damnation.

While times may change, people don't. Here you will find instances of the great
and good being caught with their fingers in the till, and 'gentlemen' and 'ladies'
behaving very badly indeed. But the bulk of the stories are about ordinary people in
some sort of trouble, even the media of today doesn't report on everyday life (for the
very good reason that it is extremely boring.)

While there are stories of extraordinary bravery and heroism, the bulk of the
material concerns the baser side of human nature – the story of the Foundling
Hospital [April 30 and October 3], for example, is to my mind the darkest stain on
the city to date.

Some interesting items have had to be left out, largely due to time constraints.
In particular the story of 'Billy in the Bowl' [*1 March 1774: 'Resolved that the man
in the bowl dish is not a proper person to be discharged from the House of Industry.'*]

and Sir William Petty's fantastical double-bottomed boat [an early European cata-maran. 23 December 1684, 'Sir William Petty's ship was tried this day week in our harbour, between Ringsend and the Bar, but she behaved so abominably, as if built on purpose to disappoint']. Others proved impossible to track down, Molly Malone remains an undated enigma and, while it is commonly believed that Fusilier's Arch contains several names of soldiers who didn't die in the Boer War, I've found no record of them.

I've always been a fan of almanacs, miscellanies and other books which appeal to the magpie mind. The more obscure and irrelevant the information, the better. Among my earliest purchases as a wage-earning adult was a battered copy of the nineteenth century *Haydn's Dictionary of Dates* which, among many curious and often breathtakingly dull pieces of trivia, provided a list of public executions, duels, strange deaths, &c. in Ireland and Britain. And, while researching this book, I found mention in the *Dublin Penny Journal* of *Finlay's Miscellany*. While I've yet to find a copy maybe the real title of this book should have been Finlay's Second Miscellany.

When I started researching this book I thought of the big events - e.g. 1798, 1800, 1803, 1916 - but as it evolved it become something else ... the end result is a 'mixum-gatherum' which, I hope, gives at least a flicker of a picture of what it was like for ordinary people who lived in Dublin over the past couple of centuries. Some of the entries raise questions which I cannot answer but one [26 January] does have at least a partial ending - when last heard of 'Magurk (or Maquirk)' was still being held in custody, but his story had been more or less accepted, The deceased was, in fact, a Sligoman who simply wanted to be buried on home soil!

Finally, if you have any comments, suggestions or corrections I would like to hear them.

Ken Finlay (kenfinlay@gmail.com)
November 2005

Chapter One

January

Every couple of decades some bright spark in Government gets the notion that the local authorities have to change in order to keep up with the times. Appropriate buzz words are thrown in to make it appear that the long-overdue change is the most desirable thing in the world.

Of course this means throwing out the old stationery, building 'better' premises, designing a new logo and generally throwing money about like a whirling dervish – not to worry, the next step is imposing a new tax or two to pay for it.

So it was on 1 January, 1930, when the citizens of Blackrock, Dun Laoghaire, Dalkey and Killiney/Ballybrack woke up to find that their township councils had been dissolved to be replaced by the bright and glittering Dun Laoghaire Borough Corporation.

Fast forward to 1 January, 1994, when the bright, glittering but now outdated Borough Corporation became a part of the brand spanking new Dun Laoghaire/Rathdown County Council, complete with new logo and motto.

The answer to the question 'where is Rathdown?' is roughly answered by one or other of the following (a) if you live outside Dun Laoghaire you are in Rathdown, (b) a medieval barony which extends from Merrion Gates to Bray and from the sea to the Dublin and Wicklow hills.

2ND JANUARY

While William Martin Murphy today is largely remembered because of the 1913 Lockout, he had other claims to fame. *The Irish Independent*, his brainchild, was published for the first time on 2 January 1905. 50,000 copies were printed and sold at a halfpenny each – cheaper than existing titles.

The editorial announced that its aim was 'to make this journal what a modern newspaper should be – the 'biography of a day', brightly written and attractively presented, free from unwholesome sensationalism' and presenting the news of the day 'without colouring or prejudice'.

The paper would be 'independent in fact as well as in its name', and 'uncompromising in its support for the restoration of the national rights of Ireland'. For the first week the Independent ran an unusual competition, offering prizes to readers for nominating the best advertisements.

Within 10 years it was the single most successful newspaper in Ireland, claiming sales of 100,000 daily. *The Irish Independent* remains the biggest selling daily newspaper in Ireland, but its freedom from 'colouring or opinion' is a matter of opinion.

3RD JANUARY

The Freeman's Journal of 3 January 1900 reported on an investigation into the possible location of the remains of Robert Emmet. 'The Trevor vault is in St. Paul's Churchyard, North King Street. Dr. Trevor was superintendent of Kilmainham Jail in 1803. This vault was accidentally discovered in 1898, and when its contents were examined by Dr. Emmet's [a grandnephew] wish . . . it was found to contain several coffins . . . One coffin was of very poor, cheap wood; the side had fallen out of it and exposed to view the skeleton within. When this was examined by medical experts it was found to be that of a young man between the ages of twenty and thirty, and, strangest of all, the head was missing! The cavity in the coffin where the head should have been was filled in with shavings.'

Dr. Trevor was cautious, but hopeful: 'It would require but a trifling corroboration from some other source to establish a complete chain of circumstantial evidence to prove at last the remains of Robert Emmet had been located.' DNA testing perhaps? And then the search for the head, reputedly taken by Dr. Petrie to make a death-mask, can begin in earnest.

4TH JANUARY

The last man to be hanged in Kilmainham Jail was Joseph Heffernan who went to the gallows on 4 January 1910. *The Freeman's Journal* reported: 'At 8 o'clock in Kilmainham Jail, Joseph Heffernan was executed for the murder of Miss Mary Walker, a telegraphist at the Mullingar Post Office.

'The only persons present at the execution were the Governor of the Jail, Mr. Michael McGann, the High Sheriff of County Westmeath, Mr. Hyde, the Chaplain, Father O'Ryan of Goldenbridge, Father Flood of James's Street, the medical officer and the warders. 'It appears that the man was very repentant and attended to the ministrations of the clergy with deep devotion. . . . At 5 minutes to 8 he was taken in charge by Pierpoint and his assistant and led to the place of execution. He was perfectly calm and delivered the responses to the Litany with much fervour.

'The morning was very cold and foggy and a crowd of about three hundred people gathered in front of the Jail. A heavy mist shrouded the whole place while the solemn tolling of the prison bell conveyed to those who were near that all was over and gradually the people went away.'

5TH JANUARY

On January 5, 1864, a statue was unveiled in College Green to commemorate a writer who was ugly, ill-mannered, a great plagiarist, gambler and inveterate

Happy Landers Concert Party, Dundrum, 25 January 1938. (Photo by Frank Corcoran)

drunkard. Oliver Goldsmith may well have been a great writer but his personal life was characterised by an unfailing ability to get himself into trouble.

He wrote a huge amount to bring in the shillings, much of it hack work which is wildly inaccurate and all but unreadable today – a two-volume *History of Rome*, his four-volume *History of England*, an eight-volume *History of the Earth and Animated Nature*.

However, his literary reputation rests on two comedy plays, *The Good-natur'd Man* (1768) and *She Stoops to Conquer* (1773), and his only novel, *The Vicar of Wakefield* (1766). His comedies are lively, witty, and humane. *The Vicar of Wakefield* is the melodramatic, but warm and humorous, story of a country parson and his family.

Goldsmith lived, played and worked too hard. His health broke and he died in London in 1774 leaving debts of £2,000. Although he earned a great deal of money in his lifetime, Goldsmith's improvidence kept him poor. He had the friendship of many of the literary and artistic greats of his day, the most notable being that of Samuel Johnson. Boswell depicted him as a ridiculous, blundering, but tender-hearted and generous creature, while Horace Walpole dismissed him as 'an inspired idiot.'

6TH JANUARY

The Lord Lieutenant ordered a Commission of Inquiry on 6 January, 1908, into the theft of the Irish Crown Jewels from a safe in Dublin Castle six months earlier. The terms of reference were 'to investigate the circumstances of the loss of the Regalia of the Order of St. Patrick, and to inquire whether Sir Arthur Vicars exercised due vigilance and proper care as the custodian thereof'.

To some extent it was an open and shut case. Security was almost non-existent and on two occasions just before the theft was discovered the door to the strong-room had been found open and unguarded. Vicars, the Ulster King of Arms, who had held the only two keys to the safe, must have known that his career was dead in the water.

Less than a month later Vicars was fired – his replacement was Sir Nevile Wilkinson (See 10 January). Almost a century later there is still debate over who actually stole the Irish Crown Jewels (which were neither as grand nor as valuable as their name might suggest). Later events showed that at least two of those involved, Francis Shackleton (brother of the famous explorer), and Francis Bennett Goldney, Athlone Puirsuivant, were thieves. Others prefer stories of drunken debauchery and homosexual orgies, either separately or together, followed by a Government cover-up. One thing is, however, certain. The Irish Crown Jewels have not been seen since 1907. (See 6 July)

7TH JANUARY

It may come as a bit of a surprise but Dublin is remarkably short on sculptures of leading politicians since the city achieved independence (dragging part of the rest of the country with it!). Older statues abound, among them that of Henry Grattan in College Green, which was unveiled on 7 January 1876 – 55 years after his death.

But why Grattan? The answer lay in his greatest speech. Having retired three years earlier, Grattan had returned to politics as the Union between England and Ireland loomed, spurred by the 1798 Rebellion and the English belief that Irish parliamentary freedom must inevitably lead to conflict between the two countries.

Though certain to lose the vote for the Act of Union in 1800, Grattan, who had overseen an element of Irish parliamentary independence only a few years before, vehemently denounced the manner in which the vote, and the Union, had been bought. 'The thing he proposes to buy is what cannot be sold – liberty,' he said. In spite of the enthusiasm which his speech aroused the vote was lost but by a narrower margin – 138 to 96 – than might have been expected given the time, money and promises devoted to it by the authorities.

8TH JANUARY

Reading old newspapers you are often amazed by the sheer amount of verbiage thrown at the page, and in the case of advertisements you were paying by the word. The death of a perfect woman on 8 January 1764 was reported by the *Freeman's Journal*: 'It is with uncommon Regret we convey the following piece of melancholy News to the Public, as it must diffuse Grief as far as the Subject's Name is known. Late last Wednesday Evening died of a Fever taken in Child-bed, Mrs. Steuart, Wife of William Steuart, Esq.; of Stafford-Street, in this City, and Daughter of Sir Richard

Butler, Bart. She enjoyed her Senses to the last, and bore a painful and distressful Disorder, with that patient Submission, which accompanies "The gay Conscience of a Life well spent", and indicates that Sweetness and Serenity of Temper, which rendered her as universally beloved in Life, as she is now lamented in Death. From a most just and exalted Sense of Religious Duties, flowed all the social Virtues in the highest Degree: For to the tenderer Offices of Society, filial Piety, conjugal Love, and parental Affection, and Friendship hardly to be paralleled, she added the most extensive Benevolence and Charity, with native Politeness, and the most engaging Affability. No wonder then, that Words cannot express the Heart-felt Sorrow which attends this Lady's Death.'

9TH JANUARY

The Report of the Mendicity Institute – its object being to take beggars off the streets and put them to work – was read in Morrison's Great Rooms on Monday, 9 January 1837. It attempted to answer some of the suggestions which had been put forward for putting their inmates to work, among them 'That a Tract of Waste Mountain Land near the City, be reclaimed by the labours of the poor of the Institution.' The Mendicity Institute wasn't impressed: 'Who is to dig and labour at it?, is it our 1,027 old women, and our equally helpless 140 old men?, for of strong men we have but 48 in the Institution, and of these 30 are requisite for the work of the house, leaving only 18 male stone-breakers for outdoor employment should opportunity offer. So long as so many professed Mendicants remain in our streets, so long will assistance be denied to our efforts. It will be remembered that within the first 18 months of establishment of the Institution, that 6,000 beggars made application for aid. The grievance is an old one in our City, for in the year 1773, 1,800 licenses to beg were granted by the House of Industry to Badged Mendicants!'

10TH JANUARY

Titania's Palace went up for auction at 12.00 noon on Tuesday, 10 January, 1978 -It was bought by Legoland in Denmark for €150,000. It was a banal end to one of the more charming, if you like that sort of thing, Dublin stories of the 20th century.

On a warm summer's day in 1907, Sir Nevile Wilkinson was sketching in the woods near his home in Mount Merrion. He was disturbed by his excited daughter, Guendolen, aged 3, who told him that she had just seen a Fairy Queen running into the base of a nearby sycamore tree.

The idea caught the imagination of Sir Nevile and he determined to build a home fit for the King and Queen of Fairyland – Titania's Palace – in which children could see the tiny treasures of Fairyland and which would raise money to help children across the world.

Miniature palaces were not a new idea, Sir Nevile had just completed a miniature model (Pembroke Palace) which was officially opened by Queen Alexandra in 1908.

Aided by Sir Nevile's detailed drawings, the palace – one inch to one foot – was constructed in mahogany in eight sections by James Hicks in No. 5, Lower Pembroke Street, aided by some of the best Dublin craftsmen of the time. The palace grew and grew, each year having more ancient and modern miniatures added – books, chandeliers, stained glass, paintings, even a tiny mouse – until it was finally opened on the 6 of July, 1922.

11TH JANUARY

Many Dubliners were shocked when they read of the death of Thomas Dudley (aka 'Bang-Bang') on 11 January 1981 – largely because they were sure he had died years before. But his absence from the streets and buses of Dublin, wielding a large brass door key, and 'shooting' passers-by with abandon had never lessened the legend of one of Dublin's great eccentrics.

Born in the Rotunda on 19 April 1906, he had led a life apart, employment held no great interest for him. He preferred to roam the streets and to visit the cinema where he had particular regard for the cowboys of the silver screen.

Perhaps it was there he picked up his shooting addiction, or maybe from a game he played as a child, but 'Bang-Bang' – though often asked – never explained why he became the 'gun-toting' scourge of Dublin.

In his later life, now preferring to be known as 'Lord Dudley', his eyesight began to fail and he had to leave his home at 80b Bridgefoot Street and move into Clonturk House for the Blind in Drumcondra, run by the Rosminian Fathers. He is buried in St. Joseph's Cemetery adjoining Clonturk House.

12TH JANUARY

It never ceases to amaze that reporters are surprised when bad people do bad things. 'Between six and seven o'clock on Tuesday evening, [12 January 1839], Mr. Gibson near the Draw-bridge, accompanied by his sister-in-law. Miss Wilkinson, was attacked near the Rope-walk by three ruffians, who not only beat Mr. Gibson and robbed him of his gold watch and other articles, but knocked the lady down twice; and one of the ruffians, while the others were robbing Mr. Gibson, kept his knees on the Lady's breast, and held a small knife or sword to her throat, threatening he would take her life if she screamed or made any noise.

They tore the lady's apparel immediately near her person in pieces in their endeavour to deprive her of them. This robbery is marked with features of peculiar ferocity; for the most wretched of the being who have hitherto, in general, been engaged in highway robbery in this country, have shown regard and delicacy towards females. From the robberies that have recently taken place in this neighbourhood, nearly adjoining the Rock-road, it is almost certain that there is a desperate banditti in that direction; and active measures should be immediately taken by the gentlemen residing on that line of road, and the police, to break up the gang before we shall have, probably, to regret the loss of some valuable member of society.' [*Saunder's News Letter*]

13TH JANUARY

It's not just U2 that can command premium prices for their performances. Back in the nineteenth century Charles Dickens, at least in terms of public entertainment.

When tickets for his January 1869 Dublin shows went on sale the police had to be called in to control the crowds.

The Dickens experience consisted of two hours solid of reading, beginning with a long and dramatic chunk from a dramatic work, such as *A Christmas Carol*, followed by a shorter and funnier piece from, for example, *The Pickwick Papers*. Afterwards, the theatre-goers could buy Dickens souvenirs in the foyer before wending their way home.

Dickens, himself, wasn't pleased with his readings in Dublin but *The Irish Times* on 13 January in its notice of his final Dublin reading said 'On this night we shall bid a long farewell to one whose name is so familiar in our homes, the occasion is one of which none will fail to avail themselves.'

The 'long farewell' predicted proved to be eternal – Dickens collapsed while on tour a few months later and died on 9 June 1870.

14TH JANUARY

The Irish Independent reported on 14 January 1922 on the gradual withdrawal of British troops: 'Two companies of Auxiliary R.I.C. numbering about 160 men left Dun Laoghaire by the mail boat last night . . . shortly before 7p.m. marched from Beggars Bush barracks to Westland Row station, carrying rifles and haversacks, their kits having preceded them. Passing along Mount Street and Merrion Street the scenes of many a bloody encounter during the hostilities they song *Goodbye* and *Are we down-hearted*. Groups of civilians gathered here and there and shouts of "Up the rebels" were responded to with cries of "Up King George". A crowd of several hundred outside Westland Row was regulated by Republican police and DMP. They seemed in good spirits and chatted gaily with friends who came to bid them farewell. As the train steamed out the Auxiliaries gave a final cheer. The band of the RIC and a guard of 80 men were present at Carlisle Pier, Dun Laoghaire. As the Auxiliaries stepped from the train the band played a few bars of their regimental march and *Auld Lang Syne*. There was much cheering among the men. Afterwards *God Save The King* was played while the Auxiliaries sang the anthem.'

15TH JANUARY

Only the language has changed, the sentiment is still expressed regularly. 'In the great hives of modern civilisation there is, unfortunately, a considerable number of persons who believe that they perform their duty to their neighbour by giving alms to every beggar who stops them with a whining tale. They will not give themselves the personal trouble of ascertaining whether his story is true or false, and, if true, of considering whether money or some other form of assistance (perhaps simple human sympathy) is what he needs. They merely put their hands into their pockets, pull out a penny or, if the tale is unusually harrowing, a shilling, and pass on in the complacent belief that they have performed a good action. What they have really done, in nine cases out of ten, is to increase the publican's receipts. It is hardly too much to say that if the practice of indiscriminate almsgiving were abandoned, the poverty and wretchedness in our great cities would be enormously diminished. The

A view down O'Connell Street from the Bridge. Note the tram and horse and carts in the foreground and the bustle of pedestrians.

undeserving would suffer, but the deserving poor would have a much better chance of securing useful assistance; for almsgiving would not cease, it would merely be directed into more beneficent channels.' [*The Irish Times*, 15 January 1902]

16TH JANUARY

Some of the imprisoned survivors of the 1798 rebellion were keeping themselves busy and getting into even more trouble. 'On an information that the Traitors confined in the different gaols of Dublin were entering into new conspiracies the several prisons were examined on Wednesday [16 January 1799], and the following discoveries made: In the apartments of Roger O'Connor, Cummins, Geraghty, & C. in Bridewell, were discovered swords, a pike of extraordinary dimensions, loaded pistols, and ammunition in abundance, and several daggers, made in the French fashion, opening like a long knife, double-edged, with a secret spring to prevent their shutting Mr. Justice Carleton was deputed to search Newgate, where he was received by the Traitors with derision Mr. Swan, on his searching the prison of Kilmainham, discovered manuscripts of great importance, in the hand-writing of Arthur O'Connor, Ivers, and others. That reported to be of the writing of Ivers, was a fair transcribed new system for the instruction of the higher and inferior societies of United Irishmen. Such is the ingratitude of these self convicted Rebels for the unprecedented acts of clemency shown them by Marquis Cornwallis.' [*The Public Register* or *Freeman's Journal*.]

17TH JANUARY

Dr. John Whalley, 'the chief quack and astrologer of his time' (Gilbert) – 'the proprietor, editor, and publisher of a newspaper, a quondam shoe-maker, an astrologer, a quack doctor, an almanac-maker, a no-Popery firebrand' (Dr. Madden) was born in London in 1653. He settled in Dublin around 1682 and poured forth volumes of abuse on his fellow-quacks, especially on one named Coats, who had rashly predicted the approaching death of his rival. Whalley survived the period assigned to him, and scourged the false prophet with such gentle epithets as 'baboon,' 'hardened villain,' and 'scandal to astrology.' In 1688 he spoke too freely and 'the Roman Catholic party being then in the ascendant in Dublin, he was put in the pillory, and pelted with rotten eggs.' When James II arrived Whalley fled to London. Around this time the Irish Bard, Feardaragh O'Daly, composed a bitter satire on the astrologer – comparing him to be in league with the devil, praying that all the diseases of earth may attend him – for which Whalley managed to get O'Daly's brother hanged.

   He died in Dublin on 17 January 1724 – his widow, Mary Whalley, continued for some time to publish his almanacs, in Bell-alley, off Golden-lane, under the title of 'Whalley's successor's almanac.'

18TH JANUARY

'Frederick Lippits, a private of the 13th Battalion Rifle Brigade, who appeared in the docks in his trousers and shirts, was charged by Constable 201C, with having on Thursday night been in Sackville street, dressed as a female. It appeared that Lippits was in the company of another soldier, and when the constable went towards him he threw off the lady's hat he was wearing, and ran towards O'Connell Bridge. There he threw off the lady's jacket, and ran as far as Fleet street, where the constable came up with him and took him into custody. He now stated that he did it for a lark. In reply to the magistrate as to where the woman's clothes were got, the witness said a woman dropped them out of a window. He also stated that the uniform was dropped somewhere in College Green when he was running away. The prisoner said that the uniform had been found, and was in the Police Station. Ultimately Mr. Mahony discharged both men.' [*The Irish Times*, 18 January 1902.]

19TH JANUARY

Within months of the Montgolfier brothers first manned balloon flight in Paris (November 1783) Europe was full of men who, with complete disregard for life and limb, wanted to be the first in their country to head for the sky in their own balloon.

Leading the charge in Dublin was Richard Crosbie, 30, described as 'of immense stature, above six foot three in height: he had a comely-looking fat, ruddy, face extremely strong and brave as a lion.'

By August 1784 he was successfully sending small animals into the sky – at least one balloon (which had started out containing a cat) was found two days later in the sea off the Isle of Man.

Come December and Crosbie was ready to go, Advertisements noted that the 'Grand Air Balloon and Flying Barge' were on view in Ranelagh, with admission a hefty one shilling.

Several delays later the big day, January 19, 1705, arrived. 20,000 spectators were on hand at the Ranelagh Gardens and the balloonist did not disappoint: 'Mr. Crosbie's dress was white satin lined with fur, and over all an oiled silk loose coat, lined with the same, red leather boots, and a superb cap, and altogether we can pronounce him one of the finest figures we have ever seen', (*Faulkner's Dublin Journal*).

At 2.30pm Crosbie ascended rapidly, disappeared into clouds, heading SE over the Bay. Rather than take any chances over water he descended at Clontarf. A large crowd brought Crosbie, 'aerial chariot' and all, shoulder-high, back into Dublin to celebrate the first manned flight from Irish soil.

20TH JANUARY

A handwritten document in the National Library recalls the difficulties, real or imagined, faced by North Dublin fishermen nearly 200 years ago: 'At a meeting of the fishermen of Baldoyle in the schoolhouse on Sunday, 20 January 1833, a full and accurate statement of the grievances under which they labour ... the decline of our trade since the period of the Union between England and Ireland. That the system of fishing called trailing has most materially injured the fishery in as much as it has destroyed the spawn and prevented the growth of the fish and that the purse net used by the English fishermen is in its construction, highly calculated for this injurious purpose. Unless the said practice of trailing be speedily abolished it will in a very short period totally destroy the Irish fishery, a calamity which will entail ruin upon our trade, starvation upon ourselves and families and be productive of serious injuries to society in general. That we appoint the three following members of our body as competent persons to become our deputies to the National Council, to submit to it these our deliberate resolutions – Messrs. Christopher and Patrick Tallon and John Coogan.'

21ST JANUARY

When reading of the launch of the 'biggest/most expensive/safest vessel ever' you have a distinct sense that Health and Safety need to called in sharpish to count the lifeboats and give the hull a couple of kicks to see if it rattles. Add in mention of 'watertight compartments' and 'maiden voyage' and a quick tenner in the bookies may well prove profitable.

The *Tayleur*, the largest iron vessel built to that date, was launched in a blaze of publicity in October 1853. There were many teething problems, and it was not until

19 January 1854, that the ship, with 650 people and a large amount of cargo, left Liverpool for Australia.

Two days later, on January 21, the *Tayleur* was anchored in storm and fog. What may have been suspected, but was about to be proved, was that the ship's compasses weren't working properly – the anchors failed, land suddenly loomed out of the fog, and the vessel was driven repeatedly onto the rocks at Lambay.

A boat was launched but sank almost immediately. Some hardy passengers made it to the island and succeeded in passing ropes to the rapidly sinking *Tayleur*. Only the fittest and bravest stood a chance – 349 lives were lost in 30 minutes.

There were several enquiries and, while the Captain and crew were criticised, blame was finally laid on the ship's erratic compasses.

22ND JANUARY

A Dubliner was once both Commander-in-Chief of the British Army and Prime Minister of England at the same time.

Arthur Wellesley, Duke of Wellington, was made Commander-in-Chief of the British Army on 22 January 1827, and exactly a year later took on the job of Prime Minister.

Though not known as a fan of Ireland, the highlight of his term was the passing of Catholic Emancipation – the granting of almost full civil rights to Catholics – which became inevitable after the landslide victory of Daniel O'Connell in the Clare election in 1829. O'Connell was legally allowed to stand as a candidate, but could not take his seat because of anti-Catholic legislation.

Arthur Wellesley, Commander in Chief of British Armed Forces, Prime Minister of England, Victor of Waterloo, Duke of Wellington, and reluctant Irishman.

Putting forward the proposal for Catholic Emancipation Wellington gave one of the best speeches of his career. 'My lords; the bill is in itself very simple. It concedes to the Roman Catholics the power of holding every office in the state, and it also concedes to them the power of becoming members of parliament.' The alternative, he argued, would be civil war in Ireland.

23RD JANUARY

The first major history of Dublin (1766) by 'the late Walter Harris' was followed nearly 40 years later by a similarly ill-fated two-volume history by Warburton (dead), Whitelaw (dead) and Walsh.

It was not until 1854-9 that the first accurate history appeared – *History of the City of Dublin* in three volumes. It was written by John Thomas Gilbert, who was born in the city on 23 January 1829. What made the difference was that Gilbert wasn't satisfied to rely on previously printed works, he insisted on rigid verification of the facts. It doesn't make for very interesting general reading but if it's the facts you want, you'll find them in Gilbert.

Somewhat of a child prodigy, he was elected to the Council of the Celtic Society when only 19, four years later he became a member of the Royal Irish Academy and secretary of the Irish Archaeological Society.

For the last 52 years of his life he lived in Blackrock and books quite literally poured from his pen, including *History of the Viceroys of Ireland* (1865), *Calendar of the Ancient Records of Dublin* (7 vols., 1889-98); *History of the Irish Confederation and the War in Ireland, 1641-9* (7 vols., 1882-91); *Jacobite Narrative of the War in Ireland, 1688-91* (1892). (See 4 February)

24TH JANUARY

'The Lord Mayor said it was a monstrous thing that the citizens had to face an annual charge for lunacy for Dublin alone of 1s. 8d. in the £. The major portion of the great cost of the asylum was outside the control of the elected representatives of the people. Anyone going down to Portrane would find it was not a building devised for lunatics, or for any of the proper public purposes of a public building, but one would think it was devised for the reception of a king, and it would stand as an eternal monument of disgrace and incompetence on the part of the Board of Control for their rash and prodigal and foolish expenditure. The cost of maintenance per lunatic, apart from the interest on buildings, had gone up enormously. They alleged naturally enough that these poor people should be wanting in nothing and the result had been that people outside who used to pay for their friends in private asylums are now sending them in wholesale to the public asylums. The increase in lunacy in this country was largely due to persons who maintained imbeciles or lunatics at their own expense; or who contributed to their expense in private asylums, had found a way of getting at the public asylums in the country? [*The Irish Times*, 24 January 1902]

25TH JANUARY

'I have arrived [in Dun Laoghaire] in the middle of the night; I have arrived on a winter's morning, and I have arrived when there have been spring showers which wet you as quickly as any rain. When you arrive at Dun Laoghaire on a winter's morning you find the pier is not properly lighted, that there are not sufficient porters to deal with the luggage and place it on the table for the Customs officers, and that there is a rush to get the newspapers into the city of Dublin. We are going to have what is called Tailteann Games this year. If people have to go through this sort of purgatory at Dun Laoghaire they will never visit the country again. At Dun Laoghaire the south-west gale from the Dublin mountains drives the rain right through the whole pier. I have seen elderly ladies there almost wet through, and an umbrella would be turned inside out immediately. The pier must be closed in if you want to attract visitors here. It is not impossibility. People say it cannot be done because they are old fashioned. We do not want that sort of people; we want to progress.' [The Earl of Mayo, Seanad Éireann, 25 January 1924] (See also 7 March)

26TH JANUARY

This story about the last journey of a Dublin resident is so strange that it just has to be true. It's the little details that convince me: 'Sligo, 26 January 1785. On Wednesday last, the following strange circumstance occurred in this town. About two in the afternoon, a fellow very much intoxicated, drove up to the abbey gate with the corpse of a man in a deal coffin, much disfigured, on the carriage of a hackney chair or noddy. The merest trifle would attract a crowd, no wonder than that such a singular appearance should beget inquiry; which the driver not giving a satisfactory return to, he was taken before the civil magistrate, to whose interrogation, we learn, he replied "that his name is Magurk (or Maquirk) drives a noddy, No. 110, Dublin, got the body of the deceased out of an house in Patrick-street; was to get four pounds for the carriage of it to the abbey gate of Sligo; and that he knew no more about the matter", which not appearing sufficiently satisfactory, he was committed to prison, until sobriety and a sense of his own situation, should render him more explicit. From the putrefied state of the deceased's body, it was perhaps not easy to form a certain opinion of the cause of his death; however, those of the faculty who have seen it, seem to think that he must have been hanged.' A short article some time later confirmed the unlikely story.

27TH JANUARY

WB Yeats was in Aberdeen on Saturday night, January 27, 1906, and Lady Gregory was running the Abbey Theatre for the first night of JM Synge's *The Playboy of the Western World*. After Act 1 Yeats received a telegram which noted: 'Play a great success.' By the end of Act 3 a second telegram arrived: 'Play broke up in disorder at the word "shift".' 'Disorder' was too small a word, by some accounts only the fact that one of the stagehands grabbed an axe and threatened to use it stopped the mob from storming the stage.

Arthur Griffiths, editor of *The United Irishman*, described the play as 'a vile and inhuman story told in the foulest language.' *The Irish Independent* noted that the riots were 'a tribute to the good taste and common sense of the audience.'

The Abbey was closed on Sunday, and Monday night saw a small audience (only about one-fifth of capacity) drown the play out with catcalls and hissing. On Tuesday things hotted up, the protesters were back, but this time Lady Gregory had her nephew and some of his friends from Trinity on hand to cheer their support for the play. To add fuel to the flames the police had been invited to patrol the theatre.

All hell broke loose, extra police were drafted in, several arrests were made and there was a fist fight outside the theatre.

28TH JANUARY

The Liverpool Mercury reported on 28 January 1814 on an inquest into the death of a murdered Dublin man: 'The first witness was the unhappy miserable mother: she stated that about seven o'clock her two sons Maurice Eaton, aged about 24, and James Eaton aged about 18 had an altercation: she turned the eldest, Maurice, out of the place and she conceived that he had gone home: about an hour after, wanting to get some bread and butter for her supper, she left her son James behind her in the house, and went to a huckster adjacent, where she stayed about fifteen minutes; on her return she found her son James lying in the passage lifeless his throat being cut from ear to ear. Surgeon Rooney [said] instant death must have been the consequence of the wound, as the windpipe was cut entirely through. Two other witnesses, a woman and a man, were next examined: the woman proved, that hearing a noise of shrieking she came down stairs and in the crowd observed Maurice Eaton: who said "it was done and could not be undone" The man also proved that Maurice said "he would submit to the law and that it was manslaughter in his own defence".'

29TH JANUARY

If there is one golden rule in local newspapers it is not to criticise amateur dramatics – if it's awful, write nothing, even if it's very good, write nothing (it will be over by the time your next edition comes out). Someone should have told the Dramatic Correspondent of the *Dun Laoghaire Borough Times* [29 January 1949]: 'My criticism of the St. Michael's Entertainers ' production of *Aladdin* appears to have represented the 'Open Sesame' for a conflict of opinions. Artistic worth is not to be assessed by the mere counting of heads, or proved by breaches of taste which on Friday evening last featured an unpleasant incident when a representative of the *Borough Times* was refused the right to discharge his duties at St. Michael's Hall ... I maintain that my criticism of the opening night of *Aladdin* was a just and lenient commentary on a performance which would have been depressingly bad even if it had been described as a dress rehearsal. A slip-shod, insufficiently rehearsed performance of indifferent material will certainly not receive my endorsement. I refuse to conceive it to be my purpose to preserve the proud illusions of players who are grimly determined not to forsake their low standards of performance.'

The stump of Nelson's Pillar after the explosion of 8 March 1966.

30TH JANUARY

Work began on building Nelson's Pillar in what was then Sackville Street (named after Lionel Sackville, eldest son of the first Duke of Dorset) on 30 January 1808. It was just over two years since news of the battle of Trafalgar and the death of the English Admiral (21 October 1805) had reached Dublin.

Of course it was only a matter of time before some public spirited individual noted the lack of a tribute to the great man. Less than a month after the battle Aldermen (senior Councillors with Dublin Corporation) of the City met to decide on something suitable. Alderman Kelly suggested an oil painting, Alderman Cope wanted a statue. The meeting agreed on a statue – they also agreed that the public should be given the chance to prove their loyalty by paying for it.

And the public eventually did – the more money raised the more grandiose the proposed 'statue' became.

The official laying of the foundation stone was 15 February 1808. A time capsule allegedly contained a variety of curios considered of interest to posterity – when opened a few years ago it was found to be empty.

After the Pillar crashed to the ground (2am, 8 March 1966) it was only a matter of time before some public-spirited individuals decided it was high time that a suitably modern emblem of 21st century Dublin should be erected on the site.

31st JANUARY

During a civil war free speech can carry a heavy price: 'Early this morning [31 January 1923] a party of armed men arrived at the partial ruins of [Senator] Sir Horace Plunkett's house at Foxrock and completed their work of destruction. The Civic Guard was on duty at the house up to 2 in the morning, and forty minutes after it had been withdrawn those parts of the premises which had escaped the flames on the previous night were utterly wrecked. A priceless collection of books and papers was destroyed by the fire. Sir Horace Plunkett's secretary, who was in bed at the time, had a narrow escape from being burned to death.

'This afternoon the residence of Caption Stephen Gwynn a former member of the Irish Party in the House of Commons, and Irish correspondent of the *Observer*, was destroyed by a land mine. Captain Gwynn's house was situated on the Kimmage road, near the terminus of the Terenure tramway line, and it was a pretty two-story building in its own grounds. Apparently it was completely wrecked.' [*The Times*]

Chapter Two

February

1st February

Proposing the adoption of the annual report of the Royal Zoological Society for 1898, Professor Mahaffy, waxed lyrical on the benefits of the Zoo: 'No city devoted to mere money making would ever attain the dignity of a city with great parks, gardens, galleries of pictures, and libraries, and a fine zoological garden wherein citizens might study the habits of creatures in nature that they could not meet with every day. An acquaintance with the inhabitants of these Gardens would cause general sympathy for animal and bird life, and people would not be so callous and cruel as they sometimes were even in the present century. It might be said that shutting up animals in cages was not a good way of showing kindness to them, but many of them were happier than if at liberty and trying to procure a precarious living. They should also consider that if by the caging of one animal they were able to preserve an entire species, it was worth while to sacrifice the comforts of a few animals for the good of the many. If they looked at the columns of *The Irish Times*, which probably represented the average intelligence of the country, they would see men boasting of having found rare birds or animals, which they immediately proceeded to shoot.' [*The Irish Times*, 1 February 1899.]

2nd February

Which Lord Mayor of Dublin once shot a councillor dead? None other than Daniel O'Connell (Lord Mayor in 1841). Twenty-six years earlier O'Connell got up the nose of the local authority when, in a public speech, he described it as a 'beggerly corporation.'

You might be forgiven for thinking that the Corporation has been called worse, both before and since, but the councillors were resolved to put O'Connell in his place, i.e. a wooden box, six feet under.

Councillor John D'Esterre spent a week trying to ambush O'Connell as he came and went from the Four Courts with the expressed intention of giving him a sound horse-whipping.

A duel was arranged and the two eventually met at Bishopscourt, near Naas, on 2 February 1815. D'Esterre, a noted duellist, fired first and missed. O'Connell's shot hit D'Esterre in the hip and he died the following day – after absolving O'Connell from any blame.

*Daniel O'Connell, orator, politician
and reluctant duellist.*

O'Connell offered an annuity to his widow. She refused any assistance from her husband's killer, but he continued to pay money to D'Esterre's daughter until his death.

3RD FEBRUARY

James Henry Reynolds was born in Dun Laoghaire on 3 February 1844. A Bachelor of Medicine and Surgery from Trinity College, he joined the British Army Medical Department (later RAMC) 1868.

The highlight of his military career was during the two-day defence against 4,000 Zulu warriors of Rourke's Drift. Reynolds later described the first Zulu assault: 'We opened fire on them from the hospital at 600 yards, and although the bullets ploughed through their midst and knocked over many, there was no check or alteration made in their approach. As they got nearer they became more scattered, but the bulk of them rushed for the hospital and the garden in front of it. We found ourselves quickly surrounded by the enemy with their strong force. They poured on us a continuous fire, to which our men replied as quickly as they could reload their rifles.'

His VC – one of 11 awarded for the action – was presented in June 1879 – the citation reads: 'For the conspicuous bravery, during the attack at Rourke's Drift on 22 and 23 January, 1879, which he exhibited in his constant attention to the wounded under fire, and in his voluntarily conveying ammunition from the store to the defenders of the hospital, whereby he exposed himself to a cross-fire from the enemy both in going and returning.'

4TH FEBRUARY

The rebellion of 1798 gave James Whitelaw, vicar of St. James, a unique opportunity to carry out a fairly complete census of Dublin. The authorities had ordered that every house should have attached to it a list of occupants – Whitelaw organised helpers to record the details. He estimated the population within the city boundaries at 170,805, and the number of houses at 14,854. [The population within the same limits in 1871 was 267,717; the number of houses, 26,859.] Some years before his death, in conjunction with Mr. Warburton, Deputy-keeper of the Records in Dublin Castle, he planned a History of Dublin. Mr. Warburton furnished documents and the ancient history of the city; Mr. Whitelaw organised the material, and wrote the modern descriptive portion of the work. It was announced in the *Gentleman's Magazine* the month before his death, as preparing for publication. He died on 4 February 1813 at the age of 64. Mr. Warburton's death soon followed, and the work was completed, chiefly from Mr. Whitelaw's papers, by the Rev. Robert Walsh, in 1818, and published as the *History of the City of Dublin, its Present Extent, Public Buildings, Schools, Institutions, etc.*, by the late J. Warburton, the late Rev. J. Whitelaw, and the Rev. Robert Walsh.

5TH FEBRUARY

The Irish Times reported on 5 February 1902 on the half-yearly meeting of the Dublin United Tramways Company. Mr. William Martin Murphy, Chairman: 'All experience has gone to show that tramway traffic must continue to grow more or less rapidly in every centre of population whose boundaries are constantly being extended by new buildings in the suburbs … As it requires somewhat less than a unit of electricity to propel a tramcar for a mile, the actual electric cost for one mile is 0.496d., or under one halfpenny. The average fare per passenger over the whole system was 1.23d. Though some few people are still found to grumble at paying the very moderate fares we charge, which in most cases are much below our authorised fares, we think we have now reached the limit of concessions on the fare question. The total number of passengers carried in the half-year was 23,816,084, a record number, equal to the moving of the whole population every three days, while the cars travel a distance equal to five times round the earth in a week. The traffic receipts per mile were 8.70d. compared with 8.48d. in 1900, and the expenses 4.728d. as against 5.02d.'

6TH FEBRUARY

The early afternoon of Wednesday, 6 February 1782, saw businessmen from around the city congregate upstairs at the Music Hall in Fishamble Street to select a candidate for Parliament. The meeting was organised by the Guild of St Luke the Evangelist (representing cutlers, painters, paperstainers and stationers). According to contemporary reports up to 400 people turned up.

The night before there had been a ball in the hall – those attending complained of 'frequent cracking and giving way of the flooring' and many had left early as a result. As the third candidate for the seat, Councillor Joseph Pemberton, gave his speech the floor suddenly gave way, dashing the crowd 20 feet to the ground below.

The Hibernian Chronicle reported that over 50 people had broken limbs and cheerfully noted that many 'will exhibit melancholy monuments, to perpetuate the memory of this dreadful event, by the loss of their legs and arms.'

Miraculously, no-one died on the spot but there were 11 fatalities recorded in the weeks following. The successful candidate was Travers Hartley of 89 Bride Street – he was one of the lucky ones on the day, suffering only severe bruising.

7TH FEBRUARY

Dublin author Joseph Sheridan Le Fanu, writer of *In A Glass Darkly*, died on 7 February 1873, in his home on Merrion Square.

After the death of his wife in 1858 he had become a recluse and his writings became darker. He was nicknamed the *The Invisible Prince* for his shyness and nocturnal lifestyle. Usually, after visiting his newspaper office, Le Fanu returned to his home in Merrion Square to write from midnight to dawn. Le Fanu's son, Brinsley, said that his father wrote mostly in bed, using copybooks for his manuscripts. He always had two candles by his side on a small table. He kept himself awake by drinking cups of strong tea, as he made the addict of *Green Tea* say – 'I believe that everyone who sets about writing in earnest does his work on something – tea, coffee or tobacco.'

He suffered from strange nightmares and used them in the scenes of terror in his stories. His writing was largely forgotten until the 1920s when ghost story writer MR James published a collection of Le Fanu's stories under the title *Madam Crowl's Ghost and Other Tales of Mystery*.

8TH FEBRUARY

Robert Southwell Bourke, three-time Chief Secretary for Ireland, was born in Dublin in 1822. In 1868 he was appointed Governor-General of India, proving one of the abler administrators. In 1872, he went to the penal settlement at the Andaman Islands, concerning which there had been reports of abuses and maladministration. Returning to embark in the dusk of the evening of the 8th February, he was assassinated by a convict named Shere Ali, who declared that 'he had no accomplices, that it was his fate, and that he had committed the act by the order of God.' He had long threatened that he would take the life of some distinguished European in revenge for having been imprisoned for murdering a man in a 'blood-feud.' The Viceroy was only able to say faintly to his secretary, 'They've hit me, Burne,' before he expired. The assassin was executed at Calcutta on the 20th of the same month. His remains were brought back to Ireland, were received in military state in Dublin, and were deposited in the family mausoleum near Naas.

9TH FEBRUARY

There's a lot of talk these days about immigration, but it was ever so! Eamon De Valera, for example, was saved from execution, because he was born in New York. Not so well-known is that Edward Carson, largely responsible for the creation of Northern Ireland, was of Italian extraction (the family name was originally Carsoni).

The Committee of the Cuala Primary Schools' League, 14 February 1938. (Photo by Frank Corcoran)

Edward Henry Carson was born in No. 4 Harcourt Street (now a hotel) on 9 February 1854. Educated in Trinity, he studied law, doing so well that he became Solicitor General for Ireland at the age of 38. Three years later he cross-examined another Trinity graduate of his own generation, Oscar Wilde, and gently led him down the path of self-incrimination until it became clear, even to Oscar, that he was doomed.

In 1910 Carson became Solicitor General in England and received a knighthood. That same year he represented a naval cadet, George Archer Shee, who had been accused of stealing a postal order. His acquittal, said Carson, was the happiest moment of his life. Terence Rattigan dramatised the events in his 1946 play *The Winslow Boy*.

Carson became leader of the Unionists in 1910 and held several wartime posts before resigning in 1918 to fight Ulster's cause again. When a Northern Ireland Parliament was established he stayed at Westminster – sitting continuously in the House of Commons for nearly 30 years before going to the House of Lords as Lord Carson of Duncairn.

Through it all he never lost his strong Dublin accent!

10TH FEBRUARY

Huge Lane received the Freedom of the City of Dublin on 10 February 1908 for his tireless work in promoting art in Dublin and for his promise to donate his personal collection to the city when a permanent gallery was set up.

Lane persuaded the architect Sir Edward Lutyens to design an art gallery which would have spanned the Liffey near O'Connell Bridge. The Corporation eventually decided against the proposal – in the process annoying Lane so much that he changed his will in 1913 and left his paintings to London instead. Two years later he changed the will again, leaving the collection to Dublin, but this time, crucially, the codicil was not witnessed. There was a condition – that a suitable home for the paintings be found within five years.

Lane drowned when the Lusitania was torpedoed in 1915. The British Government, which had possession of the paintings, later refused to honour the will (accepting the intention but noting that the art gallery had not been provided). It was not until 1959 that an agreement was reached to divide the collection in two – every five years they would commute between Dublin and London. A second agreement in 1979 gave more pictures to Dublin. The situation was further improved by a revised agreement in 1993.

11TH FEBRUARY

The Hibernian Journal was established by a printer named Mills in 1771 and within a short time became mixed up in Trinity College politics. On the night of 11 February 1775 some scholars drove in a coach to his door, and called him out on pretence of bargaining for some books. 'He was suddenly seized, thrust into the coach, and held down by the party within, with pistols to his head, and threats of being shot if he made any noise. In this way he was conveyed to the [College] pump; and, after being nearly trampled to death, he was held there till he was almost suffocated – indeed he would have expired under the discipline but for the prompt interference of some of the fellows.

'This gross outrage in the very courts, and under the fellows' eyes, which ought to have been visited by the immediate expulsion of all concerned, was noticed only by a mild admonition of the Board to a single individual; the rest enjoyed a perfect impunity, and openly exulted in the deed. The form of admonition, drawn up by Dr. Leland, actually excused the act: 'Since it appears that a body of unknown scholars committed an assault against a certain printer, named Mills, who wickedly attacked in his paper certain noble members of the college, &c.

12TH FEBRUARY

Profane History certainly sounds interesting ... 'Lately opened by Robert Brooke, in Stafford-street, a new Seminary for the Instruction of Youth in such Branches of useful Learning, as do not require a previous Knowledge of the dead languages Reading and Writing by explanatory Lectures on the best English Grammars, and Authors most approved. Arithmetic, and the Mathematics, with improvements on the most concise Methods hitherto used by Traders in Merchant's Accompts and Italian Book-keeping. The Pupils are also taught sacred and profane History, Geography, Chronology, and the Use of the Globe, with Astronomy illustrated by a new Apparatus, which renders all the celestial Appearances plain and familiar to the eyes and Apprehensions of Children. Great Attention also paid their Morals and Conduct, and their Duties, as Men and Christians, are fully and daily inoculated, in order to form their tender and pliant Minds to the Precepts of Humanity, Honour and Virtue.' [Tuesday, 12 February 1765, *The Public Register* or *Freeman's Journal*]

13TH FEBRUARY

The death of Leonard McNally in his Harcourt Street home on 13 February 1820 brought back to Dubliners memories of failed rebellions – for McNally, one of the original members of the United Irishmen, had, in his capacity as a lawyer, assisted in the defence of Emmet, Jackson, Tandy, Tone, and many others.

Then the bombshell burst – his family requested that the secret service pension of £300 a year he had received since 1798 be continued! The Lord-Lieutenant demanded a detailed statement of the circumstances under which the agreement had been made; it was furnished after some hesitation, and the startling facts became generally known. Not only had he been in regular receipt of the pension claimed, but that during the state trials of 1798 and 1803, while he was receiving fees from the prisoners to defend them, he also accepted large sums from Government to betray the secrets of their defence.

Sir Jonah Barrington, who didn't know of McNally's treachery, described him: 'His figure was ludicrous; he was very short, and nearly as broad as long; his legs were of unequal length, and he had a face which no washing could clean. He possessed, however, a fine eye, and by no means an ugly countenance; a great deal of middling intellect; a shrill, full, good bar voice. In a word, MacNally was a good-natured, hospitable, talented, dirty fellow.'

14TH FEBRUARY

It's one of the best known pictures of old Dublin – the train locomotive suspended over Hatch Street. *The Wicklow*, engine No. 17, had left Enniscorthy at 8pm on 14 February 1900. It was carrying a consignment of cattle and had a crew of three, driver Walter Hyland, fireman Peter Jackston and guard Robert Doran.

On the way to Harcourt Street from Dundrum the train began to pick up speed, despite efforts to apply the brakes. The line was greasy and the wheels were slipping. By the time it came into the station Walter Hyland had put the engine into reverse to no avail.

There were metal 'buffer stops' at the end of the station but they had never been designed to stop a speeding train. *The Wicklow* ploughed into them and pushed through the back wall before finally coming to rest.

Robert Hyland was the sole casualty – his trapped arm had to be amputated there and then.

The Wicklow was eventually lowered to street level, placed on temporary rail tracks and brought back into the station. For years afterwards schoolboys derived much innocent amusement by asking the ticketmaster at Harcourt Street for ' A single to Hatch Street!'

15TH FEBRUARY

The Right Honourable Henry Grattan, leader of the Irish House of Commons, was not given to taking insults lying down. In 1800, while discussing the Union, Isaac Corry, the Chancellor of the Exchequer, accused Grattan of encouraging revolution and consorting with the United Irishmen. Grattan, in turn, retorted with a stinging and highly offensive speech. Corry immediately demanded a duel.

The two and their seconds, met at Ballsbridge on morning of 15 February 1800. Strictly speaking duelling was illegal and a sheriff's officer was sent to prevent the shootout. Major-general Craddock, Corr's second, 'took the intruder in his arms and deposited him in a little ditch,' where he remained until the firing ceased.

At the first exchange of fire Grattan wounded Corry in the arm and Corry missed. His dander up, Corry demanded another shot. He missed for a second time and Grattan fired into the air. 'I could have killed him if I choose,' Grattan said. 'I had no enmity to him. I then went up to him. He was bleeding. He gave me his bloody hand. We had formerly been friends, but Corry was set on to do what he did.'

16TH FEBRUARY

Dr. Bartholomew Mosse, founder of the Rotunda Hospital, Dublin, died in Cullenswood House, Ranelagh, on 16 February 1759. The British Government later granted his widow £1,000, in 'consideration of the merit of her late husband in regard to the poor'. The Hospital itself was less generous, it ordered 'that she will quit the House by Michelmas'.

From the eighth day of December, 1757 (the day it was opened) to the 31 October 1764, 3,614 women were admitted. Only 51 women died during that time in the hospital. The total expense of the hospital, as it appears by the accounts for six years ending the 31st of December 1763, amounted to about or £4,500.

Before the opening of the new hospital, Doctor Mosse published a full account of the old hospital in George's Lane; whereby it appeared, that in the space of 12 years, 3,975 women were delivered there-in of 2,101 boys, and 1,948 girls, in all 4,049 children, 74 women having had twins; and that the expense of supporting the hospital, in that time, amounted to no more than 3,913£ 13s. Which was about 19s 8d. for each woman and her child.

17TH FEBRUARY

You find that your mother has committed suicide by cutting her own throat – what do you do next?

According to Edward Ball, 19, he was so concerned people might think that Lavinia 'Vera' Ball had taken her own life, that he decided to dispose of the body.

Late at night on 17 February 1936 he drove the family car to Corbawn Lane in Shankill, waited for several hours and then dragged the body into the water. Leaving the car where it was, he returned to the main road and hitched a lift back to Dublin. Mrs. Ball's body was never recovered.

In court it emerged that Edward's story was mostly true, right from the moment he decided to dispose of the body. But the prosecution argued that Mrs. Ball could not have cut her own throat and that the Gardai had found evidence pointing to a struggle in the Booterstown house. There were signs of an attempted clean-up of the premises and a suitcase left by Edward Ball in the flat of a friend was found to contain bloodstained clothing.

The jury took four hours to reach their verdict of 'guilty but insane'. Edward Ball was sent to the Central Mental Hospital in Dundrum.

18TH FEBRUARY

When the College of Physicians, Trinity College, received its charter in 1693 one of the clauses permitted the college to dissect the bodies of executed criminals. Five days later, on 18 February, the *College Journal* noted: 'the body of a malefactor, who was this day executed, was demanded. The said body was accordingly delivered to a convenient place, where Dr. Gwither, one of the Fellows of the College, is to dissect the same.'

Among those who were dissected over the years was the Irish Giant Cornelius McGrath (7 foot 5ins), whose body was taken from his wake in 1760. According to legend the lecturer Bryan Robonson told his medical students: 'Gentlemen, I have been told that some of your zeal have contemplated the carrying off of the body. I most earnestly beg of you not to think of such a thing: but if you should be so carried away with your desire for knowledge: that thus against my expressed wish you persist in doing so, I would have you remember that if you take only the body, there is no law whereby you can be touched, but if you take so much as a rag or a stocking with it, it is a hanging matter.'

19TH FEBRUARY

The curious incident of the so-called 'Bottle Riot' came to an end in a Dublin court on 19 February 1747 when Thomas Sheridan, actor and manager of the Smock Alley Theatre, and a young Galway man, E. Kelly, were each accused of assault.

There had been trouble at the theatre since mid-January when a drunken Kelly had invaded the stage during a performance of *Aesop*, interfered with a female actress – Mrs. Dyer – and said he would 'do what her husband Mr Dyer had done to her, using the obscene expression.'

Sheridan had an orange thrown at him which struck his false nose with enough force to put a dent in his forehead. After the performance Kelly followed Sheridan backstage and roundly abused him. Losing his temper, Sheridan thrashed him soundly with Aesop's stick.

Over following nights trouble escalated to the point that Trinity students got involved – at one point a band of 1,000 students, some armed, attacked the lodgings of some of those they believed were responsible for the theatre riots. The Theatre was ordered to be closed until tempers died down.

Sheridan was found not guilty of assault on Kelly. Kelly was less lucky, he was fined £500 and sentenced to imprisonment (either one or three months, depending on the report). [See 1 March]

Brooklawn Netball Club at St. Stephen's Hall, 18 February 1938. (Photo by Frank Corcoran)

20TH FEBRUARY

Oscar Wilde's play *Lady Windermere's Fan* (written over three or four weeks while he was holidaying near Lake Windermere in 1891) was first produced on 20 February 1892 at the St. James's Theatre, London. It starred Marion Terry as 'Mrs. Erlynne' and George Alexander (manager of the theatre) as 'Lord Windermere'. The first night was a great success and, responding to calls for the author, Oscar sauntered onto the stage to receive his ovation. Holding a cigarette and smiling he addressed the audience: 'Ladies and Gentlemen: I have enjoyed this evening immensely. The actors have given us a charming rendering of a delightful play, and your appreciation has been most intelligent. I congratulate you on the great success of your perform-ance, which persuades me that you think almost as highly of the play as I do myself.'

The critics felt that Oscar was far too cocky and, in the main, proceeded to denounce the author for his 'insolent effrontery'. Before the play opened he had been offered £1,000 for the rights by George Alexander, he turned the offer down and went on to make £7,000 from the original run.

21ST FEBRUARY

The Reverend Charles Wolfe, born in Dublin in December 1791, is little remembered today in his city. If it were not for a chance discovery of a letter after his death on 21 February 1823, he wouldn't be remembered at all. That letter proved that he was the author of *The Burial of Sir John Moore*:

> *Not a drum was heard, nor a funeral note,*
> *As his corse to the rampart we hurried;*
> *Not a soldier discharged his farewell shot*
> *O'er the grave where our hero we buried.*

The poem, his last, had been published anonymously, and was attributed to various authors. Wolfe wasn't one to look after himself: 'He seldom thought of providing a regular meal. A few straggling rush-bottomed chairs, piled up with his books, a small rickety table before the fire-place, covered with parish memoranda, and two trunks containing all his papers – serving at the same time to cover the broken parts of the floor – constituted all the furniture of his sitting-room. The mouldy walls of the closet in which he slept were hanging with loose folds of damp paper.'

He contracted consumption and despite the best efforts of his sister, who brought him to England and France in search of a cure, died, aged 31.

22ND FEBRUARY

Overcrowding in the Dublin workhouses was a burning issue in 1899 as this letter demonstrates: 'Girls coming from country places, persons coming to the Dublin hospitals, and unable to defray their expenses home when discharged, &c., have always contributed to swell the numbers in our workhouses. Becoming destitute here, there is no resource under the present law except to maintain them, as the guardians cannot legally expend a single sixpence towards aiding a destitute person to return to his or her native place. But of late years the influx of country admissions has been enormous. The hope of employment held out by the construction of electric tramways, Portrane Asylum, main drainage, and disappointment in obtaining work on arrival here means simply throwing a labourer, wife and family, on the rates. The present overcrowding state of our workhouses, mainly owing to this sort of thing having become a source of danger and disgrace to the city, brings the ratepayers face to face with the prospect of having to expend immense sums on auxiliary buildings. This is bad enough, but the worst has not yet been touched. I ask the public to consider the extent of our difficulties in another year or two when the works I have mentioned above shall be completed, and hundreds of strangers will have been thrown out of employment – Yours, James Crozier.' [*The Irish Times*, 22 February 1899]

23RD FEBRUARY

Mr. Minelli requests the pleasure of your company: 'It is with utmost Diffidence and Reluctance that Mr. Minelli presumes to trouble the Public but his Necessities are extreme, and no other possible Method of Relief can be contrived; the public Attention is therefore most humbly entreated to the following Particulars of his unhappy Story.'

Briefly put, Minelli had come to Ireland in charge of a company of singers, they'd done a runner and a dancer Mrs. Ricci, along with her husband, had Minelli thrown into prison until he could pay off his debts. Two years later Minelli was still trying to get out!

'Thus by a Series of severe Treatment, without any blameable or fraudulent Step on his Part, Minelli, an entire Stranger, unacquainted even with the Language of the Country, neglected and forgotten, might have perished this Winter, had it not been for the Humanity of a Fellow-Prisoner, who has hitherto in a Manner supported him.

'His distressed Situation, he hopes, will plead his Excuse for this Application to the Public, imploring their Favour and Encouragement to his Assembly on the 23 [February 1764] (at the Great Assembly Room in Fishamble-street, where Tickets may be had at 5s. 5d. each) which some Persons of Distinction have generously promised to countenance.'

24TH FEBRUARY

Sir Charles A. Cameron was made a Freeman of the city of Dublin on 24 February 1911 – the first employee of Dublin Corporation to be so honoured. As the Chief Sanitary Officer of the City he had cut the death rate from one of the highest in Europe to one of the lowest.

In 1885 Cameron had brought the Prince of Wales (later Edward VII) to see at first hand the slums of Dublin – 25 years later the then King returned and Cameron showed him where tenements had been pulled down and modern housing provided. In 1888 Cameron reported to the Corporation that: 'More than half of Dublin needs to be rebuilt. Houses must be provided for the working-class people.' He worked tirelessly to ensure that the Corporation built new housing and to prevent the outbreak of diseases which had devastated the city in the past.

In just one year (1909) he had authorised Sanitary Inspection of Tenement Houses (74,010), Other Houses (21,952), Lodging Houses (1,370), Rooms (232,513), Yards, Halls and Stairs (27,583), Factories and Workshops (4,067), Bakeries (242) Ice Cream Shops (22), Slaughter Houses (4,194), Piggeries (499), Stables (399) and Schools (56).

Presenting the Freedom of the City, Alderman Kelly (Sinn Fein) noted: 'Sir Charles had done more than a man's part in trying to combat disease in Dublin.'

25TH FEBRUARY

'Are you slaves, or are you men? If slaves, then crouch to the rod and lick the feet of your oppressors; glory in you shame; it will become you, if brutes, to act according to your nature. But you are men; a real man is free, so far as circumstances will permit him. Resign your heart's blood before you part with this inestimable privilege of man.'

So wrote Percy Bysshe Shelley in his pamphlet *Address to the Irish People* which he began to distribute on 25 February 1812 while lodging on the first floor of No 7 Sackville Street.
Initially Shelley had intended to print his broadside on large sheets which would be stuck on walls around the city. But, carried away by revolutionary enthusiasm, he had written far too much.

1,500 copies of the pamphlet were printed, some of which were dispatched to the eminent citizens and the newspapers. Shelley also amused himself by throwing copies at passers-by. 'I stand at the balcony of our window,' he wrote, 'and watch till I see a man *who looks likely*, I throw a book to him.'

The only immediate effect of the pamphlet was to bring Shelley to the attention of the Government – he was placed under surveillance.

26TH FEBRUARY

'A speaker at a recent recruiting meeting in Dublin declared that the Dublin slums were more unhealthy than the trenches in Flanders. The trenches in Flanders have been the graves of scores of thousands of young Irishmen. A very large proportion of these young Irishmen were born and reared in the slums and tenement houses of Dublin. These same slums are notorious the world over for their disease-breeding unhealthy character. All the world over it is known that the poor of Dublin are housed under conditions worse than those of any civilised people on God's earth.

From out of those slums these poor misguided brothers of ours have been tricked and deluded into giving battle for England – into waging war upon the German nation which does not permit anywhere within its boundaries such slums and fever dens as the majority of Dublin's poor must live in.

If you die of fever, or even of want, because you preferred to face fever and want, rather than sell your soul to the enemies of your class and country, such death is an honourable death, a thousand times more honourable than if you won a VC committing murder at the bidding of your country's enemies.' [James Connolly, *Workers' Republic*, 26 February 1916.]

27TH FEBRUARY

Sometimes you can be too smart for your own good – a notion which probably never occurred to one John Delahunt when he decided to turn police informer.

On the night of 27 February 1841 somebody murdered an Italian organ-grinder named Domenico Garlibrado and dumped his body at the entrance gate of Rathfarnham Castle (the Roman-styled triumphal arch which still stands, though rather forlornly, at the side of Braemor Road).

Two Rathfarnham people, a man and wife, were arrested, charged and promptly put on trial. The trial collapsed when the principal witness, Patrick Byrne, was arrested in court for perjury. Delahunt, the second informant, was not produced at the trial.

Just before Christmas the still-warm body of a boy, Thomas Maguire, was found in Pembroke Lane. Delahunt told the police that he had seen the murder and blamed the boy's mother.

It soon became obvious that Delahunt knew more than his prayers and after a mass of damning evidence was obtained, largely from his relatives, he was put on trial. Found guilty, he admitted the murder of Maguire, but denied the murder of Garlibardo. Most people, however, believed that he was guilty of both murders – his motive being the reward for giving evidence leading to a conviction.

28TH FEBRUARY

In order to combat the Fenians the Habeus Corpus Act was suspended in Ireland in 1865 and the leaders were seized and imprisoned without trial. Dr. Robert MacDonnell, medical superintendent in Mountjoy Prison, was appalled that these prisoners were submitted to a discipline more severe in some respects than a convict. 'The prisoners were confined in cells little more than six feet square, their meals were handed to them through a hole in the floor, they were kept rigidly alone, except when at religious services and at exercise.' Reporting to the Governor of the prison on 28 February 1867 Dr. MacDonnell wrote: 'Thomas Burke is showing undoubted symptoms of insanity; Finnegan has lately given way to one of those paroxysms brought on by long confinement; Sweeny is very unsettled in his mind. Barry (latterly discharged) was considered unfit, from his mental state, to go away from the prison without some one in charge of him. I have not the slightest doubt that the prolonged confinement and severe disciple are the cause of this. It would be a very grave matter if any of these untried prisoners should commit suicide.'

Too good to leave out is this notice from the *Freeman's Journal* of 28 February 1764: 'A few Days ago, as a poor Man of about 70 Years of Age was passing along New-street, he was set upon by a Cow, who took him upon her Horns and tossed him a considerable Distance off, by which he was greatly Hurt. – 'Tis remarkable that the same Man, a few Years ago, was attacked on Ormond-Bridge by an overdrove Bullock, who taking him upon his Horns tossed him into the Liffy, where he would have been drowned but for some People who went to his Assistance.'

29TH FEBRUARY

Even today cholera can be fatal, back in the mid-19th century there were regular outbreaks in the city. This report from 29 February 1832 shows some of the steps being taken to prevent an outbreak in Dublin: 'The corporation of Dublin is selling off its dung-heaps at half price to the neighbouring farmers to ensure their speedy removal, and the Boards of Health are everywhere embroiled in quarrels with the poor cotters, whose wealth and pride grows all the year round with their little dung-hill, treasured for the potato crop generally in the most ill-judged situation, beside the cabin door. These they cannot afford to part with, and have not yet learned to dread as dangerous to health, though the continued typhus fever of the country is in many cases traced to their proximity, by the first medical authorities. The fear of cholera as contagious is daily increasing in this city under the active advocacy of some medical jobbers, who are labouring unremittingly to create a panic. They have seized on the *Dublin Evening Post* as one organ of terror, and through it denounce all other journals that endeavour to keep up the spirits and maintain the health of the citizens.' [*The Times.*] Cholera broke out in the city in April and cases continued until December.

Chapter Three

March

1st March

On Friday, 1 March 1754, Thomas Sheridan, actor/manager of Smock Alley Theatre, called the cast of *Mahomet, The Impostor* together to discuss the second performance of the play. The first had been marred by an incident in which the audience demanded that a section, which they deemed politically apt ('To guard your rights, shall, for a grasp of ore,/Or paltry office, sell them to the foe'), be repeated. The country was deeply divided over the King's decision that he had power over surplus Irish moneys. Sheridan was determined that there would be no repetition and delivered a strong speech against it. The effect was undermined when he told the actor involved, West Digges, that it was up to him whether he repeated the words or not.

The following night Digges refused to repeat the words and, stepping out of character, announced that for 'private reasons' he could not do so, because 'his Compliance would be greatly injurious to him.'

The audience began calling for Sheridan to appear but he refused and left for home. After waiting for Sheridan for an hour the audience had had enough – they proceeded to demolish the theatre in a riot lasting six hours until 2am.

2nd March

The Dublin Artisan's Company provided a number of cottages in the Liberties, and held a yearly competition to find the best maintained. At the prize-giving on Friday, 2 March 1883, Lady Brabazon spoke at some length to the entrants: 'You are aware that the prizes are given for neatness and cleanliness and for window gardening, but perhaps you are not equally cognisant of the fact that the prizes are, indirectly, rewards for temperance and no prize can be given in a cottage where a person of intemperate habits resides. In some cases this rule may seem hard, and yet on the whole, I trust it may commend itself to you, for as long as intemperance continues to be so frightfully prevalent, it is clearly the duty of those who see the evil of it to endeavour to arrest its progress and to foster habits of temperance. Women could make their homes so attractive that drinking-bars shall be deserted.'

Obviously a woman with a mind like a steel trap or was she? 'Providence has decreed that an equal amount of wealth is not given to all. The rich cannot do without the poor and it has yet to be proved that the poor can do without the rich.'

3RD MARCH

On Monday, 3 March 1766, four pirates (Peter M'Kinlie, George Gidley, Richard St. Quintin, and Andrea Zekerman) were executed at Baggotrath Castle, Baggot Street, for piracy and murder on the high seas.

Their crimes were the murder of the crew of the *Sandwich* and the theft of its valuables – Spanish milled dollars, ingots of gold, jewels, and a quantity of gold dust.

The following Wednesday they bodies were hung in chains – two of them near Macarrell's-wharf, on the South-wall (the top of Thorncastle Street); and the other two about the middle of the Piles, below the Pigeon-house (around the Half Moon Battery).

About a month later M'Kinley's body fell from the gibbet and the *Faulkner's Journal* (29 March, 1767) reported that the gruesome sight was proving too much for Dubliners. 'The two pirates, Peter M'Kinley and George Gidley; who hang in chains on the South Wall for the murder of Captain Coghlan, &c., being very disagreeable to the citizens who walk there for amusement and health, are immediately to be put on Dalkey Island.'

Within a few days the two bodies were removed by sea to the Muglins, near Dalkey Island, where a gibbet had been specially erected to receive them. Richard St Quintin and Andrea Zekerman were left where they were.

4TH MARCH

Two centuries ago it didn't take much to get your neck stretched: 'Joseph Henegan, a young lad, about 24 years of age, was executed at the front of the New Gaol, pursuant to his sentence, for being concerned with others in burglariously entering the house of a shoemaker in Grafton-street, and feloniously taking leather from thence. His appearance was rather decent, and he conducted himself suitable to his unhappy situation. At the place of execution, the High Sheriffs, Kinsley and Cash, in the mildest terms, urged him to make discoveries of his accomplices for the good of society, and as some atonement to GOD for his offences; but he refused, though it appeared from his manner, he could have done so, saying 'he did not like to have their deaths upon him.' This unfortunate sufferer [declared] at his last moments, that he did not take the leather out of the house, the crime of which he was convicted; but the question being put to him 'Did he not receive, and offer it to sale, knowing it to have been a robbery?' He answered in the affirmative. Henegan had been in the Penitentiary five years ago, and was pardoned, on his enlisting; he went a recruit to England, but there left the army, and returned to his former evil ways.' [*Freeman's Journal*, 4 March 1800.]

5TH MARCH

No-one can be sure whether Buck Whalley played handball against the walls of Jerusalem – it's not impossible but is more likely to have been tacked onto the tale on his return.

But visit Jerusalem he most certainly did – now all he had to do was prove it and collect his winnings in Dublin. Buck may have been a gambler but he wasn't taking any chances on his word being accepted. He headed straight for the Convent of St. Mary and obtained a document from the Superior.

'I, the undersigned Guardian of this Convent of St. Mary, certify to all and singular who may read these presents, that Messrs. Thomas Whaley and Hugh Moore have, on two occasions, been present and resided in this City of Nazareth for the space of three days, in witness whereof-

Given in the sd. City of Nazareth,

5th March 1789.

Brother Archangel of Entraigues, Guardian and Superior.'

The Brother may have erroneously thought that Buck had some interest in religion, for the latter wrote: 'I really was pleased at the opinion this worthy man entertained of us; and felt a little inward shame, from a consciousness of demerit in this respect.'

6TH MARCH

The Dublin correspondent of *The Times* viewed the Fenians on 6 March 1867 in Dublin Castle Yard after their abortive uprising: 'Anything more miserable and contemptible than the appearance of those dwarfish, ill-clad, and starved looking wretches I never saw. They seemed to be the very dregs of the lowest operative class, such as journeymen tailors, shoemakers, tinkers, and persons with no employment, like the roughs who haunt fairs and races. Compared with the police and military, they were like pigmies beside giants; and the idea that any Government with such defenders could be overthrown by such assailants appeared absurd. They did not seem to be worth any sort of serious punishment – even supporting them in gaol would be a waste of the public resources. In all 108 prisoners were marched into Dublin today from Tallaght. They were first brought to the Upper Castle-yard, where they were detained until the police could make the necessary preparations for their reception. The prisoners were divided into three parties for conveyance respectively to the Mountjoy, Richmond Bridewell and Kilmainham Prisoners. They were marched two and two, police constables being placed at either side of each paid, in front a party of cavalry police, then a troop of the Scots Greys, and the line was closed by a party of the same regiment.' Half a century later the 'pigmies' had their day.

7TH MARCH

The Earl of Mayo, Seanad Éireann, speaking on 7 March 1924, returned [see 25 January] to conditions for travellers at Dun Laoghaire: 'Since I spoke last something has been done, and I went down yesterday in my motor to see what had been done. There has been erected what may be described as a cow-shed, or, rather, a shed that you would not put up for bullocks to protect them against the stormy winds that blow in our beloved country. I may say in passing that it was a most lovely day, without a breath of wind on the sea. You could hardly imagine that Kingstown Pier could be such a disagreeable place on a winter's morning. There is at the other end what I might describe as a calf-shed. When you put up a shed for calves you put up a shelter at the end of it, and that shelter is there. I do not think it is for passengers; I believe it is for the porters and the other officials, because I am told by my wife that she was ushered into the shed I have described, and not into this shed. That is a very nice corner to shelter in. There are no seats anywhere.'

8TH MARCH

The price of food in Dublin has always been of critical importance – there are accounts of riots when prices went through the roof in olden times. But if you could control the market, you could manipulate the price and there were those who took full advantage of any opportunity of buying up produce before it reached the city.

The Dublin Intelligence of 8 March 1709 reported on an attempt by the Lord Mayor [Sir William Fownes] to put a stop to the practice: 'Whereas complaints have been made to me that there are a sort of people called Sky-Farmers, who in truth are no other than forestallers of the corn intended to be brought to the market; who wait their opportunity at the avenues to the town and there contract for and buy up such corn under pretence of being employed by several persons in the city as servants. These are, therefore, to require all toll-gatherers, taking to their assistance the neighbouring constables, all such forestallers and all other forestallers of fish, fowl, etc. and bring them before me to be punished according to law.'

9TH MARCH

9 March

'At Night [9 March 1765] the Master of the Corporation of Bakers, attended by a Party of the Main Guard, went to the House of Mr. Christopher Moore, Publican in Cook-street, and by Virtue of the Lord Mayor's Warrant for that Purpose, there seized a Chest belonging to an Assembly of Journeymen Bakers, containing near £20 in Cash, which had been collected towards supporting unlawful Combinations against their Masters.

About nine o'Clock at Night, at some Citizens were sitting in a public House in Bridge-street, a Sharper came in under a Pretence of making a Collection for to Bury a poor Person that lay dead in an Alley in Church-street, when one of the Company took from him a Glove in which he had the Money, and desired he might shew him where the Corpse lay, which he readily agreed to, but when he came to the Place with him, the Sharper gave him the Slip, and left the Money, being 1s 9.d farth the Fruits of his Night's imposition, which was next Morning given to the Poor of St. Audoen's Parish.' [The Public Register: or Freeman's Journal.]

10TH MARCH

'Henry St. March 10 1830. An old woman was brought before the magistrates after all night in the watch house under the following circumstances, it appeared that the unfortunate woman was carrying on the preceding evening a small box from the house of her late master who was a doctor from Queen St. where he lodged to Bolton St. to which he was removing. The poor woman had the misfortune to go into a public house for some whiskey. The small box caught the eyes of some anti-resurrectionists when an alarm was immediately given. The box was opened and the skeleton of a child was found in it. This was confirmation 'strong as Holy Writ' to the mob that the old woman was not only a sack-'em-up herself but the mother and grandmother of a family of Resurrectionists and dearly she paid for the supposition for she was not only dragged out of the house but followed by two or three hundred persons pelting her with mud and otherwise ill-using her until the police arrived and for protection placed her in the watch house. It appeared on enquiry yesterday that the skeleton was 30 years in the possession of its owner who had it for scientific purposes and that the ill-treated woman had not known the contents of the box.'

11TH MARCH

It was just past one o'clock on the afternoon of 11 March 1597 when the city of Dublin experienced one of its greatest ever calamities. Down at 'The Crane', at the bottom of Winetavern Street, Stephen Sedgrave was overseeing the unloading of 144 barrels onto the quayside.

Because of a shortage of willing workers the barrels piled up. Normally it wouldn't have been a problem, but these barrels contained gunpowder. Just as the last of the barrels was lifted onto the quayside there was a huge explosion which devastated the area and severely damaged nearly a quarter of the city. An estimated 126 people died, beside 'sondrie headles bodies and heades with out bodies that were found and not knowne.'

Children had been seen playing with the barrels but it was considered most likely that the cause was a spark from a horse's foot striking the hard ground. Every catastrophe requires a scapegoat and John Alen, responsible for moving the barrels to a store, took the blame. He had skived off to 'drink a pot of ale at the house of Alderman Nicholas Barran' just before the big bang. Almost before the dust settled John Alen was on his way to imprisonment in Dublin Castle.

12TH MARCH

The Dublin Weekly Journal of 12 March 1726 carried a number of interesting, if improbably, advertisements. Among them was one for John Vennac Dufour: 'a Practitioner of Chyrurgery upwards of 30 years' which went on to state that he was: 'Famous for curing of Ruptures or broken bellies without incision. The many that has been Cured by him causes this Publication. He also cures the Venerial Distemper, without salvation or confinement with great expedition and safety to the Patient, without loss of time. He is to be spoke with at his House in Aunger's Street.'

And then there was: 'Samuel Steel Surgeon and Operator at the Golden Tooth on Ormond Key opposite the Custom House, Dublin, whose experience in drawing Teeth is very well known. He gives ease to the Thoth Ach and often perfectly cures them with out Drawing, cleans Teeth, be they never so foul, with Directions how to preserve them. He makes artificial Teeth so neat, that they cannot be discovered from natural ones and as useful to eat with as others for by a New Experiment they may be worn several Years without being taken out of the Mouth nor is it any trouble to the Person that has them and much sweeter and cleaner than the former method of tying them with silk strings.'

13TH MARCH

Dublin City Council Alderman Alfred 'Alfie' Byrne died on 13 March 1956. He was born in 1882 at Seville Place, Dublin. His father Tom Byrne was elected a city Councillor in 1901 for the North Dock Ward and was returned in every election until 1911, when Alfie was elected in his place. By then, Alfie Byrne was the landlord of the Vernon Bar, 37 Talbot Street. Byrne continued to serve as a City Councillor for the next 45 years until his death. He was MP for Dublin from 1915 to 1918. In 1922 he was returned as a TD, polling over 18,000 votes as an Independent candidate. He continued as a TD until 1928, was a member of Seanad Éireann from 1928 to 1932 and was again a TD from 1932 until his death. In 1930 he was elected Lord Mayor and re-elected every year until 1939 when he retired. He was again elected Lord Mayor for one term, 1954-55. From 1925 to 1956 he lived at various addresses in Rathmines.

A signed postcard from 'Alfie, Lord Mayor.'

14TH MARCH

Six Sinn Fein prisoners were hanged in pairs at intervals from 6am in Mountjoy Jail on Monday, 14 March 1921. Among them was Patrick Moran, 33, who had mistakenly believed that the British legal system would not kill an innocent man. Moran, Captain of D Company 2nd Battalion IRA, had fought in Jacob's in 1916 and had been imprisoned in Britain. A court-martial found him guilty of the murder of Lieutenant Peter Aimes at 38 Upper Mount Street on 'Bloody Sunday' (21 November 1921).

However, Moran's whereabouts on the day made it almost impossible that he could have done it. He had attended 8am mass in Blackrock, been seen by DMP Sergeant Connolly in Blackrock at 9am, and was, according to his landlady, eating breakfast at 9.30am. The killing had occurred at 9.30am.

So sure was Moran of his innocence that he turned down the chance to take part in an escape – on 14 February Ernie O'Malley, Frank Teeling and Moran's replacement, Simon Donnelly, walked out of the jail. His court-martial, the day after the escape, was a forgone conclusion. The remains of Patrick Moran and eight other Sinn Fein prisoners executed by the British were given State funerals and reburied in Glasnevin Cemetery in 2001.

15TH MARCH

When Dublin Corporation councillors met on the evening of 15 March 1915 there was one item on the agenda that was guaranteed to cause a ruckus – the removal of Kuno Meyer from the roll of the Freemen of Dublin.

Mayor, who was German, was a much-respected Celtic scholar who had devoted much of his life to early Irish literature. He had received the Freedom of Dublin in 1911 – Cork followed suit in 1912.

And the reason for deleting his name? Meyer had left Germany to lecture in the USA (then neutral) and was reported to have made speeches promising Ireland a 'separate and independent government' if the Irish helped Germany win the war.

The meeting was, according to reports, long and noisy. The Irish Parliamentary Party, which supported Britain in the war, took a very dim view. Councillor William T. Cosgrave, Sinn Fein, argued that it was disgraceful to remove a scholar 'who loved our country and served her soul.'

The decision to strip him of the Freedom of the City was passed by 30 votes to 16. The good news was that Kuno Meyer was restored to the Roll of Freemen in 1920 – Sinn Fein now having a majority. The bad news was that he had died the previous year.

16TH MARCH

'Patrick Murphy, 3 Hanover street, a dairyman aged 40 years, was charged by his wife with having assaulted her at Francis Street. The woman stated that her husband attacked her, knocked her down and dragged her by the hair. Mr. Hamill, for the defendant, asked that a cross charge should be entered against the woman. Her husband had given her £1 the previous night and she had spent it all with the exception of 3s. When he came home to his dinner he heard she was at a public house and went to ask if she had his dinner. She flung her shawl off and attacked him several times. Murphy was examined and said when he went to find his wife he found her drunk. She attacked him and would not let him go so that eventually he had to catch her by the hair and shove her away. Mr. Byrne sentenced her to two months imprisonment and dismissed the charge against the husband. He said that an industrious, hard-working man was to be pitied when dealing with a drunken wife, who made his home miserable and spent all his earnings in the public house.' [*The Irish Times*, 16 March 1899.]

17TH MARCH

Eliphal Dobson, author of the *Dublin Scuffle*, lived in Dundrum Castle and was recalled in Gilbert's *History of Dublin*:

'At the *Stationers' Arms*, in [No. 7] Castle Street, in the reign of James II. was the shop of Eliphal Dobson, the most wealthy Dublin booksellers and publisher of his day. "Eliphal Dobson's wooden leg", says Dunton, "startled me with the creaking of it, for I took it for the crepitus ossium [the crackling sound produced by the rubbing together of fragments of fractured bone] which I have heard some of our physicians speak of. He values no man for his starched looks or supercilious gravity, or for being a Churchman, Presbyterian, Independent &c., provided he is sound in the main points wherein all good men are agreed."

On his death, in 1719-20, he left £10 to T.C.D. and "one of the best folio bibles printed by me." Alderman Dobson was buried on 17 March in St. Werburgh's.

18TH MARCH

Any time a prisoner escapes from jail there is much speculation about the safety of the general populace – imagine then how gripped the city was by mass escape from Kilmainham in 1786. *The Hibernian Magazine* reported that, on 18 March: 'Fourteen prisoners escaped from the jail at Kilmainham. The felons, including highwaymen and two under sentence of death, had made a hole in the wall near the entrance to the prison underneath a window at which relatives and friends were allowed to talk to them and to pass them food. Two women were observed there the best part of the day sitting at the window but their design was really to cover the work of the prisoners scraping away at the walls.'

Two days later, 12 were still on the run, but 'through the activity of Mr. McKinley, the Gaoler of Kilmainham, two of the felons were retaken and conducted to their former dwelling.

Within a very short time the authorities had found their scapegoats: 'The two sentinels through whose neglect the felons made their escape from the Gaol of Kilmainham this day received five hundred lashes each in the Barracks.'

19TH MARCH

The first electric tram from Dollymount arrived at Nelson's Pillar on the morning of Saturday, 19 March, 1898. Aboard was a reporter from the *Evening Telegraph*. 'I was a privileged passenger on the first electric car to enter the centre of Dublin City. The officials of the Tramway Company had kept the fact very quiet that they intended to make their informal trial trip today before ordinary people were about but having got the necessary hint I was on the ground in good time and had the distinction of being the only unofficial passenger on the first electric car that was ever electrically propelled into O'Connell Street.

'We passed under the lee of Nelson at 7.10 am exactly and negotiated the intricate and difficult wires at the turn with the greatest ease and success, much to the delight evidently of the experts on board. Early as the hour was there was quite a crowd on the ground, principally of the early population of citizens and citizenesses on their way to work with the inevitable sprinkling of slightly sarcastic Jehus and more or less judicially critical gendarmes. The experiment was most successful and gives every promise that early next week the electric service on this line will be in full working order from the Pillar to the Bull.'

20TH MARCH

With friends like this – who needs enemies – as Jonah Barrington once found out.

At 7am on 20 March [c. 1780] he travelled to Donnybrook to duel with Richard Daly. Daly had fought 16 duels in three years – three with swords and 13 with pistols. Remarkably he, and his opponents, had escaped serious injury.

Barrington had no pistols so he and his second, Richard Crosby, had spent the previous night constructing a pair from 'old locks, stocks and barrels. At Donnybrook Daly's second, Jack Patterson, a nephew of the Chief Justice, approached Crosby explained that it was all a mistake, and asked that the two shake hands.

Barrington was in favour but Crosby would have none of it. Whipping out a duelling rule book, he pointed to rule No. 7 – 'No apology can be received after the parties meet, without a fire.'

Taking up their positions Barrington lost no time in pressing the trigger and Daly staggered back, put his hand to his chest, and cried 'I'm hit, sir.' Luckily, the ball had not penetrated but had driven part of a broach slightly into his breast-bone.

Barrington enquired why the duel had taken place. This time the rule book noted: 'If a party challenged accepts the challenge without asking the reason of it, the challenger is never bound to divulge it afterwards.'

21ST MARCH

At 8am on 21 March 1829 the Duke of Wellington, 60, Prime Minister and leader of the Tory Party, fought a duel with the Earl of Winchilsea at Battersea, London.

George Finch-Hatton, 38, was the 9th Earl of Winchilsea. A political firebrand and a staunch defender of the Protestant party, Winchilsea was also a vocal critic of O'Connell and was especially hostile to Catholic emancipation.

'My differences with Lord Winchilsea cannot be regarded as a private quarrel,' said Wellington. The reason for the duel was the passing of Catholic Emancipation – Wellington, until then opposed to concessions to Catholics, had pushed it through for reasons of state. He argued that to be described as having 'disgraceful and criminal' motives was an offence to him as a statesman.

The Dubliner was not the most prepared duellist of the day – he had to borrow a brace of pistols from his second, Sir Henry Fielding. The Saturday morning duel itself was a strange event. Wellington fired deliberately wide as he saw that Winchilsea was holding his gun at his side – his opponent then fired into the air, came forward and offered an apology, which was immediately accepted by Wellington.

22ND MARCH

'They have here [Dean Swift's Hospital for the Insane – St. Patrick's Hospital] provided modern asylum accommodation of the highest order so that the deportation of Irish patients to Scotch and English asylums in no sense superior to St. Patrick's should be discouraged and checked. The buildings are very extensive and contain drawing rooms, dayrooms, billiard-room &c. Six corridors run through the building, each 345 feet long and 14 feet wide, and provide spacious exercising rooms in severe weather. A liberal and varied dietary is provided, and no effort is spared to make the lot of the inmates as easy as possible. They are given carriage drives when required, are sent to places of amusement under the care of nurses and attendants, and are supplied with literature of various descriptions. Entertainments, both indoor and outdoor, are frequently given in the institution, and regard is always had to that privacy which the friends of the mentally ill appreciate. The Government Inspectors of Lunatics, in their latest reports speak in terms of the highest praise of the work carried on by the Governors of the hospital.' [*The Irish Times*, 22 March 1902.]

23RD MARCH

By his legs ye shall know him! 'Whereas one William Hughburn alias Moran, a Cobler by his Calling and formerly kept a Coblers-stall under Mr. Lion's in Fishamble-street, and likewise under Mr. Grime's at the Cross-Keys in Smithfield; but of late a Hackney-Coachman to the Widow Garnet on the Inn's Dublin, a middle size young Man, with thin black Hair, or a Wig, his Legs goes outwards, and his left Knee comes into his right Ham, and is also bandy Leg'd. 'Tis said now goes about the Country with a Wooden Leg having his own up; did on the 23d of March 1708-9; on the Inn's aforesaid, barbarously Murder one Henry Mac-Cullagh of the same City Brewer, first by striking him with a Coach Hammer, and afterward by striking him with a Gimlet through his Scull into the Brains : Whoever secures the said Hughburn, so that he may be brought to Justice, and gives Notice thereof to Patrick Mac-Cullagh, Gardner, at the Cherry Tree in Drumcondra-Lane, shall receive from him a Guinea Reward, and Reasonable Charges.' (*Dublin Intelligence*, 1710)

24TH MARCH

On Palm Sunday, 24 March 1689, King James made his entry into Dublin at St. James's Gate: 'And at his first entry into the liberty of the city, there was a stage built, covered with tapestry, and thereon two playing on Welsh harps; and below a great number of friars with a large cross, singing; and about 40 oyster-wenches, poultry and herb women, in white, dancing, who thence ran along to the castle by his side, here and there strewing flowers. ... At the utmost limits he was met by the Lord Mayor, aldermen, common council, master wardens, and brethren of the several companies, in their formalities, the King and herald-at-arms, pursuivants, and servants of the household, and there received the sword of state (which he gave to Tyrconnell, who carried it before him through the city), and the sword and keys of the city, and there had a speech made to welcome him to that loyal city and people, by Counsellor Dillon. And being come thus to the castle the King alighted from his horse.

And from thence he was conducted into the chapel there where Te Deum was sung for his happy arrival; and thence he retired into an apartment prepared in a new house built before in the castle by Tyrconnell, and there dined and refreshed himself.'

25TH MARCH

The Corporation of Barbers & Chirurgeons [physicians or surgeons trained through apprenticeship] Appothocaries [pharmacists] & Perukemakers set down a set of rules in 1757 to ensure that workers gave their all: 'Resolved that and Master Barber or Perukemaker [wigs] that shall employ and Journeyman, who between the 29th day of September and 25th Day or March in each year, shall refuse to work at said Trade from the hour of Six o Clock in the Morning untill nine at night, and who shall be from the 25th day of March to the 29th day of Sepr. in Each year, refuse to work at said Trade from Six o Clock in the Morning (being the usual and accustomed Hours of working the said Trade) Shall for every Such offence forfeit and Pay the sum of one pounds nineteen Shillings & Eleven pence.

Resolved That all Journeymen that are longer Employed than the usuall Time of working Shall be Constantly Paid for such Extraordinary Hours the Same In Proportion as for the Day'. And workers today think they have it hard!

26TH MARCH

The Freeman's Journal reported on the capture of a group of bandits on 26 March 1800. 'The officers of the Peace-establishment, under the direction of the Superintendant Magistrate, apprehended Neill Carr, James Lane, and William Shea, who are charged with having been of the party that robbed the houses of Dean Carleton, at Coolock, and Mr. Smith's, of Golden-bridge, a few nights since. They were brought before the Superintendant Magistrate, where, after undergoing a strict examination, were committed to prison.

William Shea is a gardener and a fiddler; Neill Carr is also a gardener; James Lane says he is a sawyer [he sawed wood!]. Shea . . . was Captain of the gang, and on him, we hear, a pair of small clothes of Mr. Smith's were identified. These offenders with others their confederates, are supposed to be the banditti that likewise robbed the house of Mr. Evan's and Mr. Meares, at the north side of the country, and of Mr. Wilkinson's steward, at Terenure, near Templeogue. The prisoner Lane, it seems, bears a mark on his side of a shot he received from Dean Carleton when attacking his house. The companion of these desperadoes who was taken up out of the canal on Sunday morning, it is stated, was named John Quinn, who was shot by one of his accomplices the night before, in the house of Mr. Smith, thro' mistake.'

27TH MARCH

Theobald Wolfe Tone, in France, was working hard on his plans for the invasion of 1798. His Diary records: 'First, as to Dublin, I did not expect, with the proposed force, that much could be done there at first; that its garrison was always at least 5,000 strong, and that the Government, taking advantage of the momentary success of the coalesced despots, had disarmed the people, taken their cannon, and passed the gunpowder and convention bills ... whose nature and operation I explained to him; that, however, if the landing were once effected, one of two things would happen, either the Government would retain the garrison for their security, in which case there would be 5,000 men idle on the part of the enemy, or they would march them off to oppose us, in which case the people would rise and seize the capital; and, if they preferred the first measure, which I thought most likely, whenever we were strong enough to march southward, if we were, as I had no doubt we should be, superior in the field, we could starve Dublin in a week, without striking a blow.'

28TH MARCH

The Battle of Hlobane against a Zulu force on 28 March 1879 was a total disaster as far as the British were concerned – 15 officers and 200 soldiers dead. For Dalkey's William Knox Leet, however, it was a good day – he not only survived, he got himself a Victoria Cross as well.

As the British forces retreated Leet and two others found themselves separated from the main body as they made their way down a mountain side. Leet and Lieutenant Dunscombe were on horseback, Lieutenant Smith was on foot.

Dunscombe was shot about half way down and Lieutenant Smith had run out of steam. He later wrote: 'I was then quite exhausted and intended to sit down and give up all chance of saving my life, as the Zulus were within a few yards of me. But Major Leet persisted in waiting for me, dragging me up behind him on the horse, which was also greatly exhausted. By good luck, he escaped from the bullets and assegais of the Zulus. Had it not been for Major Leet, nothing could have saved me'

The following day Major Leet took part in the battle of Kambula – this time the result went the other way, over 1,000 Zulus died in a four-hour battle.

29TH MARCH

Almanacs generally use a broad brush so when *Predictions for the Year 1708* by Isaac Bickerstaff appeared in early 1708, readers were surprised to find an entry foretelling the death 'by a raging fever' of the famous astrologer John Partridge. Bickerstaff predicted that Partridge would die at exactly 11pm on 29 March of that year.

Almost immediately Partridge issued a reply, claiming that Bickerstaff was nothing but a fraud. 'His whole Design was nothing but Deceit,/The End of March will plainly show the Cheat,' Partridge wrote.

Which of the predictors would be proven right? On the night of 29 March Bickerstaff published an Elegy announcing the death of Partridge. It also told the world that Bickerstaff had visited Partridge on his deathbed where, with his final breath, he had admitted to being a fraud.

A second pamphlet by Bickerstaff apologised for getting the hours wrong – Partridge, it noted, had finally expired at 7.05pm!

Partridge, however, was still alive – but having difficulty convincing people of it. Despite his best efforts, he was totally discredited. Bickerstaff, it later turned out, was none other than Jonathan Swift who was apparently annoyed by Partridge's attacks on the church.

30TH MARCH

'The want of bathing places for all classes in the [Kingstown] Township, from a sanitary point of view alone, is much to be regretted. The former site of the free bathing-place for females is now occupied by the tank of the main drainage board. As regards a bathing-place for the well-to-do, the construction of one, though very desirable from a sanitary point of view alone, seems so involved in questions of finance that it is hardly for me to touch upon it. It may, however, be permissible to point out the strange anomaly of a sea side resort so charmingly situated as Kingstown, without a respectable open sea bathing place, and this in the gangway, so to speak, for the best class of tourists on their landing in Ireland. The fact that we are unfortunately so cut off from the sea shore, in comparison, with other sea-side towns, is the reason why every effort should be made to take advantage in every way of the little open sea coast that in every way of the little open sea coast that is left us.' [J. Byrne Power addressing the Kingstown Commissioners Public Health Meeting, 30 March 1897.]

31ST MARCH

Six bodies were brought out of a Malahide mansion, 'La Mancha' on Wednesday morning, 31 March 1926 after a severe fire. Four member of the McDonnell family – Annie, 58, Joseph, 56, Peter, 53 and Alice, 46 – and two servants – James Clarke and Mary McGowan – had been killed. The blaze was nothing more than an attempt to destroy the evidence.

There were some oddities about the deaths – the women were found together, severely burned; each man was in a separate room and two of their bodies had not been affected by the fire. One man, James Clark, appeared to have been murdered several days before. Later autopsies showed varying amount of arsenic in each of the bodies.

The grim scene proved an attraction for the ghoulish. *The Irish Times* reported: 'Holiday-makers from Dublin flocked into Malahide yesterday, as on Sunday, to see the place where the deaths occurred. They came in hundreds. The Guards had considerable difficulty in preventing them from over-running the place.'

The gardener, Henry McCabe, who had raised the alarm, was later charged and convicted of murder – a verdict which was never accepted by his family. He was hanged in Mountjoy Jail on 9 December 1926.

Chapter Four

April

1ST APRIL

If you've ever wondered where Dublin got its name – the answer provided by *Haydn's Dictionary of Dates* (1852), is suitable for the day that's in it.

'This city, anciently called Ascheled, built AD 140. It obtained its present name form Alpinus, a lord or chieftain among the Irish, whose daughter, Auliana, having been drowned at the ford where Whitworth Bridge is built, he changed the name to Auliana, by Ptolemy called Eblana (afterwards corrupted into Dublana), that she might be had in remembrance. Alpinus is the first chief mentioned in history as having made this place his residence, which he did about AD. 155, when he brought the then rude hill into the form of a town.'

The origins of the original inhabitants of Ireland are equally mangled: 'It seems, however, to be satisfactorily shown that the first colonists were Phoenicians. The Partholoni landed in Ireland about 2035BC. The descent of the Damnonii was made about 1463BC. This was followed by the descent of Heber and Heremon, Milesian princes, from Gailicia, in Spain, who conquered Ireland, and gave to its throne 171 kings. Few of the kings of Ireland, during a thousand years, did more than involve the country in scenes of blood.'

2ND APRIL

The Cottage Home for Children, Tivoli Road, Dun Laoghaire, was reopened on Saturday, 2 April 1949. The orphanage had been closed for a year owing to the difficulty of securing staff, shortage of money, and because it was 'not in keeping with modern requirements for the proper upbringing of children.'

'Miss H. S. Chevenix, tracing the history of the Home, said it was founded in 1879 by Miss Rosa Barrett, as a crèche, where working mothers could leave their children for the day.

However, in the following year she recognised that there was another side of the work that she could cater for, and so established the Home. The Home was not a hospital and the children received individual treatment which was impossible in larger institutions. It catered for children from two weeks old to five years. The Home had entered on a new sphere, that of training young girls desirous of taking up nursery work and at present they had four such trainees.' [*Dun Laoghaire Borough Times*]

In 2005 the Cottage Home is again closed – and the premises are to be sold due to a combination of health and safety issues and the listed status of the building. Children are, however, cared for in two other houses operated by the charity.

3RD APRIL

On 3 April 1562 the 300-year-old south nave of Christ Church collapsed. The foundations, resting on a peat bog moved on the sloping hill-side, and the arched stone roof fell into the church, almost completely destroying the south side wall and part of the body of the Cathedral.

The debris was levelled and floored over – large portions of the ancient tiled floors were discovered during major renovation in 1871. As a result of the fall the tomb of Strongbow was very badly damaged – so much so that, in 1570 it was replaced, most likely with a monument brought by Sir Henry Sidney from Drogheda (the arms on the Strongbow tomb are those of FitzOsbert of Drogheda).

In a history of the Cathedral in 1926, Herbert B. Kennedy, Dean of Christ Church, wrote: 'The half-length figure is probably the original monument of Strongbow's son, broken by the fall of the roof and trimmed by a stone mason. There appears to be much doubt as to the truth of the tradition that accounts for its shape by saying that Strongbow cut his son in two for showing cowardice in battle.'

4TH APRIL

The Guilds of Dublin were not just in charge of merchants and shops, their influence extended as far as street sellers, as a record of 4 April 1696 records: 'That no Hawker shall be admitted to sell anything about the Towne or Citty belonging to the Corporation except as it be such as is lycenced to sell nott above a printed sheet of paper. And Every Brother that doth Imploy any of the said Hawkers shall enter their names in the booke belonging to the Corporacon and shall pay for such Hawker as they Imploy the sume of one shilling per quarter and that none of the said Hawkers shall sell any bound book or horne book primer Catechism Almanac Writting paper penns and Ink & Knives Sizors not any other goods whatsoever that belongeth to any of the ffaculties of the said Corporacon. And if any such Hawker be found to be cryeing or selling such goods as above mentioned & not entred to some Brother of the Corporacon shall Imeadiatly be taken up & punished according to Law.'

Or, to put it another way, any street seller you employed was only allowed to sell those items which you, as a Guild Member, were permitted to sell.

5TH APRIL

'Zozimus' was buried in a pauper's grave in Glasnevin Cemetery on 5 April 1846.

The Finding of Moses by Michael 'Zozimus' Moran.

> *In Aygypt's land, contagious to the Nile,*
> *The early Pharaoh's daughter went to bathe in style.*
> *She took a dip, and coming in to land,*

For to dry her Royal pelt she ran along the strand.
A bulrush tripped her, whereupon she saw
The little babby Moses in a wad of straw.
She picked him up and said in accent mild
Tarranation Jayzus girls, which iv yiz owns the child

She took him up and she gave a little grin
For she and Moses were standing in their skin,
'Bejayzus now' says she 'It was someone very rude
Left a little baby by the river in his nude.'
She took him to the Pharaoh sitting on the throne,
'Da,' says she, 'Will you give the boy a home?'
'Bedad,' says he, 'Sure I've often brought in worse.
Go my darlin' daughter and get the child a nurse.'

They sent a bellman to the Market Square
To see if he could find a skivvy there.
But the only young one that the man could find.
Was the very same young one that left the child behind.
She came up to Pharaoh, a stranger, mareyah,
Never lettin' on that she was the babby's ma.
And so young Moses got his mammy back
Shows that coincidence is enough to crack.

6TH APRIL

At 9.30pm on Saturday, 6 April 1861, the No. 7 horse-drawn bus had just pulled up at Portobello Bridge to let two passengers off. It was a very wet night and, as the bus began to move off towards town, the horses moved backwards, breaking through the barrier. The bus, horses, six passengers and the driver, Patrick Hardy, plunged into the lock. Only the conductor, Patrick Costello, who had been attempting to hold the horses at the front, remained on the bridge.

Police Constable Gaffney rescued the driver but for the occupants of the bus there was to be no rescue. The water was 10 feet deep (the lock itself was 25 feet deep) and it took some time for the lock to be emptied. Constable Gaffney and Private Smith of the 4th Light Dragoons climbed down a ladder and broke through the roof of the bus with hatchets. It was to no avail, all six people were already dead.

At the inquest it was found that the barrier was completely rotten below ground, according to one witness it 'yielded like straw.' The common belief that the lock had been deliberately flooded in a vain attempt to float the bus was found to be incorrect.

7TH APRIL

During the month of March 1836 there were three unsuccessful attempts to blow up the statue of King William on Dame Street. They must have been trial runs for the night of Thursday, 7 April: 'at a few minutes past twelve o'clock, a light appeared

Above: *The Rathmines tram and other horse-drawn vehicles at St. Stephen's Green.*

Right: *The equestrian statue of King William – a constant focal point for trouble.*

suddenly on the northern side of the statue, and immediately afterwards the figure of
the King was blown several feet into the air with a deadening explosion, extinguishing
the lamps in College Green and its vicinity. The figure fell at a considerable distance
from the pedestal in the direction of Church-lane; its legs and arms were broken, and
its head completely defaced by the fall; the horse was also injured and shattered in
several places. The mutilated figure was next day placed in a cart and conveyed to
College-street police-office, where it was deposited in the hall while an investigation
was held on a careful examination of the riderless horse a hole was found bored in its
back, between the right hip and the saddle skirt; and as there was no appearance of
gunpowder having been placed in its body, it concluded that fulminating silver had
been employed.' The King was back on his pedestal by the middle of the following
year.

8th April

On 8 April 1834 one of the great chancers of his time, Sir Jonah Barrington, breathed
his last at Versailles. After a lifetime of extravagance he had departed Dublin in 1815
– taking with him the silver dinner services of many of his friends, which he had
borrowed for a 'farewell dinner.' Even though he was gone from the country, he continued to act as a judge in the High Court of the Admiralty – and just couldn't stop
himself dipping into the till. In 1830 a Select Committee of the House of Commons
was set up to examine the question of missing money – the trail led to Barrington
and he was asked to appear before it. Pleading ill-health and a poor memory (he
wrote: 'I have not now the most remote Recollection of the Circumstance you mention; it is above Fifteen Years Age (closing 70) and much Thought have blunted my
Recollection of numerous Events.'), Barrington declined, and continued to work on
his autobiography – which, if sometimes wildly inaccurate, proves that he had all his
marbles about him at the time. Later that year, by an address from both Houses of
Parliament, he was removed from the Bench, 'in consequence of well-proven mis-
appropriation of public moneys.'

9th April

The minutes of the Royal Hospital, Kilmainham, for 9 April 1699 record: 'The committee having considered the necessitous condition of Rose Reynor, lately discharged
out of the hospital as being a papist, and it appearing she was a laborious servant
there as one of the nurses and her husband having been a protestant and a trumpet
in the army and lost a son in his present majesty's service, they recommend her case
to the consideration of the Governor and in regard there are several nasty and bed-
ridden men in the hospital who the committee think may be most fitly placed by
themselves at one end of the upper gallery in No (1) and (2) that will need particular
looking after, and the said Rose Reynor being willing to undertake the same at the
allowance of 40s. a year instead of £6.10 allowed to other nurses, the committee do
recommend the same to the consideration of the governor.

10 APRIL

Issued nearly a month previously, it took until 10 April 1764 for Lord Mayor William Forbes' command to be printed:- 'Whereas the Pavements of this City are in general in a ruinous condition, and as there cannot be a better Season of the Year for repairing the same than the present, I do thereby give the several inhabitants thereof this public Notice, that I expect they will immediately cause their several Pavements to be repaired, and to deem this Notice equal to a Summons left at their respective Houses, and not lay me under the necessity of compelling them thereto, which the Duty of my Office requires. And as great Irregularities are daily committed in this City, by many Persons causing their Pavements to be raised higher than their Neighbours, which is attended with great Inconvenience, and which I hereby particularly forbid under the Penalty of having them dug up, and obliging such Persons immediately to repair the same, as I am determined to have all the Pavements in this City carried on in a regular Manner, with a proper Level to convey the Water from the Channel of each Street to the Common Share made for that Purpose, which will be the Means of Preserving the Pavements, and keeping the Streets clean.' [*Public Register or Freemans Journal*]

11TH APRIL

An outraged Cowkeepers' Association delegation attended the Monthly Meeting of the Kingstown Commissioners on 11 April 1893. At a previous meeting Comm. Findlater said the average dairy-yards of the Township were in bad condition 'it would require the pen of a Dickens to realize the state of affairs in the matter of filth.' Comm. Scott compared conditions to those he had seen in China and India. The Cowkeepers' Association stoutly defended their premises: 'The dairy-yards can bear favourable comparison with any in the kingdom. Is it not a perversion of all reasons and common-sense to condemn the average dairy-yards of the Township from a visit paid to nine of them, there being a total of 65 dairy-yards in the Township? The Registration Books of the owners of eight out of the nine yards in questions, in which Registration Books the Dairy Inspector makes his periodical report on the state of the yards, and we challenge Mr. Findlater to tell the public, if, in each case, there is not a favourable record extending for over a year; if, on the occasion of each visit during that period, the Dairy Inspector did not report each of the yards as being clean and in proper condition. And may we further remind these gentlemen that there is no case on record of disease having been engendered or spread in this locality by the milk suppliers.'

12TH APRIL

The 'atmospheric railway' between Kingstown (Dun Laoghaire) and the quarries at Dalkey finally closed on 12 April 1854 after nearly 11 years of more or less successful operation. The atmospheric system, championed by the great Victorian engineer Isambard Kingdom Brunel, differed from a 'normal' railway in that there was no engine attached to the train – the engine was housed in a building on Atmospheric Road, Dalkey, and the power it supplied drew the train along by the suction of a plug or piston through a tube. On the down journey to Dun Laoghaire gravity was employed.

The leather flaps on the 15-inch pipe had to be kept air-tight but this never completely worked – attendants had to be employed to follow each train, press down the flaps and apply grease.

But the main reasons for closure were simpler, the atmospheric used a different gauge to the standard Irish one, and while the atmospheric railway worked, it simply didn't work as efficiently as locomotive trains. On several occasions locomotives had to be used to rescue broken-down atmospheric trains. The line, which was exactly 9,200 feet in length, was identical nearly the whole way with the course of the modern railway, diverging only at Castlepark Road.

13TH APRIL

'This day will be performed Mr. Handel's new great sacred Oratorio called the Messiah [13 April 1742]. The doors will be opened at 11 and the performance begins at 12. The Stewards of the Charitable Musical Society request the favour of the ladies not to come with hoops this day to the Music Hall at Fishamble Street. The gentlemen are requested to come without their swords.'

A report on the performance noted: 'Words are worthless to express the exquisite delight it afforded to the admiring, crowded audience. The Sublime, the Grand, and the Tender adapted to the most elevated, majestic and moving words conspired to transport and charm the ravished Heart and Ear. It is but Justice to Mr. Handel that the World should know he generously gave the Money arising from this Performance to be equally shared by the Society for Relieving Prisoners, the Charitable Infirmary, and Mercer's Hospital, for which he will ever be gratefully remembered. There were 700 people in the room and the amount collected for this noble and pious charity amounted to about £400, out of which £127 goes to each of the three great and pious charities.'

14TH APRIL

To a greater or lesser extent the Guilds controlled trade in Dublin right up to the early 19th century. The members of the Guild of the Holy Trinity were, by a charter granted in 1577, allowed to sell all types of goods in the city – with the exception of food. You could buy your way into the Guild, provided you were Protestant, but the normal method of entry was by a seven-year apprenticeship. So powerful were the Guilds that they were allowed to mete out their own punishment when apprentices broke the rules, as the following extract from the Guild's rules demonstrates: 'Certain of the brethren setting forth that whereas there are several misdemeanours committed by apprentices belonging to this Guild and that they escape unpunished by reason that there are no stocks made for the punishment of such offenders in the hall, as is usual in the halls of other corporations – It is ordered 14th of April 1656 that a pair of stocks be provided for the punishment of such apprentices as shall offend from time to time.'

15TH APRIL

Police and troops flooded into Camden Street and surrounding areas on 15 April 1920 in the wake of the killing of Detective Constable Henry Kells the previous day. The killing was the work of Paddy Daly, a member of Michael Collins' full-time IRA Squad (£4.50 per week pay). 'In all about 66 people are believed to have been taken into custody. Tonight all but five of them were released. The searches began shortly after midnight, when the curfew order came into operation, and they were continued until well into this morning. Many men were taken from the neighbourhood of Pleasant-street and Wexford-street. Twenty motor lorries carried the soldiers to the different localities, and all the prisoners were taken to Ship-street Barracks. At 3 o'clock a party of soldiers with armoured cars entered Suffolk-street and arrested two of the assistants in a public-house there. Later in the morning the military returned to the same street and placed cordons at each end of it, and an armoured car took up a position in the centre. Two offices in the street were searched. In one house, where a 'wake' was being held, several men were arrested and carried off.' [*The Times*]

16TH APRIL

Historian Austin Cooper paid a visit to Dundrum Castle on 16 April 1789 and wrote down his impressions: 'The Castle of Dundrum, three miles S. of Dublin, is inhabited and in excellent repair; at the N.E. end of it are the remains of a much older building than the present castle, which is visibly a modern addition in comparison to the old mansion. There is but very little of this ancient part remaining; some of the walls are six feet thick; about the castle are several traces of old walls, avenues, &c., proving it to have been once a very complete habitation. The whole is on the summit of a small hill, surrounded with ash trees, with a handsome rivulet running at its foot, but this shelter will soon be removed, as they are cutting away the trees.'

Artist Gabriel Beranger visited the Castle around the same time and made three sketches, describing the castle as very picturesque.

17TH APRIL

Since the time of Queen Elizabeth, Swords had the right to return two members to Parliament. To be eligible to vote you needed to be Protestant, living in the borough of Swords [for at least six months], and be up to date with your 12d yearly rent. The election in the under-populated area on 17 April 1790 was to prove an interesting one – as two candidates had come up with an ingenious method of ensuring victory: 'General Eyre Massey, some time since, cast a longing eye on this borough, which he considered as a common open to any occupant, and began to build tenements within its [Swords] precincts, in which he placed many veteran soldiers, who having served under him in war, were firmly attached to their ancient leader. Mr. Beresford, the First Commissioner of the Revenue, who had a sharp look-out for open places, had formed the same scheme; and a deluge of revenue officers was poured forth from the Custom House to overflow the place. The wary general threatened his competitor, that for every revenue officer appearing there, he would introduce two old soldiers.' In the event Beresford, along with his chosen second candidate, John Hatch, won the day.

18TH APRIL

The congregational committee of St. Michan's, meeting on 18 April 1724, to consider a pressing problem: 'That your memorialists and all others resorting to the Church and Church yard of the said Parish are greatly annoyed as are all the inhabitants thereabouts by a most abominable stench coming from Hog Court lying between Logh Boy and Church Street and bounded in the north by the said Church yard occasioned by the slaughtering of cattle and feeding of swine in the said Court. That Slaughter House and Hog Sties in so close and Populous a part of a Town can never be looked upon but a common nuisance and the authors of them worthy of Punishment; By reason whereof the ground being always saturated with blood within and loaded on the surface with stagnate Blood and dung and garbage there doth now arise from thence as there hath always done and ever must do to the whole neighbourhood a stench so offensive and detestable that the Parishioners can no longer bear it and will never acquiesce but in the entire removal of the cause thereof; which no pretence of cleaning ever did or ever can effect, but rather arise and propagate the Noisome Scent to the higher degree and farther compass.'

19TH APRIL

Trinity student John Edward Walsh had a skinfull and, with the help of an equally inebriated friend, decided to have some fun. The duo drew up a constitution for a 'The Independent Scholars and Students of Trinity College, Dublin. Then, losing interest, they left it behind them.

A few days later, on 19 April 1798, all the students were summoned to a meeting with Lord Clare, vice-chancellor of the University. 'Those who have seen Lord Clare will never forget him – the hatchet sharpness of his countenance, the oblique glance of his eye, which seemed to read what was passing in the mind of him to whom it was directed,' recalled Walsh.

Among the very few missing was one Robert Emmet – he was declared contumacious [wilfully obstinate and stubbornly disobedient] and expelled. Walsh, however, was unconcerned, he'd been at pains to stay away from any revolutionary-minded individual or group. Lord Clare gave a long speech about the need for vigilance in the face of revolution before revealing the reason for the meeting – the 'wicked paper' drawn up by Walsh. As luck would have it, the spirit of rebellion was alive in Trinity, and a number of people were expelled. The finger of suspicions never pointed to Walsh!

20TH APRIL

When the Zoological Society obtained the site the site for Dublin Zoo in the Phoenix Park there was a small cottage on it. It was occupied by a Mrs. O'Rourke, who was worried that she would be evicted. The Society, however, were in no great hurry to move her but she was proving troublesome on other grounds. On 20 April 1832, it was decided to block the entrance between her cottage and the Zoo.

The following year she was 'cautioned not to hang any more of her linen within sight of the visitors to the Gardens'. The Superintendent in November 1834 was ordered to work out for how much rent a cottage could be procured for Mrs. O'Rourke but there is no record of the result of his inquiries. Subsequently a month later Mrs. O'Rourke was offered £10 to leave the cottage but she was still in occupation in April 1835 when she was warned that 'unless she do leave the Gardens before the next meeting of the Council, she will forfeit the advantages so liberally accorded to her'.

21ST APRIL

Remember the *Helga* – last seen shelling the hell out of Dublin in 1916? On 21 April 1922 the General Headquarters of the Irish Republican Army, Beggars' Bush, issued a statement: 'At midnight last night six men boarded the gunboat, *Helga*, at Dun Laoghaire Harbour with the object of removing a 3-pounder gun form the boat. A party of Regular troops, with an officer in charge, proceeded in a rowing boat to the vessel. When they got there they found that the raiding party had disappeared, taking with them the barrel of the gun, but leaving behind the firing mechanism. The Regular Force dismantled the gun, and took it away with them. They also found a .32 revolver, with 100 rounds of ammunition, and a rifle.'

The *Helga*, renamed *Muirchu*, later became Ireland's first and, for several years, only fishery patrol vessel. It sank while under tow for scrapping in 1947.

22ND APRIL

For many hundreds of years Black Monday was remembered in Dublin – it recalled the slaughter of Dubliners (actually imported Bristolians) by the O'Byrnes in 1209: 'One party of the citizens challenged another party to exercise this recreation ['hurling of balls'] on Easter-Monday near Cullen's-wood, two miles from Dublin. The enemy, then lurking in the neighbouring mountains, marched down fell on the citizens unprepared and fatigued with the laborious diversion, and slew upwards of 500 of them.

In the following years it was the norm for the citizens to tool up, head for Cullenswood and look for a re-match. In time the muster on Black Monday was formalised and enabled city officials to judge the citizen's ability to defend the city. 'Whereas it hath binn an ancient and laudable custome that the yong men within the Cittie and Liberties trayned up for the defence of this Cittie in his majesties service the which custome hath for a long time binn discontinued by reason of the late warres and disturbances. I the Lord Mayor doe nevertheless intend to revive the said customes and in order thereunto every one of them and their men servants from sixtiene to sixtie yeares of age in their best apparell and with complete armes, doe appear with the rest of the Corporation on the first day of May next by six of the clocke in the morning dated this the 22nd of April 1665.'

23RD APRIL

The Battle of Clontarf took place on Good Friday (23 April) 1014. 'From the river
Tolka to the rising ground now occupied by Mountjoy Square, and thence to the
abbey of St. Mary's del Ostmanby, the conflict raged. The Danish king beheld the
fight from the walls of his fortress; the aged Brian, whose grandson was amongst the
combatants, remained in the rear of the Irish centre, protected by his body-guard.

'At the close of the day the Danish forces were in full flight; their ships, which had
lain along the northern shore of Dublin Bay, had been carried out of reach by the
rising tide, and the only passage across the Liffey, Dubhgall's Bridge, being covered
by the troops of Brian, a dreadful slaughter ensued. It is said by the Irish annalists
that not one of Brodar's mailed champions escaped alive, while Prince Dubhghall,
son of Aulaf, and 3,000 of his troops were also amongst the slain; and on the Irish
side, Prince Murchadh and his son had fallen.

'Brodar, probably in attempting to force his way to Dubhgall's Bridge, came on the
tent of Brian, and slew the aged king, it is alleged, while engaged in prayer, and was
himself slain by the bodyguard.'

24TH APRIL

Did you hear the one about the man who went into the GPO during the Easter
Rising to get some stamps?

F. J. Cronin, President of the Preston Irish Literary Society, was home in Dublin
to visit his parents. He went into town on Easter Monday, 24 April 1916, where, after
noticing that something was up which involved men with guns he made his way to
the GPO to see what it was all about.

'I got off at the Post Office, where there was a small crowd gathered outside. On the
steps were three Sinn Feiners armed with rifles. Then I realised there was something
doing, and I thought I would get into the Post Office and look around. The three fellows did not stop me, and I got through the swing doors, but a fellow inside pulled
me up. Who are you? he asked, and I tried to look innocent, and said I had come to
get some stamps. He said, Get out of here, and gave me a push and ran me out at the
front of a revolver. That man was very like Connolly, but I won't swear to him.

'By the time I got out again the windows were being smashed with the butt-end of
rifles. That was about 12.30. They were giving out handbills, and I thought it wiser not to
put one in my pocket. The trams had then ceased running, but I managed to get home.'

25TH APRIL

There were very few students in Trinity College during the Easter Rising, it was, after
all, a holiday period. One who had remained on campus anonymously described the
events of Tuesday, 25 April, in *Blackwood's Magazine* (July 1916)

'The great event of Tuesday was the recapture of the *Daily Express* offices by the
military. We were at the time in ignorance of what was actually happening; for we
were possessed with the idea that the Sinn Feiners held the Castle.

'When, therefore, we saw at the head of Dame Street men in successive waves
rush across the street from the City Hall towards the *Express* offices, we thought

they represented the enemy in process of expulsion from the Castle. As a matter of fact the waves of men were composed of the troops.

'From our position in front of the College we could see that a terrific fire was being directed against the *Daily Express* building: plaster and powdered brick were flying in showers from its facade. This fire was to cover the advance of our soldiers.

'But in spite of this we saw, more than once, one of the running figures pitch forward and fall. It was expensive tactics; and later a better method of dealing with the Rebel strongholds was found when the artillery came into the City.'

26th April

After three days of fighting the military cordon around the city was being tightened and the 'rebels' found their communications increasingly difficult. But there was still a chance for reckless Dubs to rubberneck – among them Miss Lilly Stokes. Her memories of that week were published in *Nonplus* (1916).

'We heard [26 April] the soldiers had had nothing to eat since they landed. They had had a long march from Kingstown carrying their heavy packs. They looked weary, so Maive, Pauline and I came back and Mother gave us two grand cans of tea, which we took to them by the Elgin Road lane.

'They had cleared the Rebels out of Carrisbrook House at the corner of Pembroke and Northumberland Roads – there were eight dead inside it. One soldier was killed.

'The noise of the firing and bombing was tremendous. They took the corner house in Haddington Road after an obstinate fight – they bombed it. They say there were 36 dead men, women and children in it who had all been fighting.'

Irish Rebellion - May 1916.
A group of Officers with the captured rebel flag.

The fighting over, a group of British officers take time for a posed photograph at the Parnell Monument with the flag which had flown over the G.P.O. during Easter Week.

'There was heavy fighting about Mount Street Bridge. The Sinn Feiners were in the School House and had a machine gun in the corner house of Lower Mount Street and Clanwilliam Place. 'The Sherwood Foresters stumbled into the trap and were mown down, over 100 of them on the bridge. They finally bombed out the four Clanwilliam Place houses.'

27TH APRIL

By Thursday, 27 April 1916, Dublin had become a very dangerous place and the body count was mounting. A nurse working in Dublin Castle wrote her account of the week (*Blackwoods Magazine*, December 1916).

Thursday: 'The windows overlook the Castle garden, where all day about 20 men were digging graves. The nearest were for officers, each made separately; then two large graves for Tommies and civilians, and, far away by themselves, the Sinn Feiners.

'There were over 70 buried in the garden: most of them were removed when the Rebellion was over, but some of the officers are there still. Only a very limited number of coffins could be obtained: most of the bodies were buried sewn into sheets. The funerals took place each evening after dark: more than once the burying party was fired on.

'Towards the end of the week the dead were so many, they were brought in covered carts instead of ambulances. I saw a cart open once – about fifteen bodies, one on top of the other. It took time to carry them round to the Mortuary, and sometimes as one passed two or three bodies would be lying near the side door, dressed in khaki, but so still, so stiff, the hands so blue, and the faces covered. One wondered if they were the men who had shouted 'Gangway!' that morning, and laughed and talked so cheerily.'

Sackville Street (Now O'Connell Street), featuring the Imperial Hotel.

Suffolk Street decorated for the arrival of Queen Victoria in April 1900.

28TH APRIL

On Friday, 28 April 1916, O'Connell Street was in flames. Warre B. Wells, Assistant Editor of *The Irish Times* wrote: 'How it [the fire] originated – whether through the shelling from Trinity College, the explosion of a rebel ammunition store, or some accident of looting – will probably never be known.

'It broke out on the west side of Sackville Street, immediately in rear of the rebel fortified post fronting on the bridge, and raged and spread without ceasing from Thursday evening throughout Friday and Saturday, until Sunday.

'The military operations made it impossible, except at long intervals, for brief periods, and at certain points, for the Dublin Fire Brigade to attempt to cope with the conflagration. The fire, fanned by a breeze from the sea, spread from the west side of Sackville Street, where it had devastated a wide area, across to the east side.

'The whole of the west side of Sackville Street, comprising forty-seven buildings, was gutted. In all, here and in the surrounding streets, some two hundred and thirty buildings were demolished.

'Fortunately, few residential houses were within the devastated area, although it contained some tenements, and the loss of life directly due to the fire was small.'

29TH APRIL

As the fighting drew to a close on Saturday, 29 April, Warre B. Wells, Assistant Editor of *The Irish Times* wrote dramatically of unfolding events. 'Of the fighting which attended this final phase of the rebellion no clear account is possible. It was a confused and desperate affair of ambuscades and sniping in streets and alleys where the glare of the fires paled the sun and the crash of falling masonry mingled with the roar of artillery and bombs, the vicious knocking of machine-guns, and the rattle of musketry.

'The rebel remnant, surrounded by the soldiers and the flames, fought with the courage of despair.

'The inevitable end came early in the afternoon, when PH Pearse went out under a white flag and agreed to unconditional capitulation.

'The "cease fire" was sounded, and one by one, as the news of the surrender at headquarters was confirmed, the various detached bodies of the rebels about the city made their submission.

'By nightfall although single snipers still haunted many roofs, all organised resistance to the forces of the Crown was at an end, and Dublin emerged from a week of revolution to contemplate its destruction and bury its dead. The Irish Rebellion of 1916 had passed into history.' Or had it?

30TH APRIL

The minutes of the Royal Dublin Society record that £34 2s. 6d. was voted to Lady Arbella Denny on 30 April 1767 to be used by her to reward the most deserving children in the Foundling Hospital. That institution aspired to prevent the 'Exposure, death and actual murder of illegitimate children' and also to raise those children 'in the Reformed or Protestant Faith, and thereby to strengthen and promote the Protestant Interest in Ireland.'

It had an abysmal record with up to half those lodged there dying in childhood. During Lady Arbella's twenty years of hands-on involvement from 1758 to 1778 there were dramatic improvement – the figures for the ten years to 1770 show that out of 8,726 children taken in, 1,990 had died. After her retirement the figures soon changed for the worse – in 1790, out of 2,180 foundlings received 2,087 were dead or unaccounted for. In the previous ten years, out of 19,368 entered, 17,000 were dead or missing.

Lady Denny, according to Wadsworth's *History of the Foundling Hospital*, was 'singularly free from sectarian religious bigotry, her ladyship was bigoted only where abuses were to be reformed and improvements introduced; when she brooked no delays, shortcomings, or interference.'

Chapter Five

May

1st May

In days gone by Stoneybatter, on Oxmantown Green, was the place where the May-day Festival was annually celebrated by Dubliners. This custom was eventually abolished, the cause being a riot in connection with a May fete.

This riot is reported in the papers of the day as follows: 'On the 1st May, 1773, there was a great riot at Stoneybatter in consequence of the setting up of a Maypole, which was attempted to be pulled down by some soldiers, on which a violent quarrel ensued, the populace of Stoneybatter attacking the soldiers, driving them into their barracks, and breaking the windows of same, whereupon the soldiers returned, some with their muskets, and fired upon their antagonists.

'Some of the inhabitants, to prevent further mischief, called on Sheriff Jones, who ordered the picket guard to attend him in this affray, and took seven soldiers, who went to the barracks; owing to the great courage and activity of Major Digby, who took three of the soldiers prisoners, and to Major Marsh, who was also very brave on this occasion, the riot was suppressed, but before it was over most of the houses in that place and neighbourhood had their windows smashed, and had it not been for these two worthy officers much more damage would have ensued.'

2nd May

First things first! With the city in a state of chaos after the Easter Rising, the authorities knew that it was essential to restore some sense of normality. One of the first area to be tacked was that of the mail. 'The authorities have had under consideration the question of restoring such Postal facilities as will meet the pressing requirements of the public. It is obvious that any arrangements made for the present must be of a temporary character. It will be a long time probably before the General Post Office premises in Sackville Street can be restored and the several departments put in working order. It is desirable that the new building selected should be in a central part of the city, and it is suggested that the Rotunda would, when the necessary alterations were made, be the best adapted to serve the purpose. The College Green premises already in possession of the Postal Authorities may be capable of extension, and it is not unlikely the authorities may decide upon their adoption.' [*The Irish Times*, 2 May 1916]

3RD MAY

Dublin actress Margaret Woffington, better known as 'Peg' was one of the acting stars of the eighteenth century in Ireland and Britain. Reputedly the 'handsomest woman ever to appear on stage', Woffington was supreme in comic parts but was also celebrated for her Shakespearian roles. She performed at Covent Garden and Drury Lane and in Dublin, and appeared opposite David Garrick, with whom she had an affair, in *King Lear* and *Richard III*.

She was known for her love affairs and for her bitter rivalries with other actresses; while performing with Mrs Bellamy, she drove her off the stage and stabbed her. She was ill but decided to press ahead with a charity performance of *As You Like It* on 3 May 1757 at Covent Garden, London. She struggled through the performance until the fifth act, breaking down when she came to the lines in the epilogue:

'If I were a woman, I would kiss as many of you as had beards that pleased me.'

As she struggled with the lines, her voice gave out and she was completely overcome. With the mournful cry of, 'Oh God! Oh God!' She staggered to the wings where she fell unconscious, or as one writer put it 'walked into the shadow of death.' Peg Woffington died an invalid the following year.

4TH MAY

The Irish International Exhibition was opened on a 52-acre site at Herbert Park, Ballsbridge, at 2pm on 4 May 1907, by the Lord Lieutenant, the Earl of Aberdeen.

The opening was held in grand style and attended by the Prince of Wales along with various English Mayors and delegations from English local authorities. The exhibition was centred in a large building which had eight wings – each was 164 feet long and 80 feet wide. Pavilions were provided for the British Colonial and Foreign

A bust of Queen Victoria, a visitor to the Irish Industrial Exhibition in 1853.

An postcard advertising the opening of the Irish International Exhibition, May 1907.

exhibits, Motor Cars, Electric Lighting, Gas Lighting, Irish Industries, Machinery and Power Houses. The Fine Art Gallery, which had all the latest refinements in fireproof construction and security, contained Modern Art from all over the world.

Apart from the technical exhibits there were ample opportunities for amusement and refreshment. Visitors could listen to vocal and instrumental performances in the Concert Hall as well as trying out the delights of the Canadian Waterchute (now the duck pond) and Switchback!

Curios included the writing desk of Sir John Moore (died at Corunna), the copy of Chateaubriand's works which Napoleon took to St. Helena, old photographs of the Irish College in Paris and a list of the Irish casualties at the battle of Fontenoy. Admission was one shilling for adults and six pence for children under twelve. The Exhibition closed on 9 November.

5TH MAY

The Rev. John Wesley, founder of Methodism, visited Dublin in 1783 and, as his diary records 'spent two or three weeks with much satisfaction' – even though he had to walk from Dun Leary into Dublin 'not being able to procure a carriage.'

On Monday, May 5, he was ready to leave: 'We prepared for going on board the packet; but as it delayed sailing, on Tuesday 6, I waited on Lady Arbella Denny, at the Black Rock, four miles from Dublin. It is one of the pleasantest spots I ever saw. The garden is everything in miniature. On one side is a grove, with serpentine walks; on the other, a little meadow and a green-house, with a study (which she calls her chapel) hanging over the sea. Between these is a broad walk, leading down almost to the edge of the water; along which run two narrow walks, commanding the quay, one above the other. But it cannot be long before this excellent lady will remove to a nobler paradise.'

In this Wesley proved mistaken – the redoubtable Arbella outlived him by a year, dying at the age of 84 in 1792.

6TH MAY

On Saturday, 6 May 1882, Lord Frederick Cavendish, just arrived in Ireland to take up a position as Chief Secretary to the new Lord Lieutenant, Earl Spencer, walked toward his home, 'Deerfield', (now the U.S. Ambassador's residence) in the Phoenix Park. He was joined by Thomas Henry Burke, the Under-Secretary.

What neither knew was that Burke, a Catholic, was judged by the optimistically, if inaccurately, named Invincibles (an offshoot of the IRB) to be a traitor to Ireland because of his long service for the British Government. Suddenly, and without warning, the two were viciously attacked and stabbed to death, the assailants fleeing in two horse-drawn vehicles.

They were quickly caught and their leader, a former councillor, James Carey turned informer, as did three others: Richard Farrell, William Lamie and Michael Kavanagh.

Five were hanged (Tim Kelly had to be tried three times and up to the very last minute there were hope of a reprieve) and three were sentenced to penal servitude.

But it didn't quite end there, James Carey was to have another small note in history (see 4 July) and Charles Stuart Parnell, who had condemned the murders was to be accused of supporting them.

7TH MAY

Lord Ardilaun sits comfortably on his lofty seat inside the railings of St. Stephen's Green and facing the Royal College of Surgeons. Many's the Dub who's passed by and idly wondered who was he and why is the statue there?

In the ninteenth century the Green had become a public nuisance and it was handed over to Commissioners representing local householders. They promptly repaired the damage and enclosed the area – denying entrance to the public.

In 1879 Ardilaun, a member of the Guinness family, arranged for the Green to be made a Royal Park, *i.e.* the Board of Works took it over, personally funded the restoration and cleared the debts which had accrued. It opened to the public two years later.

It took eleven years for Ardilaun's generosity to be noted, with plans for a triumphal gateway (similar to the later Fusilier's Arch) quietly dropped. The foundation stone of the Ardilaun Monument was laid by the Lord Mayor, Alderman Meade, on 7 May 1891, following a grand procession by trades unions and their bands – union members had greatly contributed to the cost – to the west side of St. Stephen's Green. The statue was unveiled on 18 June 1901.

Lord Ardilaun, who paid the bulk of the cost for completing St Stephen's green to its current state.

8TH MAY

Thomas Amory (1692-1759) wrote a strange and at least partly fictional autobiography, *The Life of John Buncle, Esq*. In it he recalled a visited to Ringsend in May [6-9] 1725. 'The Conniving House, was a little public house, kept by Jack Macklean, about a quarter of a mile beyond Ringsend, on the top of the beach, within a few yards of the sea. Here we used to have the finest fish at all times; and in season, green peas and all the most excellent vegetables. The ale here was always extra-ordinary which, with its delightful situation, rendered it a delightful place of a summer's evening. Many a delightful evening have I passed in this pretty thatched house.'

Amory would doubtless have enjoyed the following close shave: 'On Sunday, 8 May 1743, a sailor was brought up from Rings End to Irish Town Churchyard to be buried; but when they laid him on the ground, the coffin was observed to stir, on which he was taken up; and by giving him some nourishment, he came to himself, and is likely to do well.' [*Dublin News-Letter*]

9TH MAY

On 9 May 1945 when Seanad Éireann was discussing the establishment of a compulsory arbitration tribunal it was hardly surprising that the strike at Downey's pub in Dun Laoghaire (demolished for Dun Laoghaire Shopping Centre) should be mentioned. It had, after all, continued for the past seven years.

Senator Duffy: 'I know of a strike in Dun Laoghaire that has been going on for years and that, I believe, has gained international notoriety. There is a story told that when an Irish ship was held up somewhere at sea by a German submarine one of the men who came on board to examine the papers, when he discovered that the ship came from Dublin, said to the captain: 'I see that you live near Dublin. Is Downey's strike over yet?' *

Not only was it still on, it would continue until the death of the owner in 1953. The strike, which had started out as with ill will on both sides, soon settled into a more amicable mode – with Downey allowing the picketers to store their placards in the pub, sending out hot drinks during bad weather and, during the hard winter of 1947, clearing the snow from the path outside the pub to allow them to walk safely.

* In an article by the late Robbie Brennan in Vol. 11, 2002, of *Dun Laoghaire Journal*, the ship is named as the *Irish Elm*, the submarine as *U-638*, and the date of the encounter as March 1942.

10TH MAY

The punishment meted out to Oscar Wilde for his homosexuality is well known. Harsh though it may have been, his 'crime' could have proved more personally damaging had it happened in the eighteenth century.

The Dublin Journal of 10 May 1726 reported: 'Tomorrow will be published by the printers hereof the remarkable tryal of the notorious and detestable Sodomites, who have been detected within the city of London with a full account of the proceeds and moral reflections on that heinous and brutal sin, which pulled down Divine Vengeance on the city.'

A week later *Faulkner's Dublin Postboy* returned to the subject with a letter proposing a solution: 'There is an expedient humbly offered to the Legislature for suppressing sodomy *viz.* that when any person is convicted and sentence pronounced that the Common Hangman should tie him hand and foot before the Judge's face in open court, and a skilful surgeon take out his testicles and then the hangman sear up his scrotum with an hot iron.'

Before the Judge's face? The thought brings tears to the eyes.

11TH MAY

The Liberty Boys – tailors and weavers from the Coombe – and the Ormond Boy – butchers lived in Ormond-market on Ormond quay – often battled each other ferociously. 'On May 11, 1790, one of those frightful riots raged for an entire Saturday on Ormond-quay, the contending parties struggling for the mastery of the bridge; and nightfall having separated them before the victory was decided, the battle was renewed on the Monday following. It was reported of Alderman Emerson, when Lord Mayor, [in 1776] on one of those occasions, that he declined to interfere when applied to, asserting that 'it was as much as his life was worth to go among them.'

'These feuds terminated sometimes in frightful excesses. The butchers used their knives, not to stab their opponents, but for a purpose then common in the barbarous state of Irish society, to hough or cut the tendon of the leg, thereby rendering the person incurably lame for life. On one occasion, after a defeat of the Ormond boys, those of the Liberty retaliated in a manner still more barbarous and revolting. They dragged the persons they seized to their market, and, dislodging the meat they found there, hooked the men by the jaws, and retired, leaving the butchers hanging on their own stalls.'

12TH MAY

The Irish Industrial Exhibition, organised by William Dargan, was held in a temporary crystal palace erected on Leinster Lawn (then the home of the Royal Dublin Society). It was opened on 12 May 1853 by the Lord Lieutenant, the earl of St. Germains, after a procession from Dublin Castle to Merrion Square. The main building measured 265,000 square feet, one third the size of the Crystal Palace of 1851.

On 29 August the exhibition was visited by Queen Victoria – she had dragged along her 12-year-old brat of a son – Albert Edward, later Edward VII – who refused to take a catalogue because it wasn't as well bound as his mother's. His copy can be found in the National Library – 'Presented to the Prince of Wales on the occasion of Her Majesty's visit but declined, not being bound in the same manner as the copy presented to her Majesty.'

When the Exhibition closed several months later it was judged a success for Irish industry – not so for Dargan who lost £19,000 of his own money. It may have been some consolation to him that the National Gallery was built some years later as a result of a testimonial collection taken up for him – and he got his statue in the forecourt!

13TH MAY

You could be forgiven for thinking that making professional people responsible for their actions is a new idea. But no, the Victorians were well able to tackle their peers. 'An action, which raised a serious question as to the liability of medical men under the Infections Notification Act terminated this afternoon [13 May 1895]. It was brought by

A view of the Irish Industrial Exhibition on Leinster Lawn. It opened to the public on 12 May 1853.

Mr. Mason, a draper, of Rathmines, against Dr. Hadden, of the same place, for damages sustained; it was alleged, in consequence of this having negligently, improperly, and unskilfully diagnosed as smallpox a disease from which a shop girl, named Hawkins, was suffering. The girl was removed to the hospital, and it was there ascertained that the disease was not smallpox. The plaintiff gave evidence that his business had fallen off in consequence of the report. Medical witnesses were examined on both sides [including] Dr. Thornely Stokes (president of the College of Surgeons), and Dr. JW Moore, through whose hands 3,000 cases of smallpox had passed, gave evidence to justify the notice, the symptoms being such as showed themselves in the incipient stages of smallpox. The jury, however, found a verdict for the plaintiff, with £100 damages.' [*The Times*]

14TH MAY

If it had succeeded it would rank for daring with Sarsfield's destruction of the Williamite Siege Train, even in failure it was one of the most audacious jailbreaks ever conceived.

Sean McEoin, leader of the Longford Flying Column, was being held in Mountjoy Prison, under sentence of death. Michael Collins wanted him out and came up with a plan which, while simplistic in outline, faced coming apart at the seams at every turn.

1. Capture a British armoured car. 2 Drive into Mountjoy and get McEoin (he was to arrange an interview with the Governor at the appointed time). 3. Get away.

'The Squad', a full-time part of the Dublin Brigade, took up the challenge with gusto and on the morning of Saturday, 14 May, 1921, captured an armoured car after a brief gun battle at the Dublin Corporation Abattoir. Donning British uniforms they gained admission to the prison, but were turned away from the wing where McEoin was being held and brought to the Governor's office.

All went well until Governor Malone decided to ring Dublin Castle to confirm the order to remove McEoin. The game was up – the Governor and several staff were quickly tied up and the IRA men made for the gate, escaping as firing began. When the excitement had died down McEoin was finally given his interview.

15TH MAY

Dublin newspapers reported on 15 May 1921 on an over-the top response by Her Majesty's armed forces to the rehearsals of a Dublin band.

'An extraordinary arrest took place on Sunday, when Crown forces placed in custody all the members of St. James's Band and conveyed them to the Royal Barracks. The band was at practice in their rooms at Bridgefoot St. preparatory to their departure to take part in the May Procession at the Oblate Church, Inchicore.

Lorries containing military drove up and stopped in the vicinity of the rooms. Armed guards were placed in strategic positions, while the main body made a descent on the musicians. After some time the Crown forces emerged on the street, brining with them the band.

Forty-seven of the musicians were accommodated in the lorries and carried away to custody. The charge against them is not known. They were first taken to the Richmond Barracks, but were removed from there to Arbour Hill Barracks where they are at present detained.'

The musicians were released without charge on the Monday. St. James' Brass and Reed band, the oldest in Dublin and one of the oldest in Europe, continues to this day.

16TH MAY

A Court of Enquiry was set up on 16 May 1916 to examine the alleged shooting of civilians by British soldiers during the Easter Rising. Not surprisingly, the eleven-day sitting proved to the authorities' satisfaction that any shot civilian deserved to be and absolved the troops of any wrongdoing.

Heading the enquiry was Colonel EWSK Maconchy CB, CIE, DSO the very same who had headed some of the Field General Courts Martial for trying rebels in the aftermath of the Rising.

In '59th Division 1915-1918' Maconchy recalled: 'During the enquiry a party of women had to be taken out in taxis to Straffan to endeavour to identify men of the Staffordshire Brigade against whom charges were brought. Two thousand men were paraded. One lady, arrayed in a fur coat evidently looted during the burning of Sackville Street, wished to be supplied with whisky before she started, and shouted for it when passing public-houses. When passing along the ranks she remarked: 'Shure, I feel just like Queen Victoria reviewing the troops'. Col. Maconchy, a Longfordman, was promoted to Brig. Gen. on 6 June 1916.

17TH MAY

Lord Edward Fitzgerald had a narrow escape on 17 May 1798. His nemesis, Major Sirr, had earlier received a letter from Edward Cooke: 'Lord Edward will be this evening in Watling Street. Place a watch in Watling Street, two houses up from Usher's Island; another towards Queen's Bridge; a third in Island Street, at the rear of the stables near Wailing Street, and which leads up to Thomas Street and Dirty Lane.'

Thomas Moore, in 1830, wrote an account of Sirr's version of events. '[He] divided his forces, and posted himself, accompanied by Regan and Emerson, in Watling Street, his two companions being on the other side of the street. Seized the first of the party, and found a sword, which he drew out, and this was the saving of his life. Assailed by them all, and in stepping back fell; they prodding at him. His two friends made off. On his getting again on his legs, two pistols were snapped at him, but missed fire, and his assailants at last made off.'

What Sirr neglected to mention that the reason he survived was because of a coat of mail he was wearing. One of his assailants, Gallaher, had delivered at least seven stabs, not one of which produced more than bruising.

18TH MAY

Sir Robert King, 2nd Earl of Kingston, must have been a very worried man on 18 May 1798 – behind him stood a man with a raised executioner's axe!

Sir Robert was on trial for the murder of Colonel Henry Fitzgibbon who had abducted his daughter. A friend of the family, Major Wood, had previously duelled with Fitzgibbon over the abduction – standing just 10 paces apart they exchanged six shots, missing each and every one.

That Sir Robert had tracked Fitzgibbon down and shot him wasn't in much doubt, but perhaps a plea of self-defence would be entered – after all, Fitzgibbon had been aiming two pistols at Sir Robert at the time.

The raised axe was all part of the panoply of a full trial before his peers – the House of Lords, College Green. During the trial the supposed executioner raised the axe to neck level, but with the edge averted. If the verdict was death, the blade was instantly turned towards the prisoners, indicating his sentence and his fate.

In the event the trial was a damp squib – none of the witnesses turned up – and after less than an hour the Earl was found 'Not guilty.'

19TH MAY

'Dublin, May 19th [1733], the Right Honourable the Earl of Orrery, the Reverend Dr. Swift Dean of St. Patrick's, and the Reverend Dr. Sheridan, rode from Dublin to Tallow Hill to take a prospect of the adjacent country. As they were mounting a rock, they observed a stream running through the middle of it, which fell into a natural basin, and was thence conveyed through some subterraneous cavities; but they could not anywhere discover by what secret passage it was conveyed out again; so that they concluded the waters were still in some reservoir within the bounds of the hill, which must infallibly come to burst forth in time, and fall directly upon the city. The Doctor sent for a milking-pail to compute what quantity ran out, which held two gallons, and it was filled in the space of a minute, so that it runs in twenty-four hours 2,880 gallons. This multiplied by 365 produces 1,051,200, and shows the quantity that runs from the rock in a year; so that in three years, about the 15th of November, he computed that it must burst the body of the mountain, and emit an inundation which will run to all points of the Boyne, and greatly endanger the city of Dublin.' – [Scott's *Works of Swift*]

20TH MAY

Sometimes the news from the past can be startling, but this next piece appears particularly callous: 'This day [20 May 1799] three men, or rather more descriptively speaking, two men and a body [sic] (the latter about 14 years of age), were executed in front of the New Prison, pursuant to sentence of a Court Martial held on them last Friday at the Barracks. They were tried for the murder and robbery of a man near Swords, and it appeared in the course of the evidence, that the most horrid cruelty was exercised by them towards the victim of their barbarity – they having – shocking to relate, literally roasted him alive.'

Four dead, one of them a 14-year-old boy [if it had been a girl, you can be sure it would have been yet another fact 'shocking to relate.'], and the writer doesn't think it worthwhile to mention a single name.

21ST MAY

At the beginning of the nineteenth century one way of making a living was highway robbery. Areas around the city organised regular armed patrols to ensure the safety of the coaches, not always with success.

Sir Richard Colt Hoare wrote: 'In the evening I sailed from Holyhead in the Union packet, Captain Skinner; and after a rough and tedious passage of twenty-three hours landed at the Pigeon-house; from whence a vehicle, very appropriately called *The Long Coach* (holding sixteen inside passengers, and as many outside, with all their luggage), conveyed us to Dublin, distant about two miles from the place of landing. A most daring attack was made a short time ago (21 May 1806) upon this coach by a large gang of robbers, who ordered the passengers (Lord Cahir, George La Touche, Esq., and six more) to dismount, and plundered them one by one; the mail carrier was also fired at by the same people. When this vehicle is known to convey so many of the principle nobility, gentry, and merchants from Dublin to the Packet-boat, a regular horse-patrole to attend the coach from the office, could be attended with no inconvenience to Government, and would ensure the property of many individuals.'

22ND MAY

Mrs. Margaret O'Brien, owner of a brothel in Cope Street, had taken the day off – Sunday, 22 May 1803 – to visit her country house in Baggot Street [Dublin was a much smaller city then]. In the evening there was trouble in Temple Street and Cope Street and a mob broke into a numbers of brothels in the area, including Mrs. O'Brien's, and did a lot of damage. Some of those responsible were brought to trial and acquitted – not least because Mrs. O'Brien turned up drunk on the day and threatened one of her own witnesses that she would have him charged with involvement in the riot. Down, but not out, she turned to the civil courts and claimed £2,000 from the city for malicious damage, engaging John Philpott Curran to represent her. One would have thought that her chances were slim as there was no question about the nature of her business – evidence being provided by William Cumberland Shea, Inspector of the St. Andrew's Watch, and Constable William Harrison. Lord Kilwarden, however, took a different view, finding that her business had, indeed, been damaged (her beds had been broken up and thrown into the street). The jury found in her favour and she was awarded damages of £173-11-4½d with sixpence costs.

23RD MAY

On 23 May 1798 the Belfast mail [coach] on its way to Dublin was stopped in Santry village, by nine or ten armed men, who had placed carts across the road; they told the driver and guard that they were friends and stopped the mail, 'fearing it might fall into the hands of a large body of the insurgents nearing Swords; the guard and driver, believing them, dismounted, and entering a house, were there detained while the coach was filled and covered over with dry furze and set on fire, except a small remnant of the letters, which were brought half-burnt to the Dublin Post Office. None of the passengers were ill-treated, nor anything taken from them. In the fields about were assembled not less than one thousand persons, as the coachman calculated. The Attorney Cavalry Corps, who happened to be patrolling that evening in the neighbourhood, captured five men suspected of being concerned in the foregoing transaction and brought them into town.' (*Saunders News Letter*).

The following day martial law was proclaimed in the city and county of Dublin and troops were sent 'through all that tract of country called Fingall attacked the enemy with great vigour and everywhere dispersed them with great slaughter.' (*Dublin Journal*)

24TH MAY

During 1798 rebel troops from South County Dublin took the field on 24 May, assembling at the Pond, Rathfarnham, under the leadership of David Keely, Edward Keogh, James Byrne and Ledwich. They defeated a force of yeomanry under Lord Ely – Ledwich and Keogh had been members of his corps. They intended to move on and join with another group of United Irishmen at Fox and Geese near Clondalkin.

Word was conveyed to the Castle, and a force of regular troops was sent to Rathfarnham, where at Whitehall a stiff encounter took place. Keogh was severely wounded and taken prisoner with Ledwich – both were taken to the Castle with other prisoners. The prisoners, with the exception of the two leaders were publicly exhibited in the Castle Yard, and the macabre spectacle was visited by the Lord Lieutenant, among others. Ledwich was executed on Queen Street.

The surviving United Irishmen, after being mauled and losing their remaining leaders at the Turnpike on the Rathcoole Road moved on to Kildare, where they joined the forces continuing to operate under the command of one of the more successful leaders, Alymer.

25TH MAY

Early in 1921 the IRA Army Council met in Herbert Park to discuss a major action in the city – one big enough to let the world know that the British were no longer in control. There were two suggestions, the HQ of the Auxiliaries in Beggar's Bush Barracks and the Custom House (an important part of the British Civil Service in Ireland). Beggar's Bush was quickly ruled out (too many men with guns inside!). The Custom House, however, had no armed guards inside, was only lightly patrolled outside and was full of highly inflammable documents.

Just before 1pm on 25 May a large force of the IRA Dublin Brigade, led by Oscar Traynor (later Minister for Defence) rushed the building, cut telephone wires and began soaking the rooms with paraffin. The mission was planned to last 25 minutes, but was delayed slightly, just long enough for British troops to arrive in force. A fierce but one-sided, battle ensued – five IRA men were killed and over 100 captured.

The fire in the Customs House was out of control – it blazed for five days – melting the dome and destroying hundreds of years of public records.

26TH MAY

Even today this appeals to the part of me that eternally hopes for painless dentistry. 'The most violent Tooth ach, effectually cured in a few Minutes without drawing the Tooth – No Cure, No Pay. – The above Cure is performed by a few Drops of Hamilton's famous Tincture, for curing the Tooth-Act, by applying in on a small Bit of Cotton, to that Part of the Gum where the Pain lies; and at the same Time putting a little Bit into

The Customs House in flames following the IRA attack on the building on 25 May 1922.

the Tooth; if rotten or decayed, and by repeating the same 2 or 3 times in Occasion; by which means the most racking Tooth-Ach may be cured, either in young or old People. Likewise by applying a little of this Tincture outwardly, it will entirely remove and take away all Kinds of Swellings in the Cheek, or Pain in the Ear or Temples. Any Person in the least doubtful of the real Virtue and Efficacy of this Tincture, by applying to Mr. Hamilton, at his Lodgings at Mr. Tyrril's at the two Blue Posts in Britain-street, opposite Granby Row, Dublin, may see a List of near 306 Persons Names, and their Places of Abode who have been effectually cured thereby within these few Months, besides many poor People Gratis.' [26 May 1764, *The Public Register*, or *Freeman's Journal*.]

27TH MAY

Albert, the first giraffe to be born in captivity, Europe was presented by the London Zoological Society to Dublin Zoo on 27 May 1841 – eleven years after the Zoo opened. The charitable Londoners weren't just handing over any old giraffe: 'They selected this animal with the kindest consideration, as the most portable and hardiest of their stock, although from its being the first ever reared in Europe, being so far acclimated; and a personal favourite and pet of very many of the Society, he was the most valued, and probably the most invaluable giraffe in London.'

Albert, aged three, needed proper housing and the Zoo promptly appealed for funding to build: not only a house suited to the wants of the Giraffe, but one which would accommodate the elephant and camel, both fine animals imperfectly lodged and whose present houses are much wanted for other animals'

The public, however, proved unwilling to build the proposed structure which 'combined with all the desired requisites, the advantage of a lookout tower,' and a smaller, less expensive building was erected.

*The very first Aer Lingus flight, from Dublin to Bristol, took place on 27 May 1936.
EI-ABI, a deHavilland Dragon DH-84, was named the 'Iolar' (Eagle). The company
restored a similar plane for mark its 50th anniversary in 1986.*

28TH MAY

The Volunteers liked dressing up as soldiers, but even toy soldiers need weapons and
ammunition. So it was that on 28 May 1782 the foundation stone of a gunpowder mill
was laid at Moyle Park, Clondalkin, by the first Earl of Charlemont. The ceremony
was attended by a number of the Volunteers, who had marched to Clondalkin from
the Phoenix Park, where they had been reviewed, and who, after the stone was laid,
were entertained by Mr. Caldbeck in his garden on 'every substantial dish fitting for
soldiers, with abundance of wine, Irish porter and native whiskey.' The mills, inau-
gurated with so much splendour, blew up in their turn five years afterwards with an
explosion of the most terrific character. Only two lives were lost, but it is said that
pieces of the building several tons in weight were found six fields away, and that the
concussion was felt so severely even in Dublin that it caused the fall of a stack of
chimneys on Usher's Quay.'

Clondalkin was the choice for an earlier gunpowder mill. In the year 1733 it is
stated that: 'the gunpowder mills near Clondalkin were blown up, by which several
persons received much damage.'

29TH MAY

Madame Tussaud is remembered for her famous waxworks in London, what is less
well known is that the famous wax modeller spent four years in Ireland and was
based in Dublin, lodging at 16 Clarendon Street (demolished).

Her first known exhibition in Dublin was on Tuesday, 29 May 1804 when the following advertisement appeared in the *Dublin Evening Post*:

Shakespeare Gallery, Exchequer Street near Grafton Street

'To be seen this and every day, the most beautiful collection of FIGURES, executed from life, consisting of ACCURATE MODELS IN WAX, of the invention of the celebrated CURTIUS, than which nothing can be a closer resemblance of nature. – The Figures being elegantly dressed in their proper costume are scarcely to be distinguished from life; and have been exhibited at the Lyceum, London, and at Edinburgh, with the greatest applause.

The Exhibition is open from eleven o'clock till four, and from five till dusk. Admission – two British Shillings. Permanent tickets, not transferable, at 7s each. Ladies and Gentlemen may have their Portraits taken in the most perfect imitation of Life; models are also produced from persons deceased, with the most correct appearance of animation.'

The exhibition was a success. She wrote 'When I am in Dublin, the takings can reach £100 a month. People come in crowds every day.'

30TH MAY

Report on the Health of the Kingstown Township, for the Four Week period ending 30 May 1896: 'The number of births registered was 20, being 10.8 below the average during the previous seven years, and represents an annual rate of 14 per 1,000 persons living. The number of deaths registered was 26, being 2 below the average for a corresponding period during the previous seven years, and represent an annual death rate of 18.2 per 1,000 persons living. The death rate during the same period was 22.3 for 16 of the principal Towns in Ireland, 24.3 in Dublin, 14.7

Dublin's North Strand after an accidental bombing by the German air force in 1941.

in Rathmines, 14.6 in Blackrock, and 17.6 in London; of the 26 deaths in Kingstown one was an infant under one year of age, and seven were of persons of 60 years of age and upwards. There was one death from typhus fever, and one from diphtheria, registered during the period. There were 10 deaths form consumption, registered during the period, which is double the average of such deaths. I have frequently called attention to the insanitary condition of the water-closets in the Town Hall, they have been very offensive of late.'

31st MAY

The Rathdown Dispensary for the 'relief of the sick poor' was set up in 1812. The Ninth Annual Report for the year ending 31 May 1821, had a few words to say about interfering know-it-alls: 'Oftentimes after the doctor's visit a consultation of old women and imposters is held, each of whom has innumerable nostrums to propose, all equally infallible; and although they may dispute the superiority of their own individual plans, they invariably and unanimously agree in overruling his injunc-tion. Notwithstanding these obstacles and discouragements to the efficient practice of a Dispensary physician in this country, the proportion of deaths this year has not materially increased from that of former years; and, notwithstanding the existing prejudice s among the lower classes before stated, the growing confidence of the poor in your Dispensary is fully evinced by the progressively increased number of patients relieved during each succeeding year, so as to be in the last [year] nearly double that of 1815.'

The Dispensing Doctor whose opinions were being disputed was Thomas Arthurs MD.

The statement above, of course, may be read in two ways; the death rate remained constant because of 'modern' medical treatment, or because patients opted to stick with the old methods.

Chapter Six

June

A Dublin Metropolitan Police report of rioting in O'Connell Street. 'At about 10.15pm on 1 June 1917, a crowd of about 3,000 persons assembled in Sackville Street, outside the old GPO, waving Republican flags and singing seditious songs. They smashed open a [side] door and entered, hoisting a Republican flag on the parapet. Bonfires were lit, and great disorder ensued. The two constables on duty to protect the building were powerless against such a mob. Superintendent William Patrick Bannon, accompanied by an inspector and a constable entered the building unobserved. Hearing footsteps and voices the superintendent waited until three rioters appeared, and promptly placed them under arrest. Just then a rush was made by about 100 of the rioters into the main passage. Spt. Bannon succeeded in giving the impression that a force of police supported him, and firing his revolver over their heads, forced the mob back into the street, and then endeavoured to secure the broken door. The crowds however soon discovered there were only two officers supporting them, and tried to affect a re-entry. The superintendent forced them to retire again with his revolver, and resisted all further attacks until 1am.'

Supt. Bannon was later awarded the King's Police Medal – one of 24 to the DMP between 1909 and 1922.

2ND JUNE

Underwater diving was in its infancy in the eighteenth century but, while the risks were high, the profits could be large enough to outweigh the obvious dangers. Among those who practised this dangerous trade was Charles Spalding from Edinburgh. A contemporary newspaper noted: 'He at length became so proficient in this aquatic act that he could remain, if necessary, for a whole day in water of 12 to 14 fathoms deep.'

He had a number of successful recoveries from wrecks when he was sent to the Kish Bank by the underwriters of the *Count Belgioso* (an East Indiaman) which had gone down with all hands. The cargo was valued at £150,000 of which £30,000 was in silver and lead. He was to have a fourth of any metals raised and half the value of any of the rest of the cargo.

On 2 June 1783, while making his third trip down to the ship it all went wrong. They [he took workman with him] remained one hour under water; two barrels of air were sent down to them, and no apprehensions were entertained for their security. After some time, however, the signals from below were not repeated as usual – the bell was drawn up, and the unfortunate philosopher and his assistant were found dead.

3RD JUNE

The Freeman's Journal reported on an event which had necks craning in O'Connell Street on 3 June 1881: 'Yesterday morning, about 11 o'clock, a most exciting scene was witnessed in Sackville-street at Nelson's Pillar. A boy succeeded in getting up the stone stairs without paying the usual sixpence fee. He was not noticed until he came out on the top, where he commenced to rush quickly around, until he attracted the attention of the passers-by in Sackville-street, Henry-street, and Talbot-street. A large crowd collected. The young boy then ascended to the top of the railings and got outside, running around quickly, with one hand holding the top rail. This daring proceeding was continued for fully ten minutes. Two police-constables waited at the trap-door for the boy, while the man in charge of the Pillar ascended the steps and took him down. He was given into custody of the two police, and marched to the Red Lamp Police-Station, Store-street.'

The following day the errant newsboy, John Connolly, 15, was charged with obstructing the thoroughfare in Sackville Street by his conduct. It must have been his lucky day – the magistrate, Mr. M'Blain, noted that while Connolly had been very stupid, he wasn't guilty of the charge.

4TH JUNE

In olden times the authorities certainly knew how to make their point – i.e. insurrection does not pay! 'This day [4 June 1798] Thomas Bacon, an eminent tailor, and formerly a Major of Brigade in the old Volunteers, was hanged, pursuant to sentence of a Court Martial, on Carlisle [O'Connell] Bridge. From the barracks to the place of execution he was conveyed in a cart through several principal and populous street, as in terrorem to the multitude, and such a melancholy and ignominious fate attending a man of his rank in life, would in no other person excite more public interest, or have more effect, as he was very generally known.'

Of the same day *The Times* reported: 'At two o'clock this morning, Lord Edward Fitzgerald died in the New Prison, where he was confined. For some hours before his death he was outrageously mad, but more calm in his last moments. An inquest sat upon his body, which pronounced his death, to have been in consequence of an effusion of water from the left side of the thorax, and an inflammation in the lungs, occasioned by a fever, aided by two wounds inflicted on his right arm by pistol balls found lodged over the scapula of that side.

An aerial view of O'Connell Street in the early 1920s. Large areas remain vacant and without replacement buildings after 1916.

5TH JUNE

When Sir Boyle Roche, master of the mixed metaphor and of schizophrenic bird fame ('How can I be in two places at once unless I were a bird?'), died at his home in Eccles Street on 5 June 1807, the event was surely marked by recollection of his many eccentric remarks. Even today, a brief trawl through the internet will quickly turn up a vast collection of Roche's quotes, many of dubious heritage.

Here's a selection. 'Mr Speaker, I smell a rat; I see him forming in the air and darkening the sky; but I'll nip him in the bud. The cup of Ireland's misery has been overflowing for centuries, and is not yet half full. Ireland and England are like two sisters; I would have them embrace like one brother. I answer in the affirmative with an emphatic 'No'. All along the untrodden paths of the future I can see the footprints of an unseen hand.'

Jonah Barrington described him: 'a bluff, soldier-like old gentleman. He had numerous good qualities; his ideas were full of honour and etiquette – of discipline and bravery. His lady, who was a 'bas bleu' prematurely injured Sir Boyle's capacity, it was said, by forcing him to read Gibbon's *Decline and Fall*.'

The inauguration of Douglas Hyde, the first president of the Irish Republic in 1938.

6TH JUNE

Captain J. C. Bowen-Colthurst, Royal Irish Rifles, had cold-bloodedly murdered three innocent men in Portobello Barracks during the Easter Rising – journalists Francis Sheehy Skeffington, Thomas Dickson and Patrick McIntyre.

Skeffington, a pacifist, had been trying to prevent looting when he was arrested. That night he was taken as a hostage on a raiding party during which he witnessed Capt. Bowen-Colthurst, shoot dead an unarmed 17-year-old boy who was returning from church.

Bowen-Colthurst reported to H.Q. that the three journalists had been shot because of 'fears that the prisoners might be rescued or escape'.

And there the matter might have ended except for the demands for a full investigation by another officer, Major Sir Francis Fletcher-Vane. When he got nowhere in Ireland he went right to the top and arranged interviews with Prime Minister Asquith and Field Marshal Kitchener.

Bowen-Colthurst, who was from Cork, was arrested and court-martialled on 6 June 1916 at Richmond Barracks. He was found guilty but insane and sent to Broadmoor Criminal Mental Asylum. He was released in 1922, emigrated to Canada, and died in 1966.

Major Vane, the whistle-blower, was thrown out of the British Army.

7TH JUNE

Dr. Loftus, Archbishop of Cashel, was hanged on a gallows in Stephen's Green on 7 June 1584 (there are differing dates) – which must have come as a tremendous relief to him. A few weeks earlier he had been tortured in a savage manner. 'The Bishop was bound hand and foot, was thrown on the ground, and tied to a large stake. His feet and legs were encased in top-boots (a kind of boot at that time common, made of leather, and reaching above the knee), filled with a mixture of salt, bitumen, oil, tallow, pitch, and boiling water. The legs so booted were placed on iron bars, and horribly and cruelly roasted over a fire. When this torture had lasted a whole hour, the pitch, oil, and other mixtures boiling up, burned off not only the skin, but consumed also the flesh, and slowly destroyed the muscles, veins, and arteries; and when the boots were taken off, carrying with them pieces of the roasted flesh, they left no small part of the bones bare and raw, a horrible spectacle for the bystanders, and scarcely credible. When, however, in this savage way, the tyrants had failed to break the unconquerable spirit of the martyr [he was] brought back to his former prison, a foul place, filled with a dense fog, ready to endure worse torments, if such could be devised.'

8TH JUNE

'Sir – Having at eight o'clock, taken a third-class ticket to Dublin, I was entitled too, and received one for three pence. On arriving at Sydney-Parade, as I live convenient, I got out of the train, and was proceeding from the station, when I was called on by the railway official to pay an additional penny, as the ticket which I held was for Dublin. Now it appears very strange to me that if the fare be paid for the full journey, that the Directors of this railway should in their wisdom ordain and order that any person getting out at any intermediate station, should be obliged to pay more for the ticket than if he continued the journey to Dublin. I have travelled on all the principal railways in England and Ireland, and the rule invariably adopted was to charge according to the distance – the greater the distance the greater the pay. I have travelled by other conveyances, stage-coaches, omnibuses, and cars, and they, by certain regulations often charge as much for a short distance as a limited longer one, but I have not, on any occasion, known or heard of any public conveyance charging more for a short distance than the entire, and full sum demanded for the longer journey. A Lover of Fair Dealing.' [*Kingstown Evening Journal*, 8 June 1868.]

9TH JUNE

A Dublin prostitute Lizzie O'Neill, also known as Honor Bright, was brought by two men one evening to Lamb Doyle's. The following morning, 9 June 1925, her body was found on the roadside near Ticknock Crossroad – she had been shot through the right breast. The two men, a doctor and an ex-Garda were later charged with her murder – the verdict, on 1 February 1926, was 'Not Guilty.'

The murder was recalled by Sara Fagan in *Madams, Murder and Black Coddle*: 'I remember that poor, unfortunate girl, Honor Bright. Everyone was talking about her, the way she was murdered up in the Dublin Mountains. She was shot dead up there. A policeman, a big shot in the police force, and a dispensary doctor were charged with her murder but they got off. Poor Honor. She lost her job in a big clothing shop when she became pregnant. I remember some of the women talking about her. They said the reason why she was murdered was she was going to name the father of her baby'.

As no-one claimed the body, Lizzie O'Neill was buried in a pauper's grave in Kilgobbin graveyard.

10TH JUNE

On Friday, 10 June 1768, someone attempted to steal the poor box from Santry Church, failing only because it was fastened to the floor. The clerk of the church, Paul Tanner, was not a trusting man and figured that the thief would be back – presumably armed with the tools he needed. *The Dublin Journal* reported that 'Fearing it would be repeated, [he] placed two of his sons, well armed, the night following to watch. They remained on the porch until break of day, when they went home for half and hour, and on their return found a window of the Vestry-room broken open. They heard the noise of a saw in the church, and going in, with the turnpike [the turnpike was the eighteenth century equivalent of modern-day road tolls] man, they found a villain taking the money out of the box, which he had cut with a saw. They secured him and brought him before the Rev. John Jackson, Justice of the Peace for the county of Dublin, who committed him to Kilmainham Gaol, on Sunday morning'.

Presumably this was the same 'box with three locks' which had been bought by the church nine years earlier for the sum of eleven shillings and four pence.

11TH JUNE

Garrett Óg Fitzgerald, Earl of Kildare and Lord Deputy of Ireland, left his son, Thomas (aka 'Silken Thomas' because his followers wore silk on their helmets), in charge when he was summoned to London in 1533.

False reports were circulated Garrett had been executed in the Tower of London and Silken Thomas, 21, made a disastrous decision – open revolt!

On 11 June, he arrived in Dublin accompanied by 1,000 troops and a personal bodyguard of 140 horsemen in coats of arms. Heading straight for the Chapter House of St. Mary's Abbey he threw down his Sword of State: 'Now I need of my own sword, which I dare trust. I am none of Henry's deputy; I am his foe'.

He laid siege to unsuccessful siege to Dublin Castle and later to Dublin itself.

The rebellion finally petered out 14 months later when Silken Thomas, after a promise of pardon, surrendered unconditionally to Lord Gray. He, and five uncles, were taken to the Tower of London, and hung, drawn and quartered at Tyburn. Silken Thomas's unfinished signature can still be seen carved into the wall of his cell – 'Thomas FitzG'.

12TH JUNE

J. Byrne Power, Kingstown Medical Officer, hit the roof after the Sanitary Committee changed the brand of disinfectant used by the local authority. 'At a meeting of the Committee on 12 June 1904, a resolution passed at the previous meeting, accepting the tender for Jeyes' preparations was rescinded, on the ground that they were not found satisfactory as regards price, and the preparations of another company, of which, I much regret to say, I cannot approve, were adopted instead. I again recommend the original acceptance of Jeyes' preparations because I know that recent scientific experiments have proved them to be, for practical disinfecting purposes, the most efficient, and therefore the cheapest in the market. Now bacteriological experiments have proved Jeyes' Fluid is about 8 times as strong as carbolic acid when in emulsion with 99 per cent of water, which emulsion will cost less than one halfpenny per gallon, and it is therefore the cheapest and most effective disinfectant for our purposes in the market, as far as I can ascertain. I cannot but think that it would be well if the Sanitary Authority would be guided by me in such matters.'

13TH JUNE

Irish suffragettes wanted the vote for women to be included in the Home Rule Bill and the Irish Women's Franchise League had sent a letter to the British PM reminding him. No reply from Mr. Asquith forthcoming they decided to focus attention on the injustice. So it was that early on 13 June 1912 a small group of women made their way into the centre of Dublin. Most, if not all, carried large handbags – filled with stones! The well-planned operation saw simultaneous attacks on a number of Government buildings – the Custom House, Ship-Street Barracks, Land Commission offices, and the GPO – which lost four large plate-glass windows worth £32. Eight were arrested – Mrs. Hannah Sheehy-Skeffington, Miss Margaret Murphy, Mrs. Palmer, Miss Jane Murphy, Miss Hilda Webb, Miss Maud Lloyd, Miss Marjory Haslar, and Miss Kathleen Houston. Arrested and tried, a number were sentenced to two months in prison – four weeks later they were joined by other IWFL members who had followed their example. Their escalating campaign, many went on hunger-strike, led to the introduction of the 'Cat and Mouse' Act – weakened hunger-strikers were released from prison, only to be brought back when they had recovered.

14TH JUNE

The Dublin Penny Journal of 14 June 1834 reported on a curious case of sleep-walking: 'Edward Harding, a student of Trinity College, Dublin, who inhabited an attic was in the habit of walking upon the roof in his sleep. One night, having taken a relation, who was locked out, to sleep with him, they had not been in bed more than two hours, when the latter saw him deliberately get up, put on his clothes, strike a light, and sit down, apparently to study. In a few moments he observed him opening the window, and immediately proceeding to walk out of it upon the roof. He pursued him cautiously. The day was just dawning, and he could see him distinctly walking along the parapet with destruction within an inch of him. Seizing him suddenly by the arm, pulled him into the gutter, there holding him by force, notwithstanding his violent exertions to disengage himself, until at last he became quite awake. He never afterward walked in his sleep, although he used to get out of bed at night, and mope about for a moment or two; but he would awake in the greatest terror, which, however, soon dissipated, and he rested well the remainder of the night.'

15TH JUNE

1932 saw a breakdown in law and order – sanctioned by Government! Preparing for the Eucharistic Congress, various laws were brought in on 15 June (Eucharistic Congress (Miscellaneous Provisions) Act) which, today, would cause an outcry.

Specifically, the Minister for Justice could allow any person to drive any or all motor vehicles without a driving licence! For the duration everybody could act as a taxi without a taxi plate. The only exception was those who were already disqualified from driving.

Pubs, with the approval of a Judge, could open as long as they liked (including during the Holy Hour!) Anyone planning a once-off event could apply for a drinks licence – they could even get rolling licences, each one coming into effect as the last expired.

The only exception was June 26 between the hours of 2pm and 6pm – the time of the Pontifical Mass in the Phoenix Park – when no alcohol was allowed to be sold. Your only chance of a legal pint at that time was as a bona fide resident of a vessel moored in Dublin Bay!

16TH JUNE

By the mid-eighteenth century the Blue Coat school, housing 170 boys, was not in good condition – the Registrar of the School noted that it was only kept together by patchwork and had to be rebuilt – he estimated the cost at £12,789. 'Wednesday last, when his Excellency, Lord Harcourt, arrived at the Blue Coat School, he was received by all the officers of that house, who showed his Excellency several of the apartments, which were in a most ruinous condition. from whence his lordship, attended by the Lord Mayor and other governors, went through one of the Courts which was lined with two rows of the children, very clean and neatly dressed, who made a most pleasing appearance, and sang psalms in a most harmonious manner. His Excellency passed down through a guard of the army into Oxmantown Green, and laid the foundation stone with a silver trowel, with the Lord Lieutenant's arms engraved thereon, with the following inscription: 'This stone was laid by H.E. Simon Harcourt on Wednesday, 16th June, 1773, in the thirteenth year of the reign of HM George III. Right Hon. Richard French, Lord Mayor; James Sheil, James Jones, High Sheriffs; Thomas Ivory, Architect.'

17TH JUNE

A letter from Dr. Mullen of Trinity College to Sir William Petty of the Royal Society of London, describes the accidental burning of an elephant in Dublin: 'The Booth where the elephant was kept took fire at 3am on Friday 17 June 1681. The city became alarmed and multitudes gathered about the place, many becoming very excited trying to procure a small part of the animal for a souvenir. As the entrance fee to see him in life had been rather stiff, few had seen him. To prevent a riot, Mr. Wilkins, Manager, procured a file of Musqueteers to guard the remains until such time as a shed could be built, where the remains could be disjointed in order to preserve the skeleton. The work had to be done very speedily and Dr. Mullen had to call in a number of butchers to assist him, whom he describes as being 'unruly'. However, as the carcase was emitting very 'noisome steams' it had to be disjointed by candlelight. Some parts of it were burned and some more or less defaced by being parboiled. Finally the skeleton was carefully preserved and sent to London.'

18TH JUNE

Senator O'Farrell was among those who addressed the wretched condition of O'Connell Street in Seanad Éireann on 18 June 1924. 'I know that though there are thousands of visitors coming to the country this year, there is now no hope of having these wretched ruins in O'Connell Street cleared away by the 1st August; but there is every possibility that in two years from now the same wretched spectacle will be presented to any visitors to our city. We have, since 1916, ruins left untouched and the people are only just now considering the question of rebuilding. Some owners of premises in O'Connell Street are trying to sell their premises evidently at a price that would please them. But they are in no hurry to complete that bargain, seeing that they have two whole years to wrangle over the price. I sincerely hope the Seanad will take the view that twelve months from now – three years after the destruction – is quite sufficiently long to give those people to make up their minds whether they are going to rebuild or not. Surely if they have not made up their minds they ought not to be any longer allowed by the Corporation or whoever is in charge of the city to have these sites as they are. The Corporation, or whoever is in charge of the city, should step in and set those sites to someone who would build on them.'

19TH JUNE

Dublin Corporation considered a report on 19 June 1893 on Artisans and Labourers' Dwellings in Benburb Street: 'At the close of the year 1892, there were 136 dwellings in occupation, leaving eight unoccupied. The number of persons in occupation were 463, viz., 248 males and 215 females. There were 17 deaths – four from bronchitis (two females, aged 62 and 68 years) and two children (2.5 years and 2 years); four from consumption (two men, aged 25 and 45, and two females 34 and 45); one man, aged 40, asthma; one girl, aged five years, pneumonia; one man, aged 38 years, tumour in stomach; three children, two 6 weeks and one 2 years, convulsions; one boy, 3 years, gastric; a boy aged 11 years and girl 4 years, measles. Of these death all those of bronchitis, asthma and consumption occurred during the first three months, during the influenza epidemic. There were 19 births – 9 males and 10 females.'

A further report on Bow-Lane tenements noted that they were fully occupied – by 335 persons – 164 males and 171 females. 'There were five deaths in them – one man, aged 26, typhoid; two children from teething; one child, bronchitis; and one from croup. There were 15 births – 8 males and 7 females.

20TH JUNE

James Clarence Mangan, poet, born in Fishamble Street in 1803, died in the Meath Hospital on 20 June 1849 – a victim of the cholera epidemic then raging through Dublin – after a life of 'unrelieved poverty and unhappiness'.

He worked for a time in a legal firm as a scrivener [a person who drafts document], and did not enjoy the experience. 'Those who knew him in after years can remember with what a shuddering and loathing horror he spoke, when at rare intervals he could be induced to speak at all, of his labours with the scrivener and the attorney.'

Found a job by his friends in the cataloguing department of Trinity, he appears to have made a eerie impression there. A contemporary records: 'It was an unearthly and ghostly figure in a brown garment; the same garment (to all appearance) which lasted till the day of his death. The blanched hair was totally unkempt; the corpse-like features still as marble; a large book was in his arms, and all his soul was in the book. Here Mangan laboured mechanically, and dreamed, roosting on a ladder, for certain months, perhaps years; carrying the proceeds in money to his mother's poor home. All this time he was the bond-slave of opium.'

21ST JUNE

The Pavilion and Winter Gardens in Kingstown (Dun Laoghaire) were officially opened by the Earl and Countess of Longford on 21 June 1903. The highly ornate building contained a roof-top garden, four viewing turrets, reading, smoking and tea-rooms, and a large theatre (also used as a cinema and skating rink). Outside the gardens had a waterfall, a bandstand and a lawn area which was used for bowling, tennis and badminton.

The venue, close to the railway station (there were cheap fares at the weekend) ensured its success, and it rapidly became the premier suburban entertainment venue.

The heyday of the Pavilion lasted just 12 years until it was completely gutted by fire. When it was rebuilt it had lost much of its 'fairytale' character and became a cinema with seating for 850. It was again destroyed by fire in June 1919. In 1939 the Pavilion was given an overhaul and became an unimpressive concrete structure. It closed its doors for the last time in 1984.

22ND JUNE

The Hibernian Auxiliary Church Missionary Society held their first meeting at the Rotunda on 22 June 1814. Within a few years it had established several schools in Africa – annual subscribers of £5 had the right to adopt an African child and give him/her a name. In the space of a few years donations amounting to £1,000 and annual subscriptions to about £200 had been built up.

By 1817 the society was planning a new settlement in New Zealand. *The History of the City of Dublin* (1818) pulled no punches when describing the dangers it expected such a mission would face: 'In physical and intellectual energies the New Zealander far surpasses all the savages of the Pacific Ocean. He is, however, ferocious, treacherous, and vindictive, a cannibal and devourer of human flesh from appetite and choice. Such a being must be treated in no ordinary way. Already have some considerate

Kingstown pavilion, Dun Laoghaire.

traders introduced the potatoe [sic] into New Zealand, and the culture of this nutritious root in some degree has weaned the native from his thirst for human blood.'

23RD JUNE

A conference of ministers met in London on 23 June 1921, the day following the assassination of Sir Henry Wilson by two IRA members (one-legged Joseph O'Sullivan and Reginald Dunne, both aged 24).

Longford-born Wilson, 58, had been a Field-Marshall in the British Army, was MP for North Down and was Sir James Craig's military adviser. His killing may have been authorised by Michael Collins.

The conference decided on a policy of immediate military retaliation. It was planned that troops would take over the Four Courts using armour, artillery and aircraft. General MacReady, who attended the conference, felt that the attack should pose no great military difficulty but expressed concern at the political consequences of the proposal and the attendant civilian casualties. The Royal Navy was ordered to arrange for ships to be sent to Kingstown to transport prisoners to Great Britain when the operation was completed.

On the day of the proposed operation [25 June] the order to attack was rescinded. It appears that General MacReady had developed stronger doubts than he had expressed in London, The naval vessels which were on their way to Kingstown were ordered to return to their home port.

24TH JUNE

'A great famine afflicted all Ireland in this and the foregoing year, and the city of Dublin suffered miserably. But the people in their distress met with an unexpected and providential relief. For about the 24th of June [1331] a prodigious number of large sea fish, called Turlehydes [most likely bottle-nosed whales], were brought into the bay of Dublin, and cast on shore at the mouth of the river Dodder (This is now called Donebrook river, and falls into the Liffey at Ringsend). They were from 30 to 40 feet long, and so bulky, that two tall men placed one on each side of the fish could not see one another. The lord justice, sir Anthony Lucy, with his servants, and many of the citizens of Dublin, killed above 200 of them, and gave leave to the poor to carry them away at their pleasure.'

Scarcity of food was not uncommon and prices could rise quite dramatically over a very short period of time. Twenty-one years earlier it is reported that 'The bakers of Dublin were drawn on hurdles at horses tails through the street, as a punishment for using false weights, and other evil practices. This happened in a year of great scarcity, when a cronoge of wheat sold for 20 shillings and upwards.'

25TH JUNE

The Dublin Penny Journal pulled down the shutters for the last time with its issue of 25 June 1836. It had lasted for four years and, though not a newspaper, had provided extensive coverage on the building and running of the Dublin to Kingstown Railway, as well as extensive notes on antiquities and curiosities both in Dublin and further afield. 'The hand of disease has so paralysed our energies, and affected our general health, as to render it necessary that, for a considerable time to come, we shall abstain from making any exertion in which the powers of the mind may be occupied. For the information of those interested in such details we may here observe, that a publication of this kind, to succeed in this country must be carried on by one individual, who will have the profits of Editor, Printer, and Publisher, to repay his trouble, and who can allow from £1500 to £2000 to remain in the concern. A circulation beyond 11,000 or 12,000 cannot be calculated on; while the capital engaged is scattered over England, Scotland and Ireland, in small sums, sometimes not easily got in. That there is very considerable talent in the country there cannot be a doubt; what we want in Ireland is a little more national and public spirit.'

26TH JUNE

'Tuesday night last [26 June 1764] between the Hours of Twelve and One, the Watch of St. Mary's was attacked by a Number of Rioters armed with Cutlasses &c. They wantonly assailed them, and wounded several of the Watchmen; amongst the latter, was the Sergeant, whom it's said, received several Cuts in his Head, and had his Back broken, and whose Life is despaired of. These Miscreants, exceeding twenty in Number, all escaped, the Watchmen having Fled to their Garrison, in Mary-street, where they took Shelter, and suffered their Antagonists to go off in Triumph, seeking whom else they could destroy

WHEREAS the Watch of St. Mary's Parish have been grossly abused by a great Number of Rioters The Supervisors of the Watch of said Parish, do hereby offer

Vast crowds attended the Pontifical Mass in the Phoenix Park on 26 June 1932

a Reward of ten Pounds Sterling to the first Person who shall discover and prosecute to Convictions any one or more Persons concerned in the said Riot, and if any Person concerned will discover any of his Accomplices, he shall not only be entitled to said Reward, but Application shall be made for his Pardon.' [*The Public Register*, or *Freeman's Journal*]

27TH JUNE

After the killing of Field Marshall Sir Henry Wilson in London by two IRA men [See June 23], the British Government demanded that the Irish Free State take immediate action against the Anti-Treaty forces or the Treaty would be declared void.

On 27 June, five days after Sir Henry's murder Free State artillery (loaned by departing British regiments) opened fire on IRA forces who had occupied the Four Courts since April. The commanding officer in the Four Court, IRA Major General Rory O'Connor, smuggled out a statement: 'At 4.40 this morning, we received a note from Tom Ennis demanding on behalf of "the Government" our surrender at 4am, when he would attack. He opened attack in the name of his "Government", with rifle, machine and field pieces. The boys are glorious, and will fight for the Republic to the end.'

It was a one-sided battle but the garrison held out for three days. 170 prisoners were taken.

Fire had already taken hold and Dublin Fire Brigade fought the flames in the Four Courts and the Public Record Office for three hours until a mine exploded.

The statue of Lord Gough, which formed the backdrop to one of Winston Churchill's earliest memories.

28TH JUNE

Work on the deceased John Foley's equestrian statue of Lord Gough was ending, and the foundry was pressing the organising committee about where to deliver it. The committee, in turn, was trying to get Dublin Corporation to go back on their decision to place it in relative obscurity in Foster Place – they wanted to see the statue placed in a more prominent position in Westmoreland Street. A special meeting between the committee and councillors was held on 28 June 1879: 'A letter was read from the committee, in which it was stated that a site had been offered in London. The opponents of any more liberal grant than that of Foster-place appeared to take umbrage at this as implying a threat, and resisted the resolution. It was warmly supported, however, by Alderman Tarpey, the High Sheriff, who, though one of the most pronounced Nationalists in the assembly, showed a generous appreciation of Lord Gough's claims to respect and honour from his countrymen, and it was finally adopted. The effect is to leave the Council free to grant the site in Westmoreland-street, but it is not at all sure that it will be ultimately given.'

In fact, Lord Gough's statue ended up blocking the road in the Phoenix Park. Among those at the opening was the very young Winston Churchill who later wrote of it as his first coherent memory.

29TH JUNE

By 1941 petrol rationing was beginning to bite – even for good causes! 'On Sunday morning next [29 June 1941], starting at 8 o'c., the LSF and Red Cross will co-operate in moving the entire equipment of the Orthopaedic Hospital and all its intern patients from Merrion Street to its new home at Blackheath, Clontarf. Announcing this at the Dublin Rotary Club today, Mr. WB Conyngham, Chairman of the Hospital Board, appealed to the Rotarians for assistance in obtaining petrol to carry out the removal. The Government, he said, had given an allowance of petrol for this purpose to the L.S.F. who were in charge of moving the hospital beds and other equipment, but they had been unable to obtain a grant of petrol for the Red Cross side of the removal work, which included the moving of the patients, many of whom have to be taken in ambulances.

'We are going around,' he said, 'scrounging a gallon here and a gallon there. So if any of you can find a couple of gallons for us between now and Saturday, please let me know about it.' (*The Evening Herald*, June 23rd 1941.)

30TH JUNE

As the leader of the IRA you have reason to fear many people, but perhaps those you need to watch most carefully are your own fellow-travellers. So Stephen Hayes found out when, on 30 June 1941, he was kidnapped, tortured and 'court-martialled' by Northern-based IRA members.

Things had not been working out for the IRA, and operations organised by Hayes had an annoying habit of being raided by the Gardai. When Hayes met German spy Herman Goetz in Dublin in 1940 the police recovered details of the German plan 'Operation Kathleen.' In August, a meeting organised by Hayes for senior IRA men, including Paddy McGrath, Tom Harte and Tom Hunt, was also raided.

In captivity Hayes was moved from house to house before, a week later, ending up in No. 20 Castlewood Park. His 'court-martial' lasted over 24 hours. He was sentenced to death.

Hayes thoughtfully offered to write a full confession. Taking as long as possible, he waited until his single guard left the room, grabbed a revolver left on a mantelpiece, and jumped through a window.

It was just another quiet day in Rathmines Garda Station – right up to the point that Hayes burst through the doors, bound hand and foot in chains, badly beaten and clutching a revolver.

Chapter Seven

July

1ST JULY

Second in command of the Williamite forces at the Battle of Boyne on 1 July 1690 (the change to the Gregorian Calendar in 1752 moved the date to 12 July), Frederick Herman Schomberg, seeing the Williamite foothold on the south bank endangered near the village of Oldbridge, he led his fellow Huguenots to reinforce them, only to be hacked twice by sabres and fatally shot in the back – either by one of his own troops or by a deserter to the Jacobite side, depending on the various accounts.

After the battle he was buried in St. Patrick's Cathedral with an epitaph later supplied by Jonathan Swift. DA Chart describes it as: 'A characteristic piece of work, intended rather to libel the living than to praise the departed. It is in Latin, and records how the cathedral authorities often entreated, to no purpose, the heirs of the great marshal to set up some memorial, and, in despair, at length erected this stone, that posterity might know where the famous Schomberg lies. 'The fame of his valour,' Swift sums up, 'was more effective with strangers than his nearness of blood was with his kinsmen.'

2ND JULY

After the Battle of the Boyne King James was almost the first to convey the news of his own defeat to Dublin. Lady Tyrconnell met him on steps of Dublin Castle. 'Madame,' he is reported to have said, 'your countrymen can run well.' 'If so,' she replied, 'I see your Majesty has won the race.' At six o'clock on 2 July 1690, James summoned the Lord Mayor and some of the principal inhabitants to the Castle, advised them to submit to William's army, not to let the French troops injure the city, and then unkindly pointed out to the people who had put their lives and property at risk for his cause: 'I came to this kingdom, and found my Roman Catholic subjects here equipped and prepared to defend my cause as their ability could bear, I found the fatal truth of what I had been so often precautioned, and though the army did not desert me here, as they did in England, yet when it came to a trial they basely fled the field and left the spoil to the enemies, nor could they be prevailed upon to rally, though the loss in the whole defeat was but inconsiderable; so that hencefor-ward, I never more determine to head an Irish army, and do now resolve to shift for myself, and so gentlemen must you.'

3RD JULY

Thomas Grubb, described in detail the casting of a 48 inch diameter mirror reflecting telescope for Melbourne Observatory throughout 3 July 1866, at Grubb's premises on Observatory Lane, Rathmines. In part it reads: 'The room was small (35ft x 16.5ft). Besides the monstrous red-hot pot and its glowing contents, there were the melting furnace, the open furnace and lastly the fifty tons of red-hot brickwork that formed the annealing oven. I'm a strong man, but the moment I did reach the open air, I fainted away.'

All went well until near the end of the process. 'The mirror wouldn't come off its bed in spite of the efforts of six individuals. If that metal disc had remained there much longer, with its temperature running down, it would be worse than useless. Some metal had got into the interstices and formed solid pins that kept it in the beg. At last someone jumped upon the taut chain, Blondinlike, and a second or two later the mirror was in the annealing oven.'

In 1868 the completed telescope arrived in Australia, reaching Melbourne in November of that year; it was ready for work by the end of June 1869, and observations commenced in August of the same year.

4TH JULY

A great crowd was gathered in Glasnevin Cemetery on Friday morning, 4 July 1890 to witness the burial of five members of the one family.

The previous Tuesday James O'Connor, a journalist on the staff of *United Ireland*, had returned home from work to find his wife, three of his four daughters, and a female servant in distress. They had been poisoned by diseased mussels from the seashore beside the family home at 1 Seapoint Avenue.

Mr. O'Connor gave each an emetic and two doctors quickly arrived. Their combined efforts were to no avail as just after 9pm the deaths began – first Annie, 13, then her mother, Molly, quickly followed by Alieen, 11, Kathleen, 7, and Norah, 5.

The coroner's court revealed that the pond where the mussels were taken had been condemned by Doctor Pollock, the medical officer, 15 years earlier. It was also pointed out that three people had died nearby from cholera, that the area was not served by sewers and that 'the sewage comes back into the pond during flood tides. County Coroner Davys returned as verdict of death by poisoning. James O'Connor died in 1910 and was buried in the family plot at Glasnevin. His sole surviving daughter, Moya, was later a friend and helper of Michael Collins.

5TH JULY

On the afternoon of Wednesday, 5 July 1922, Free State troops, backed by artillery and armoured cars, had pushed back the last remnants of the lightly armed 'Irregulars' into a final position on O'Connell Street – the Granville Hotel.

It was held by Cathal Brugha, 17 men, and three nurses – a much larger force had been evacuated by Cmdt. Oscar Traynor on Monday night. Brugha's token force had been intended to keep the attackers occupied as the evacuation took place, but Brugha had then refused to accept any order for retreat.

By 5pm the end was in sight with the Granville Hotel in flames. He ordered his men to surrender but himself remained inside the building for a time. Cathal Brugha emerged, revolver in hand, and was promptly shot – dying in hospital two days later just short of his 48th birthday.

It was a fitting end, Cathal Brugha had denounced the Treaty in bloodcurdling terms: 'If our last bullet had been fired, our last man were lying on the ground with his enemies howling round him with the bayonets raised ready to plunge into his body, that man should say if they say to him "Now, will you come into our Empire?" – he should and he would say "No, I will not".

6TH JULY

The Irish Crown Jewels, then valued at £50,000, were discovered to be missing from the safe in which they were kept in Dublin Castle on 6 July 1907. The stolen jewels, including the Star and Badge of the Order of St. Patrick, were never recovered, nor was anyone convicted of the theft.

The Granville Hotel, Dublin, the last hold out of the anti-treaty forces in central Dublin and the scene of Cathal Brugha's last stand. In this image firemen are dealing with the last stages of the blaze.

The King, Edward VII, head of the Order, was due to visit Ireland for three days, starting on the 10 July, and some of the jewels would have been worn by the Lord Lieutenant at a variety of functions over the three days.

The Order of the Knights of St. Patrick dated back to 1783 and the insignia had come into existence in 1829 on the order of King George IV. By statute of 1905 it had been ordered that the insignia, collars and badges be kept in the strong-room in the Office of Arms.

There were seven keys to the room, held by Sir Arthur Vicars (the Ulster King of Arms), Mr. Burtchaell the Secretary, Stivey, a messenger, Mr. O'Mahoney, the office-cleaner Mrs. Farrell, Kerr the castle detective and O'Keefe a servant of the Board of Works.

The loss was discovered by Stivey at around 2.15pm when putting a box containing a gold collar in the safe. The safe had not been picked, nor in the opinion of locksmiths, could a duplicate key have been used. Although a £1,000 reward was offered, no concrete evidence of the identity of the thief was ever found. [See entry for 6th January]

7TH JULY

Dubliner Richard Brinsley Sheridan, 65, died in London on 7 July 1816 – his home was taken over by the bailiff's and his body had to be moved to a friend's home. It was ironic that just a few days later he was buried with great ceremony in Westminster Abbey.

But Sheridan's life had always been a matter of ups and downs and in matters financial he had a remarkable talent for failure. Married twice to wealthy women he managed to lose their money. A successful playwright – *The Rivals*, *The School for Scandal*, etc. – he gave up writing for a career as a not too successful politician. He had invested his money, and more, in Drury-lane Theatre and its destruction by fire in 1809 brought him financial ruin. He was called out of the House of Commons on the occasion, and is reported to have said to a friend who remarked on the philosophical calmness with which he sat in view of the fire taking some refreshment: 'A man may surely be allowed to take a glass of wine by his own fire-side.'

In the spring of 1815 he was arrested and placed in prison. A newspaper appeal raised enough to get him out. Only the insistence of a doctor prevented his return to prison during his final illness.

8TH JULY

Speaking on the Dublin Boundaries Bill in Mr. TW Russell MP, strongly supported the annexation of the suburban townships [i.e. Pembroke, Clontarf, etc.]: 'Take the question of sewage. The river Liffey had been nothing more than an open sewer. All of the drainage of Dublin and all the trade refuse of Dublin poured into it, whilst not one of the townships pretended to have any efficient system of drainage at all. Clontarf poured crude sewage upon the slob lands, and it was then washed back by the tide to the estuary. Rathmines and Pembroke, too, simply poured what amounted to crude sewage, without any treatment, into the estuary. The Corporation, however,

Richard Brinsley Sheridan, a playwright, politician, failed investor and philosophical about loss.

were now carrying out an efficient system of main drainage, and if the townships were brought in to participate in it there would be a wonderful change in the state of the locality. Towards the close of last century Dublin was largely occupied by the nobility, and the houses which used to be kept up by them were still standing. But the houses devised for the accommodation of one family were now occupied by six, seven, and even ten different families. There were no adequate sanitary facilities conveniences in those houses and the result was that a great mass of people were living under conditions simply appalling. The infant mortality in Dublin was nothing short of a public scandal.' [*The Irish Times*, July 9 1899.]

9TH JULY

When Douglas Corrigan landed his OX5 Robin monoplane at Baldonnel on 9 July 1938 there may have been nobody more surprised that him! After all he had left New York the previous day after filing a flight plan for California.

He claimed that after taking off in fog from Floyd Bennett Field in Brooklyn he had misread his compass heading for 26 hours – only realising his mistake when he dropped out of the clouds to see an ocean below him.

There were few who believed him, after all Corrigan had been applying for permission for fly to Ireland since 1935 – the authorities turned him down

Wrong Way Corrigan. The man who flew the wrong way or did he. Whatever way he did it he flew non-stop across the Atlantic in 1931 and had a ticket tape parade for his trouble on his return home to New York.

repeatedly because his plane was considered incapable of non-stop transatlantic flight. Corrigan, in turn, had modified the plane to make the flight, in his opinion, possible.

Oddly, too, Corrigan had passed over Belfast before making his landing – he didn't see an airport. But he found Baldonnel? 'Having studied the map of Ireland two years before, I knew this was Dublin,' he told anyone who asked.

The unlikely story, his good-humour, and the sheer madness of it all eventually won the day for Corrigan. His only penalty was a suspended pilot's licence, which ended on August 4, the same day he returned to the USA (by ship). A ticker tape parade in New York attracted 1,000,000 people.

10th July

Kevin O'Higgins, Minister for Justice and External Affairs, was assassinated by Republicans as he went to Mass in Monkstown on 10 July 1927. *The Blackrock College Journal* noted: 'At 11.45am this peaceful neighbourhood was startled by the sound of shots and almost immediately the report was spread that Mr. Kevin O'Higgins, Minister for Justice and External Affairs, had been shot down in a most brutal and cowardly manner on his way to 12.00 Mass in the Parish Church of Booterstown. At about 5pm he passed away having died a glorious and happy death.'

The killing came as a total shock as the wounds of the Civil War were believed to be healing. But O'Higgins held a special place in the bitter hearts of the defeated IRA – he had personally signed the death warrants of 77 Republican prisoners between 1922 and 1923. He forgave his killers before he died. He was given a state funeral – the cortège stretched for 3 miles.

Many years later the identity of the killers was revealed – Timothy Coughlin, Bill Gannon and Archie Doyle. Their story was that, travelling by motor car to a match in Dublin, they spotted O'Higgins and decided to kill him on the spot. An explanation which ignores the presence of the gun!

11TH JULY

The Daily Express of 11 July 1903 reported on the loss of a film of the Phoenix Park Speed Trials: 'The management of the Empire Theatre, having secured the speed trials in the Phoenix Park on Saturday last for cinematographic purposes, have been very much disappointed in the result of their elaborate arrangements, owing, it is alleged, to the treatment meted out by the Post Office to a parcel containing the negative film which was posted for despatch to London for development. We understand that on the evening of the trials in the Park the operators of Mssrs. Edison's pictures, securely packed 165 feet of film in a light, air-tight box, which was well covered and tied with twine, and handed it in any the College Green Post Office. In the course of post twine and label were delivered to an address in London, and three days later the box containing the film was returned to the sender, who, on examination, discovered that in the meantime the box had been opened in ordinary light, and of course the complete strip of sensitive film was destroyed. As this film was the only one exposed at the interesting event, it need scarcely be said that the loss of such a monopoly is keenly felt by the management of the theatre, and also be the owners of the cinematograph.'

12TH JULY

Mr Harney 'the son of a respectable citizen of Dublin' was lodging in Dublin with Mrs Mary Byrne – 'known in the gay world by the distinction of the splashing Widow Byrne, otherwise Buck Byrne.' One evening Mr. Harney was set upon by highwaymen and, while defending himself, fractured his leg. Surgeon Carmichael set the leg and told him to get a nurse. But the only young woman that he could think of was one who had lodged in Mrs. Byrne's house sometime previously. Winny and a male friend of Mr. H were tending to his wounds one night when 'this Amazonian, attended by her daughter, a more violent termagent than herself, and accompanied by two savage butchers' broke into the room, assaulted Winny, calling her a thief and a street-walker, and insulted Mr. H with 'epithets of the most gross and vulgar description.' Next on the scene were the watch, they having been summoned by Mrs. Byrne to arrest the 'prostitute.' In the ensuing chaos Mr. Harney did his leg in again. The whole sorry tale came out in court on 12 July 1811. Mrs. Byrne said she believed that Harney had seduced the young woman, that she was in a passion at the time, and that she was willing to pay for any other nurse. The judge seems to have felt that Mr. Harney may have been at least partly at fault – finding Mrs. Byrne guilty, he awarded only sixpence damages.

13th July

They say that there is no such thing as bad publicity – it's a maxim which doesn't always hold true. Take the case of John Sinnott, charged with stealing fresh fruit from a garden in Dun Laoghaire and placed on remand. On August 13 1863 he was brought back before Judge M'Dermott: 'He [Sinnott] stated that he lived upon Albert Road, where his father and stepmother resided, but that the latter used to beat him, and that he could not stop at him. The magistrate said that this was the case which had been so erroneously reported in some of the Dublin papers, in which it was said that the lad was only eight years old, and that he was sent to a reformatory for stealing three pence worth of fruit. Now the fact was that he was near sixteen years old, and that he had been in a reformatory before for three years.

Instead of being an innocent lad as was insinuated, it appeared from the records of the prison that he had been convicted and committed to jail on seven different occasions and four out of these seven was for felony. He was considered so incorrigible that he would not be received again into the Glencree Reformatory, and the mangers of the Upton Reformatory declined to admit him also. He was now sentenced to one month's imprisonment.'

14th July

At St. Michan's, itself one of the great curiosities of Dublin, can be found the mortal remain of two brothers, John (34) and Henry (32) Sheares, both of whom were executed in on 14 July 1798.

Along with most of the Dublin leadership of the United Irishmen, they had been arrested in late May 1798. Quickly convicted for treason, the two brothers – a soldier and a barrister, both had been educated at Trinity College – faced the gallows together before a large crowd outside Newgate prison.

Ironically, Lord Kilwarden, was killed by a mob during Emmett's failed rebellion of 1803, because they mistook him for Judge Carleton who had condemned the Sheares brothers. Over the years their wooden coffins gradually decayed and the bodies were exposed to all comers.

A visitor of 1832 found it too much: 'I confess I was in as great haste to leave this horrid place, as I had been to enter it. My friend called me back to see the spot where the two ill-fated Sheares rest. The common jail shells in which they repose sufficiently identified them, and – the headless trunks! I could stay no longer, but rushed into the open air.' Both of the bodies were later placed in lead and oak coffins by the historian of 1798 Dr. Madden in 1853.

15th July

'The Hibernian Society in Dublin' (for maintaining, educating and apprenticing the orphans and children of soldiers in Ireland) was granted a Charter on 15 July 1769.

An imaginative engraving of the attack on Lord Kilwarden in Thomas Street on Saturday, 23 July 1803. The costumes seem to date to a previous century and the scene appears rural. [History of Ireland, by Thomas Wright]

Their bye-laws show that the inmates didn't have it easy: '[The Master] is to reside constantly in the hospital. He is to cause the children to rise at six in the morning from the 25th March to the 29th September, and at half an hour after seven from the 29th September to the 25th March. He is to allow one hour to the boys to brush their cloaths, clean their shoes, wash their face and hands, and to have their heads combed. He is then to read prayers in the schoolroom, in a clear and distinct manner, and to cause one of the boys to read one of the lessons in the same manner. He is then to proceed to the school business of reading, writing, arithmetic, &c. previously examining each boy, to see that they are washed clean, and dressed in a proper manner. He is to keep the boys at their school-learning in the afternoons, until six in the evening in the summer, and until dark in the winter. He is to see that the boys are all in bed and well at eight o'clock in the winter and nine in the summer, and that no candle or fire be left in their rooms.'

16TH JULY

Whenever Dublin genealogists and local historians get together the destruction of the records held in the Four Courts and the Custom House is sure to be mentioned.

The Calendar of the Ancient Records of Dublin demonstrates that there were always people who were willing to dispose of ancient papers: 'Gentlemen – Having agreeably to your desire compleated the searches amongst the City's Ancient Records for evidence respecting the Tolls and Customs, I am to request you will be placed to report me to the assembly for some compensation. On this very laborious business, I was engaged for forty-six days and had the satisfaction to find a vast quantity of decisive evidence from the reign of Henry the Seventh down to the present time. I also carefully separated into different classes the Records of the Crown side, those of the Pleas side, and the City Papers, so as to avoid confusion in future, and cleared out above six cart-loads of old fragments and rubbish, but not until after previous careful examination. Timothy Allen, 16 July 1818.' The Council, no doubt ecstatic at the destruction of the fragments, voted him £50.

17TH JULY

Jonathan Swift, keenly aware of his troubled mind and mortality, wrote on 17 July 1735: 'I have now finished my will in form wherein I have settled my whole fortune in the city on a trust for building and maintaining an hospital for idiots and lunatics, but which I save the expense of a chaplain and almost of a physician.' After various alterations, Swift ordered that the premises should be near Dr. Steven's Hospital (a general hospital which could treat the physical ailments of his patients) or, if that wasn't possible, near to the centre city: 'Large enough for the purpose and in building thereon an hospital large enough for the reception of as many idiots and lunatics as the annual income of the said lands, and worldly substance, will be sufficient to maintain, and I desire that the said hospital may be called St. Patrick's Hospital.' Swift also went to the trouble of drawing up a constitution for the management of the hospital – it was shaped by his own experiences as a governor of the Bedlam Hospital in London. In the event a suitable site was leased in 1748 and St. Patrick's Hospital opened in September 1757.

18TH JULY

The pillory was a device designed to inflict punishment through public humiliation. Often a placard detailing the crime was placed nearby: these punishments generally lasted one or two hours. Time spent in the pillory could be dangerous as it used hinged boards, raised on a post, to clamp around the offender's neck and wrists, forcing the prisoner to remain standing and exposed. After that it all depended on the mood of the crowd – and they could prove fickle!

Take for example the case, reported in *Whalley's Newsletter* of 18 July 1720: 'Thomas Delaney, convicted of perjury in the King's Bench, and one Martin from Cork (hired to be a clerk in the Sugarhouse in Caple Street) for seditious words against his Majesty, stood in the pillory before the Tholsel [on the corner of Nicholas Street and Christchurch Place] on Wednesday last. The first, his ears nailed to the pillory, was pelted so with eggs it was doubted whether he would recover but, if he does, it is believed he will lose at least one, if not both his eyes but Martin had not one egg thrown at him.'

19TH JULY

The Battle of Landen in the Netherlands on 19 July 1693 was an extremely bloody affair – the French losing 9,000 men and the British 19,000. Among those mortally wounded was Dubliner Patrick Sarsfield, Baron Roseberry, Viscount of Tully, and Earl of Lucan, who, as his seniors were killed one by one, became commander of the French left flank. Struck by a bullet in the chest, he was taken to the town of Huy 20 miles away, where he died three days later. His final words are reported as: 'Oh, that this were for Ireland.'

He is buried in the grounds of St Martin's Church, Huy, where a plaque on the wall marks the approximate location of his grave. He is best remembered today for his surprise cavalry attack on a Williamite siege train during the siege of Limerick. At Ballyneety eight heavy battering cannons, five mortars, eighteen tin pontoons, and 200 wagons loaded with ammunition and supplies, fell into his hands. The artillery was spiked, and the other supplies were collected together and destroyed. After brokering the Treaty of Limerick he sailed for France in December 1691, being appointed Captain of the second troop of Irish Life Guards on his arrival.

20TH JULY

On 20 July 1898 the first radio sports broadcast and the first 'public' broadcast was made from Dublin Bay by Italian Guglielmo Marconi, the inventor of wireless telegraphy. The event was the Royal St. George Yacht Club Regatta and Marconi had been asked to cover the event by two Dublin newspapers, the Evening Mail and the Daily Express.

He installed a transmitter on boar a steam tug – *The Flying Huntress* – and based his receiver in the Harbour Masters House (now Moran Park House) where a telephone had been specially installed and linked to the *Daily Express.*

It all went without a hitch, with Marconi giving wireless reports to the mainland from distances of 5 to 10 miles out in Dublin Bay. He was also sending Queen Victoria reports concerning the health of her son, the Prince of Wales, who was recovering from a knee injury as he watched the regatta from the royal yacht. It was all done through Morse code – radio speech wasn't possible until 1921.

When Marconi died in Rome in July 1935 he was accorded the unique tribute of a two-minute silence by radio stations across the world.

21ST JULY

'Mrs. Mary Mitchell, of Fair Hill Road, Galway, was charged by Caroline Howard, matron of the Bird's Nest Institution [Dun Laoghaire], with assaulting her by tearing her face with her hands, and endeavouring to force and take away a child named Ann Mitchell, eleven years of age, an inmate of said institution, while proceeding to church on Sunday. The assault was witnessed by several constables. The Rev. Mr. Brownrigg, also connected with the above institution, deposed that he knew the father of the girl to have been a member of the Church of England. It appears that the mother of the child was always a Catholic, but it was alleged on the other side that when the father was dying he appointed certain trustees who were to take care of his child, which,

A picture of the royal party on their visit to Ireland in July 1903.

however, was denied by the mother. The child, however, after her father's death was given up to some lady who said she would provide for her, and she was then sent to the Bird's Nest, but after some time she became disillusioned with her treatment there, and wrote to her mother requesting her to come and fetch her away. The mother was informed by some one that she had a right to take the child away by force, and acting upon that advice she committed the above assault. [*Kingstown Journal*, 21 July 1868.]

22ND JULY

One of the strangest hangovers of Imperial Britain was the large statue of Queen Victoria in front of Leinster House – perhaps a reminder to TDs that Britain was never that far away. By 1948 it was looking like a permanent fixture until Mr. Con Lehane asked the Taoiseach if he was 'aware that the national feelings of the majority of Irishmen are outraged by the failure to remove the statue of a foreign monarch from the Quadrangle at Leinster House, and if he will state whether it is proposed to remove this statue at an early date.'

At which point the Taoiseach, John A Costello, sprang his surprise. 'A scheme, which was approved in September last, for the provision of parking accommodation for motor-cars at Leinster House involves the removal of the statue to which the Deputy refers, and it is anticipated that the work on the removal of the statue will begin early next month.'

The statue was finally transported off the premises on 22 July 1948 and transported to the Royal Hospital, Kilmainham. In the 1970s Victoria was shipped off to Daingean where the statue languished until it was transported to Sydney, Australia, where it can be found in front of a shopping mall.

23RD JULY

One of the great mysteries of Dublin is the location of the body Robert Emmett – another is what possessed him on the night of 23 July 1803? It was not so much an insurrection as a street brawl ending in tragedy.

Dr. Madden later described the scene as the crowd moved through Thomas Street after wounding a Mr. Leech: 'a private carriage was seen moving along that part of Thomas-street which leads to Vicar-street It was stopped and attacked; Lord Kilwarden, who was inside, with his daughter and his nephew, the Rev. Richard Wolfe, cried out: 'It is I, Kilwarden, Chief-Justice of the King's Bench.' A man, whose name is said to have been Shannon, rushed forward, plunged his pike into his lordship, crying out: 'You are the man I want.' His lordship, mortally wounded, was dragged out of the carriage, and several additional wounds inflicted on him. His nephew endeavoured to make his escape, but was taken, and put to death.'

'A detachment of the military made its appearance at the corner of Cutpurse-row, and commended firing on the insurgents, who immediately fled in all directions. The rout was general in less than an hour from the time they had sallied forth.'

The Bank of Ireland building on college green, previously the Irish House of Parliament, lit up for the royal visit in 1903.

24TH JULY

The annual report of the Royal Hospital Donnybrook for 1904 recorded the visit of royalty, in the person of Queen Alexandra, on 24 July: 'This was the first occasion on which a Queen Consort had visited and the ceremony was consequently a very interesting and important one and was attended with the most favourable impressions of Her Majesty's gently and womanly nature and of her touching and queenly sympathy with those in deep affliction. Her Majesty was presented with a large bouquet of flowers by a youthful patent. The queen visited several of the numerous wards and amongst them the female consumptive patients, where Her Majesty with her usual sympathy for the suffering, briefly conversed with each patient and presented each with a bunch of flowers, which were much appreciated by the objects of her solicitude. Before leaving the hospital Her Majesty commanded the presentation of the members of the Managing Committee, who were introduced into the Queen's presence in a body by the Chairman [Mr. Fry].'

25TH JULY

'Wednesday [25 July 1764] a Man at Finglass drawing a Charge from his Gun, it went off and wounded him so desperately that his Life is in danger; he was carried to the Inns-Quay Infirmary. One hundred and eleven Pounds of Tea, seized by Messieurs Draper and Byrne, were lodged in his Majesty's Stores. Being Election Day with the Corporation of Bricklayers and Plasters, Mr. Richard Gilbert Plummer of Abby-street, was elected Master, and Messrs. John Adams and John Keating were elected Wardens for the ensuing Year; which Corporation will ride the Franchises as usual. The Corporation of Cutlers, Painter-stainers and Stationers, resolved that they would ride the Franchises of this City in a decent uniform Manner, and that the Cloth to be worn by them on this Occasion, should be of Irish Manufacture Only.' [*The Public Register*, or *Freeman's Journal*]

26TH JULY

The Illustrated London News reported on June 26 1875: 'An extraordinary scene took place at a great fire in Dublin at Reid's malt-house and Malone's bonded warehouse, in the Liberties. The former had above £2000 worth of malt in it, and the latter, which immediately adjoins it, had 1800 puncheons of whisky, the property of various distillers, and worth £54,000. The burning liquor, running down Ardee-street, Chamber-street, Cork-street, and Mill-street, spread the flames with great rapidity. In two hours all the houses on one side of Mill-street and several in Chamber-street were destroyed. The fire brigade could not use their engines lest the water should carry the flames through the city, but they tore up the pavement and used sand and manure carried from a depot in a neighbouring street . . . Crowds of people assembled, and took off their hats and boots to collect the whisky, which ran in streams along the streets. Four persons have died in the hospital from the effects of drinking the whisky, which was burning hot as it flowed. Two corn-porters, named Healy and M'Nulty, were found in a lane off Cork-street, lying insensible, with their boots off, which they had evidently used to collect the liquor. There are many other persons in the hospital who are suffering from the same cause.'

27th July

When it came to the naming of a new street Councillor Timothy Daniel Sullivan came up with 'Lord Edward Street'. It might get up the noses of a few of the more 'loyal' types, but he was quite surprised to be warned off by the Irish Republican Brotherhood: 'With regard to the Re-Naming of the Streets of Dublin, there are in Ireland, and elsewhere, a considerable number of men who have a very earnest respect for the memory of all who have striven for Ireland, but who do not believe that the proper time has yet arrived for removing the names of the Hirelings of the Oppressor. Whatever names you may use, we warn you not to use the names of any of the men of 1798, or 1803, of Thomas Davis, or of the men of 1848, except Gavan Duffy or D'Arcy McGee. Let the proposer and seconder of the changes look well to this warning, as we will hold them responsible, and take such action with regard to them as their conduct shall deserve.'

Sullivan was also visited one night be three men 'who came, as they told me, to still further impress upon me the caution I had already received.' As Lord Mayor, Sullivan performed the opening of the street on 27 July 1886.

28th July

During the rebellion of Silken Thomas in 1534 the Protestant Archbishop of Dublin, John Allen, wisely decided to get out of Dublin and hot-footed it onto a boat at Dames gate – destination England. His luck was out and the boat was stranded at Clontarf, whereupon he headed for Artane and the 'safety' of Mr. Hollywood's house. Early next morning, 28 July, Silken Thomas arrived before the house in hot pursuit of him. The Archbishop was dragged out in his shirt, and, falling on his knees, begged for mercy.

Open caskets in the crypt of St Michan's, Dublin.

'Take away the churl,' exclaimed FitzGerald to his followers 'but the attendants wilfully misconstruing their master's words, beat out the bishop's brains, and thus committed as monstrous an act of sacrilege as Irish History records. It was observed that Archbishop Allen, as the perpetrator of sacrilege, deservedly became its victim; and that he who was the ready tool of Henry's spoliation of the monastic establishments in England, met in due recompense his murderous fate; at all events his assassins left a revenge on themselves, for the two actual perpetrators shortly died of most loathsome diseases.'

29TH JULY

Witness protection schemes are not a new phenomenon to Ireland. James Carey, leader of the 'Invincibles', killers of Burke and Cavendish in the Phoenix Park, was a marked man after turning informer on his comrades. His evidence had sent men to the gallows while he walked free for turning Queen's Evidence.

It was decided to relocate Carey almost as far away from Ireland as was possible. He was secretly sent to South Africa. On board the *Melrose Star*, travelling from Durban to Cape Town, he (under the alias James Power) became acquainted with another passenger, Patrick O'Donnell.

At Cape Town O'Donnell was shown a photograph of the informer Carey and immediately recognised 'Mr. Power'. On 29 July 1883 the two men met in the refreshment saloon. O'Donnell drew a revolver and fired three shots into Carey's body killing him almost instantly.

It was believed that O'Donnell sailed with Carey in order to kill him, but O'Donnell's ticket was bought at a steamship agency in London a fortnight before the Irish Government made up its mind to send Carey to South Africa. The murder, therefore, could not have been the result of premeditation. O'Donnell was brought to London for trial and hanged (See 17 December).

30TH JULY

On 30 July 1947 two young men were brought in front of Justice O'Sullivan – their alleged crime being that 'in sight of a place which the public habitually passed' [the Forty Foot] they 'did act in such a way as to offend modesty or cause scandal or injure the morals of the community'. Or, to put it bluntly, they had been sunbathing in the nude!

The *Journal of Criminology* [1948] reported on the case: 'The prosecuting solicitor urged that the place was still a public place, in that 'anybody, any lady could walk in'. To this the District Judge replied that 'for that matter, a lady could walk into the men's lavatory over there', and in holding that the prosecution was 'ill-founded and unfounded and one which should never have been brought', he dismissed the case with the hope that 'such stupid cases' would not be brought before him again.'

The *Evening Herald* noted: 'We trust that this famous swimming place will be free in future of any further vexatious proceedings of the kind, and that future generations of swimmers will be able to enjoy its amenities unhampered, as did their fathers before them.'

Fusiliers Arch, St Stephens green.

31ST JULY

The Dublin Fusiliers and four other Irish regiments in the British Army were offi-cially disbanded on 31 July 1922. In June, the flags of the Regiment had been handed over to King George V who promised to hold them in trust until the regiments were re-established.

It had come into existence as far back as the mid-1600s as part of the East India Company garrison – the 102nd Royal Madras Fusiliers – the Dublin Fusiliers date from the merging of two Indian regiments after the Indian Mutiny in 1857.

The Dubs (also nicknamed 'The Old Toughs') were mauled during the Boer War. In November 1899, a party of Dubs, along with *London Evening Post* reporter Winston Churchill, were captured by the Boers. On his escape two months later Churchill telegraphed their Colonel: 'My earnest congratulations on the honour of the Dublin Fusiliers more than any other Regiment have won for the land of their birth. We are all wearing the Shamrock here.'

During WWI a total of 4,777 Dubs died during the battles of Gallipoli, Salonika, Somme, Ypres and Passchendaele. The regiment's lasting memorial is Fusilier's Arch at the Grafton Street end of St. Stephen's Green – it records casualties suffered during the Boer War.

Chapter Eight

August

1st AUGUST

One of the earliest surviving records of the Ouzel Galley Society, known to have been in existence since 1705, is a receipt issued to John Macarell Esq, Captain of the *Ouzel Galley*, by John Morris, owner of the Ship Tavern, Chapelizod (where the society held its meetings). Dated 1 August 1753 Morris promised to return a portrait of the ship to the society on demand – in fact it went AWOL until 1870.

The Ouzel Galley Society, forerunner of Dublin Chamber of Commerce, came into existence for very practical, though highly unusual reasons. A Dublin ship, missing since 1695, returned to port five years later – laden with treasure. The ship obviously belonged to the insurers (who had paid out to owners Ferris, Twigg and Cash), but who owned the cargo? The crew told tales of piracy, slavery, hardship and final escape – but there was agreement that it would be giving a bad example to other seamen to share it between them. Five years into litigation – with the cost likely to exceed the value of the cargo – all parties agreed to arbitration by a number of Dublin merchants.

The money was given to charity and the merchants formed the Ouzel Galley Society to settle other business disputes. The Society was finally wound up in 1888.

2nd AUGUST

The last meeting of the Parliament at Dublin was on 2 August 1800, when the Lords chose 28 of their members to represent the peerage of Ireland in the Parliament of the United Kingdom. Lord Cornwallis delivered a speech from the throne, and the prorogation of the Parliament was announced.

As compensation for the abolition of their appointments, pensions amounting to just over £32,000 pounds were granted to the officials and servants connected with the House of Peers and Commoners, the amounts being based on salaries and benefits paid over the previous three years – among them Mrs. Albinia Taylor, keeper of the Parliament House who received £877 18s 9d.

After the Act of Union Government officials asked John 'Speaker' Foster for the return of the Speaker's Mace. He decline, saying that 'until the body which had entrusted the mace to his keeping demanded it, he would preserve it for them.'

It remained in his family until 1933 when it was sold for the Bank of Ireland. It can be seen in College Green – not in the House of Commons which has not survived, but in the Chamber of the House of Lords.

3RD AUGUST

Dubliner Roger Casement, 51, was hanged for treason in Pentonville Prison on 3 August 1916. Born in Sandycove, he had spent 20 years working in Africa, and later in South America, for the Consular Service of the British Foreign Office. In 1911 he was knighted for his work on exposing the exploitation of natives in Peru.

Returning to Ireland in 1913 he became involved in the fight for Irish independence. He travelled to Germany to arrange arms supplies but, shortly after the Aud sailed with its lethal cargo, returned to Ireland on board a submarine, U-19, hoping to persuade the leaders that a rising could not succeed.

He was arrested after landing at Banna Strand, brought to London and imprisoned in the Tower of London, tried at the Old Bailey and sentenced to death. Calls for clemency were muted – something which was later explained by the 'Black Diaries' – containing torrid descriptions of homosexual adventures. Some of the more lurid sections were shown by the British Government to influential people who ordinarily might have called for leniency.

Whether the diaries are authentic is still hotly debated – but his sexuality should not detract from his humanitarian and nationalist exertions. Casement's body was returned to Ireland and buried in 1965 in Glasnevin after a state funeral.

Roger Casement, a decorated British Foreign Service official who fell foul of the British Authorities following his involvement with the Irish Freedom struggle and was executed in 1916.

4TH AUGUST

Wednesday, 4 August 1747, was eagerly looked forward to in Dublin as it marked the third day of racing at Kilmainham. But complaints had been made, probably by a Mr. King, whose lands adjoined the area where the races were being held, and the authorities decided that the races would not be allowed to take place: 'On Wednesday last, the Sub-Sheriff of the County of Dublin, attended by a party of constables and a detachment of soldiers from the Poddle Guard under the command of a sergeant, went to the Commons of Kilmainham to prevent the assembly of people to see the races to be run there that afternoon as had been done the days preceding. To do this effectually orders were given to pull down the booths and break the barrels in which strong liquors which was punctually executed. The populace, however, expressed their disapproval of such proceedings by crying out '"Shame, shame," or as some say a stone having been thrown, the soldiers were commanded to fire which they did and killed one man on the spot and wounded three others who died soon after.'

5TH AUGUST

The Medal of Honor is the highest award for valour in action against an enemy force which can be given to an individual serving in the US Armed Services. It is normally presented by the President. During the American Civil War 126 Medals of Honor were awarded to soldiers of Irish birth or descent. Just one was from Dublin – Sergeant James S. Roantree, US Marine Corps, who was born in Dublin in 1835.

Sgt. Roantree's moment of glory came on 5 August 1864. His Citation reads: 'On board the *USS Oneida* during action against rebel forts and gunboats and with the ram *Tennessee* in Mobile Bay. Despite damage to his ship and the loss of several men on board as enemy fire raked her decks and penetrated her boilers, Sgt. Roantree performed his duties with skill and courage throughout the furious battle which resulted in the surrender of the rebel ram Tennessee and in the damaging and destruction of batteries at Fort Morgan.'

The *Oneida* was the last in line of 18 Federal ships entering Mobile Bay, and sustained heavy damage from the Confederate ironclad *Tennessee*.

6TH AUGUST

Queen Victoria was in chipper form when she wrote her diary entry for Monday, 6 August at the Viceregal Lodge (Aras An Uachtaran).

'Dublin is a very fine city; and Sackville Street and Merrion Square are remarkably large and handsome; and the Bank, Trinity College, &c. are noble buildings. There are no gates to the town, but temporary ones were erected under an arch; and here we stopped, and the Mayor presented me the keys with some appropriate words. At the last triumphal arch a poor little dove was let down into my lap, with an olive branch round its neck, alive and very tame. The heat and dust were tremendous. We reached Phoenix Park, which is very extensive, at twelve. Lord and Lady Clarendon and all the household received us at the door. It is a nice comfortable house with a pretty terrace garden in front and has a very extensive view of the Park and the fine range of the Wicklow Mountains. We are most comfortably lodged, and have very nice rooms'

A sketching of George IV's visit to Dublin in 1821.

A few days later, she was still enthusiastic: 'I intend to create Bertie 'Earl of Dublin', as a compliment to the town and country; he has no Irish title and this was one of my father's titles.'

7TH AUGUST

There was breathless anticipation for a sporting event scheduled for 7 August 1899. *The Evening Telegraph* reported: 'The [R.I.C. Depot Sports] will come off at Ballsbridge on Monday the entries for nearly event in the programme are exceptionally large, and class is well represented. In fact almost every cyclist and athlete of any note in Ireland will be present, and a goodly sprinkle of first-rate men from over the water are coming also.

'The ladies; bicycle race is attracting widespread interest, and no less than nineteen riders are to face the starter. There may be some startling performances by some of the fair contestants. The prizes for this event are the best we have ever seen offered at any meeting, the first being a new ladies' safety, the second a gold hunting watch, and the third a very beautiful ornament for the dressing table or drawing room.'

Huge crowds on the day turned the meeting into somewhat of a shambles and though the *Telegraph* reporter did his best, he admitted failure. No fewer than 164 took part in the Boys' Race. And then there is the peculiar note: 'Mooskey won the Niggers race, George Laverdale second, Tippo Baskool third.'

8TH AUGUST

The Dublin Penny Journal of 8 August 1832 had its economics right – *The Big Issue* is sold today in just the way predicted: 'So far from thinking that the demand for these [penny] publications will subside, we think it will increase, and that a change will be produced by them upon the state of public feeling as extraordinary as it will be beneficial. Say there are forty thousand penny magazines sold in all Ireland weekly; (perhaps there are more) this brings in upwards of one hundred and sixty pounds per week, and the profits resulting from this sum give employment not merely to paper makers, to printers and to booksellers, but to a great many honest poor people, who not having a trade, or unable to exercise it, through various causes, are finding a means of subsistence by hawking the cheap publications. Now, if every gentlemen in Ireland were to encourage all his friends, servants, and dependants to buy each, say one a week, there would soon be upwards of an hundred and fifty thousand sold of the cheap publications, treble the number of poor people would be employed in selling them, a vast mass of information would be diffused, thought would be awakened, the public mind would receive a prodigious impulse, and the very face of society would be changed.'

9TH AUGUST

On 9 August 1738 a wild young nobleman, Lord Santry, and other rich but rowdy gents, were drinking at a tavern in the village of Palmerston. Santry was, not to put too fine a point on it, drunk and irritable.

Annoyed at one of the servants, he attempted to draw his sword but couldn't co-ordinate himself enough to do it, a fact which only inflamed his anger.
Heading down a passageway towards the kitchen he bumped into Laughlin Murphy, the pub's pot-boy and messenger. Giving him a push, Santry swore he would kill him if he said a word. Murphy didn't take the hint, said something under his breath, and was promptly run through by the excitable peer. Santry gave the inn-keeper some gold as recompense for the commotion and left the premises.

Murphy, however, inconsiderately died in Hammond's Lane in late September and Lord Santry found himself charged with murder in front of his peers in the House of Lords. He was found guilty but later reprieved – the story goes that his uncle, Sir Compton Domville, threatened to divert the Dodder (chief supply of drinking water for the city), unless he was let go.

10TH AUGUST

The Irish Times reported the death of a student at the Forty Foot, Sandycove, on 10 August 1897.

'Yesterday between 11 and 12 o'clock a young gentleman named Michael Nolan, aged about 20, was drowned while bathing at Sandycove. Mr. Nolan got in at a spot opposite what is locally known as 'Ring Rock.' He was subsequently seen to be in difficulties, sinking beneath the surface and reappearing at intervals. A young gentleman named Henry Moore of Newtownsmith, who is an accomplished swimmer, was obliged to dive in order to secure the deceased. Mr Weir was then enabled with the help of another swimmer, Mr. White, to bring deceased ashore whose every

A busy day a Blackrock Baths

effort was made to restore consciousness, but without avail. Dr. Hartford and Dr. McCullough who were summoned to the spot as quickly as possible tried every means professionally known to induce respiration, but unfortunately could not succeed. It is supposed that the poor young fellow became weak in the water and could not gain the shore some 20 or 30 yards away.'

Five years later, in June 1902, William Coleman, a seminarian of the Vincentians, St. Joseph's, Temple Road, Blackrock, was drowned at the Forty Foot. In October 1910 Fr. William English, a Holy Ghost Father, was also drowned

11TH AUGUST

A tablet in Christchurch Cathedral recalls the life of Sir Samuel Auchmuty, Commander-in-Chief of HM's forces in Ireland: 'died the 11th August 1822. He was brave, experienced and successful officer, and victorious whenever he had command. The capture of Monte Video in South America and of the Island of Java in the East Indies added both to his fame and his fortune.'

While Auchmuty and his deeds are all but forgotten today a story connected with his passing is still well-known in Dublin. For it was at his funeral that a lieutenant lost his way in the crypt, and was locked up by accident, to remain there until he was found, a skeleton, but still grasping his sword, while all around the poor fellow were discovered numbers of dead rats which he had killed before the hosts of surviving vermin which swarmed from the great sewer which led from the cathedral to the Liffey overcame and devoured him.'

The version I heard as a child overcame one the inconsistencies in the story by explaining that he was overcome only after his light died. Another problem with the story is the lack of a name – such an event is extremely rare and would have been widely reported in the papers of the time.

12TH AUGUST

Magee, the proprietor of the *Dublin Evening Post*, published a series of satires in his paper and was jailed for his troubles. On his release, he decided to take some measure of revenge on the judge who had sent him down – Lord Clonmell. On 12 August 1789 he invited his fellow citizens to a day of great amusement – to be held in his fields immediately adjoining Lord Clonmell's marine residence, 'Neptune,' Temple Hill, Blackrock. Sports were arranged; there was 'grinning through horse-collars,' asses dressed up in wigs and scarlet robes, dancing dogs in gowns and wigs as barristers. When the crowd had reached its maximum the great scene of the day took place; a number of pigs, with their tails shaved and soaped, were let loose, and it was announced that each pig should become the property of anyone who could catch and hold it by the slippery member. A scene impossible to describe took place. The pigs, frightened and hemmed in by the huge crowd, rushed through the hedges which separated the grounds of 'Neptune' and the open fields; the pursuers followed in a body, and continuing their chase over the parterres and shrubberies, soon revenged Magee on the noble owner, who could do nothing as the assembly was held in Magee's own fields.

13TH AUGUST

Towards the end of the eighteenth century there was much concern about conditions in Dublin prisons. There was particular disquiet about overcrowding and of the peculiar practice of refusing to release acquitted detainees until they had paid the iniquitous 'charges' imposed by the prison authorities.

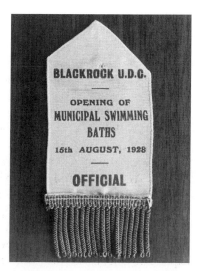

A badge from the Blackrock baths opening ceremony in 1928.

A 1784 report on Old Kilmainham Jail noted: 'There was not so weak or ill conceived a jail as the County Dublin one, and it was hoped that a new one would be built on a proper construction and site'.

Shortly afterward work commenced on the new Kilmainham Jail. However, it was not until 13 August 1796 *Faulkner's Dublin Journal* could report: 'That the new County Gaol was completely finished and fit for the reception of prisoners', the several persons confined in the old were conducted to the New Gaol under a strong military guard.

'The first occupancy of this great building which for safety, healthfulness, convenience and compactness is said to be superior to any Prison in Europe, was attended by the High Sheriff of the County, the High Sheriffs of the City, several Justices of the Peace and a great number of other gentlemen who afterwards dined by invitation at Harringtons in Grafton Street.'

14TH AUGUST

'A singular memorial from a person named Aspel was read by the Town Clerk before the close of the meeting [Dublin Corporation, 14 August 1871]. It prayed the Council to supply the applicant with the means of emigrating, upon the grounds that he was constantly in the habit of getting drunk and committing assaults when drunk, and he consequently had been in prison 67 times. It was impossible for him to reform in Dublin, and he saw no prospect here except to end his days in prison or a lunatic asylum. The Council were visibly impressed by the frankness of the confession, and resolved to aid the penitent in turning over a new leaf in America. At the recommendation of the Board of Superintendence his fellow prisoners were made instrumental in promoting his reformation, the expenses of his journey were defrayed out of the profits realized by the sale of their work.'

Why Aspel felt he could avoid the demon drink in America (Prohibition not arriving until 1917) was not discussed. Not, indeed, was the desirability of sending a habitual drunk and criminal to another jurisdiction.

15TH AUGUST

On 15 August 1898 the centenary commemorations of Wolfe Tone and the United Irishmen were held in Dublin. The vast procession first filed past Tone's House in Stafford Street. Michael JF McCarthy recalls the route: 'It then pursued its way, with bands and banners, to St. Michan's Church [burial place of the brothers Sheares and Oliver Bond] Lower Bridge Street was next visited, in which are the Brazen Head Hotel at which meetings of the United Irishmen used to be held, and the house which was once Oliver Bond's. Next in order came the site of Robert Emmet's execution in Thomas Street; and the house, No. 151, in the same street in which Lord Edward Fitzgerald was arrested also the birthplace of Napper Tandy. Back Lane, the site of Tailor's Hall, was next visited, where the Irish Catholics assembled in 1792, and the United Irishmen in 1793 and 1794. Then came High Street, where the remains of Wolfe Tone were 'waked' for two nights, prior to his burial at Bodenstown and finally College Green, the site of the Irish Houses of Parliament, now the Bank of Ireland. The foundation stone of a projected monument to Tone and the United Irishmen was laid with great ceremony at the Grafton Street corner of Stephen's Green.'

16TH AUGUST

The Dublin Intelligence reported in 1726 on an boating accident which had occurred on 14 August in Dublin Bay:- 'On Sunday last a most Unfortunate Accident happened, a Boat full of People coming between Dublin and Rings End, were by the Carelessness of the Boatmen drove in to a Great Current which is there and Over set and many of the Passengers were lost, among whom we are inform'd were one Mrs. Sands of Phenix street's, 2 Children, and a Nurse, also one of Mr. Sands of Christ Church-yard his wife and Child, the Child tho' only was quite lost, for he in striving to throw it on shore unhappily drop'd it in, tho' he and his Wife were brought off, with them was one Mrs. Lamb, a Young Woman of Essex-street, a GentleWoman in Sheep-street, a Coach-Harnisser in George's-Lane, a Sailor, a Confectioners Maid on the Blind Quay, and several others.

There were many who were Sav'd, by the Help of Ropes, and Boats, and the Endeavours of several well dispos'd Persons.'

17TH AUGUST

As the Famine took hold the British Government announced on 17 August 1846 that the price of grain would not be regulated – the price promptly went up and stayed high for a year.

Thousands, wasted by famines and consumed by fever, flooded into the cities. The Census Commission reported on 'mournful and piteous scenes At the gate leading to the temporary fever hospital erected near Kilmainham, were men, women and children, lying along the pathway and in the gutter, awaiting their turn to be admitted. Some were stretched at full length, with their faces exposed to the full glare of the sun, their mouths open, and their black and parched tongues and encrusted teeth visible even from a distance. Some women had children at the breast who lay beside them in silence and apparent exhaustion while in the centre of the road stood a cart containing a while family who had been smitten down by typhus. Inside the fever hospital, was a small open shed, in which were 35 human beings heaped indiscriminately on a little straw thrown on the ground. Several had been thus for three days, drenched by rain, &c. Some were unconscious, others dying; two died during the night.'

18TH AUGUST

On 18 August 1828 'when the Derry mail [coach], on its way from Dublin, was about two miles from Santry, James Fagan intentionally drive his cart against it and broke one of the lamps. The guard gave the horse and cart in charge of the police at Santry, who, when conducting them to Santry Pound, were attacked, near Coolock Bridge, by Fagan and seven others. The police fired two shots, severely wounding a man, named Wade, in the thigh, and another in the heel, and, arresting them and Fagan, brought them before the Police Court, Dublin, where Fagan was committed for further inquiries, and the wounded men were conveyed to Jervis Street Hospital, where they lie dangerously ill.' (*Saunders' News Letter*).

The following year a robber was shot on the road near Santry and, according to the Churchwardens' MS.) was buried in the churchyard. Tradition has it that the body was taken up by resurrectionists or body-snatcher, and his head taken away for the sake of his teeth.

19TH AUGUST

The Dublin Publication Supplement to the Warder reported on some of the court
cases of the day, including the following rather strange case: 'Anne Dunne was
brought up in custody, charged with having violently assaulted Edward Maguire,
at 15 Ship-street. From the evidence, it appeared that the complainant was standing
on the stairs of his house at about twelve o'clock on the night of the 19th of August
[1870], when he received a blow on the head, which caused him to fall to his knees.
He rose to his feet, and was again struck on the temple. He called for help, and a
candle was lighted. The prisoner was then found standing on the landing having
a battered can in her hand. The injured man was removed to Mercer's Hospital,
whither the prisoner followed him; and, while he stood upon the doorsteps of the
hospital, she again struck him. She subsequently assaulted him in the hospital and
also in the Chancery-lane Police-station, while the charge was being taken. The prisoner was sentenced to two months imprisonment, with hard labour.

20TH AUGUST

On 20 August 1775 George Faulkner, 76, went out for dinner with some of his friends.
The tavern had been painted very recently and Faulkner experienced breathing
problems. Later he developed severe hiccupping and other problems – he was dead
ten days later.

His own newspaper, the Dublin Journal, printed a brief notice. 'Yesterday morning at six o'clock died Alderman George Faulkner, who was printer of was printer of
this journal upwards of 50 years.'

Jonathan Swift's publisher and friend was buried in the 'Cabbage Garden' in
Cathedral Lane.

His tombstone, transcribed in 1876 by Richard Robert Madden reads in part: 'a man
of superior benevolence of mind and goodness of heart. He was esteemed by the Great
which honour he never sought; and by the Poor, who were the constant objects of his
munificence. In fine, he earned the esteem of all the country – of none the hatred.'

A bust of the Dean which was to have been placed in a niche in front of Faulkner's
house in Parliament- street, was presented to St. Patrick's Cathedral by his nephew,
where it was placed over the Dean's tomb.

21ST AUGUST

Just over a month after Emmet's failed rising the Lord Lieutenant, on 21 August
1803, authorised a type of police force in Dublin – the 'Conservators of the Public
Peace.' The city was divided into 53 wards or districts – a number soon cut down to
a more manageable 21.

Ten or more inhabitants, of unquestionable loyalty, in each district were encour-
aged to form a committee which would keep the peace. They were to 'keep registers of
every house in their area, the number and quality of the occupiers, with their means
of livelihood and to give notice of any unusual number of strangers coming to the city.
They had a regular office in each district, elected a president, and met once a day; and
each citizen was sworn a constable, so that no one might questions their authority.

The only problem was that with the rebellion beaten down there really wasn't much for them to do – they dissolved within a year though not without first preparing a census of the city – it reported that there were 6,480 houses on the northside (population 61,049) and 9,754 on the southside (pop. 172,042)

22ND AUGUST

1. How many areas of Dublin end in 'o'?
2. Where is the other O'Connell Bridge?
2. In which year was Kevin Barry shot by the British?
4. Where can you find Lord Nelson's head?
5. What day did the Battle of Clontarf take place?

On the morning of 22 August 1791 Dubliners were bemused – the entire city seemed to have been vandalised during the night, the word 'quiz' was chalked almost everywhere that could be reached.

Who had done it and what did the strange word mean? The answer to the first part was Richard Daly, manager of the Smock Alley theatre. The previous day, Daly had made a bet that he would introduce a new word into the English language. Not one to do things by half, he had hired a team of men, equipped them with chalk, and set them loose.

The answer to the second part is that not even Daly knew what 'quiz' meant, but it entered the language anyway.

5. Good Friday.
4. The Civic Museum.
3. He was hung.
2. St. Stephen's Green.
1 Portobello, Marino, Rialto, Pimlico, Phibsboro (opinion is divided, there are those who say that it's only a contraction of Phibsborough).

23RD AUGUST

The body of Bridget Gannon was discovered in the Dodder, between Herbert Park and Londonbridge, on the morning of 23 August 1900. She was naked to the waist and the remnants of a flower she had been wearing the night before were found on the river bank. Initially unidentified, an inquest reached a verdict of 'death by drowning' and she was buried in Glasnevin.

And there the matter would have rested had not Margaret Clowry reported that a friend of hers was missing since the night of August 22. The body was exhumed and formally identified by her brother, Patrick.

Clowry said that she and Bridget had gone for a walk that night and had met Constable Henry Flower. The three had walked as far as Carrisbrook House when, after a heavy hint from Flower, she left him and Bridget.

Constable Flower denied knowing the dead woman, but was arrested on 14 September. Three days later his Sergeant, John Hannily, cut his own throat. Flower was tried, found not guilty, and left Ireland for Australia.

On her deathbed 40 years later Margaret Clowry confessed to the murder to a solicitor, John Cusack. She said that she had met Mridget again that night, after Flower had left, they had argued over money, she had pushed Bridget into the river and robbed her.

24TH AUGUST

'This morning about 5.20am one of the Vartry water mains burst close to the Crampton statue which is between the cross ways of College Green and Great Brunswick Street. The pressure was so powerful that an immense jet of water was shot straight up in the air, high as the house tops. This striking spectacle attracted the attention of Constable Kelly, 200B, who are one informed the occupiers of the [houses]. It was 6.25am before any particular official notice was taken of the matter. At that time a man was despatched from the depot, who turned off the water. The street around was flooded, about 3 square yards of it turned up by the violence of the sizeable deluge. The cellars of the houses, No. 7, 8, and 9, occupied by Mr. J. Berry, Dyer, Mr. Flynn, Boot and Shoe Maker, and Mr. Hennessey, Grocer, were also flooded, water reaching to the ground floor of the premises. Mr. Hennessey's shop was flooded and so was the cellar of Mr. Doyle, Publican, 28 Fleet Street. A number of Corporation workmen have been employed during the morning in effecting necessary repairs to the main and the street.' (*Dublin Evening Mail*, Monday August 24th 1896)

25TH AUGUST

Even the fantastical Kingdom of Dalkey suffered its share of tragedy! *The Dalkey Gazette* of August 26, 1793 reported: 'Her Most Affable Majesty [has] departed this life. Her last moments were marked by firmness and resignation. The greater part of her personal property she has left in different donations to the poor. Her five millions in the Bank of Amsterdam are to return to the island from which they were produced, and to be expended in Christmas beef for such manufacturers as are at present destitute of employ. On this calamitous event the court has been thrown into the profoundest grief. The Marchioness of Mushroom, shut herself up with no other company than her Prayer book and 'Hoyle upon Gaming'. Lord Periwinkle forgot to feed his pet monkey, and the dear creature expired through the neglect. Six Commoners – Oyster, Scallop, Kelp, White Rock, Muglin and Surge – who were said to be engaged to vote against their country in the evening, could not, through decency, appear in public. The Chamberlain has issued orders from the Royal Court at Armagh for a suitable dress. Full dress: Black calimancoe, trimmed with sea-weed. Undress: Grey frieze, and weepers of the muslin of fish skin.'

26TH AUGUST

Somehow I don't think this one would work today, maybe if you replaced hats with trousers

'On Monday night [26 August 1822] about 9 o'clock, 15 or 20 ruffians collected in Stephen's-green, at the corner of Harcourt-street, all bareheaded. They had previously deposited their hats in a place of safety, and were assisted in the execution of their plan by a number of women. They assailed every person who passed, pretending to have lost their hats, and desiring to see the hat worn by those who alighted from the cars which came from the fair. As soon as the unsuspecting passenger gave his hat for inspection, one of the females snapt it from the bareheaded robber, who pretended to have no knowledge of her; the female fled, while one of the robbers called out 'Stop thief!' but with what success may be imagined. In this way about 20 hats were taken from different persons.' [*The Times*]

27TH AUGUST

By 27 August each year Donnybrook Fair was going at full speed, as the *Dublin Penny Journal* reported in 1833: 'Yonder a tent crowded with lads and lasses, tripping it on "the light fantastic toe", or gazing in admiration on some heavy legged bog-trotter, footing a horn-pipe to the music of a pair of bagpipes, or the notes of a half-drunker scraper on three strings; while thickly studded round may be seen tents crowded with the drinking and the drunken – the painted prostitute, or the half tipsy youngster lovingly caressing 'the girl of his heart', who flushed cheek and glancing eye, too plainly indicate that she herself has already had a potion of the intoxicating draught; while in the distance in various directions may be seen the waving of the shillelah and heard the brawling of a party … the orgies of the night, when every species of dissipation may be better imagined than described. It may be sufficient to say that it has been calculated, that during the week of Donnybrook fair there is more loss of female character, and greater spoliation of female virtue among the lower orders, than during all the other portions of the year besides.'

'It has been calculated ' – that must have been fun!

28TH AUGUST

Sometimes justice has to be felt to be believed. *The Evening Telegraph* of 28 August 1899 reported on the treatment meted out in the courts to young offenders: 'James Smith, a respectably dressed lad of about ten years of age, was charged with throwing stones at 'The Salvation Army' yesterday afternoon near Leeson Street Bridge. The guardian of the boy appeared in court and made an appeal for him, and the matter was eventually compromised by Mr. Byrne discharging Smith and the guardian promising to thrash him when he got home. This arrangement appeared to suit everyone but Smith.'

'Nicholas Meade, another small boy, was charged with breaking glass in one of the public lamps by sending a potato through it. Mr. Byrne sentenced him to a whipping and appointed Mrs. Meade the executioner.'

A few days later the same newspaper reported on a narrow escape by three youths: 'A big constable charged three small boys, the eldest about 8, with bathing in the Grand Canal. The constable seemed a little ashamed of his case. Mr. Swifte at once discharged the criminals.'

29TH AUGUST

In 1903 the Kingstown Urban District Commissioners were dealing with an outbreak of smallpox – 21 cases were reported between January and September. Just as cases declined typhoid broke out. The Medical Officer, J. Byrne Power, described the steps taken: 'I had been informed by a leading doctor in the township that a number of cases of fever could be traced to the supply of milk from Ward's Dairy. [The Sub-Sanitary Officer] visited the premises and found on the premises a girl stricken with typhoid fever. He destroyed the milk on the premises and had the patient removed to Monkstown Hospital. The house was disinfected at once . . . As regards the source of infection there can be no doubt that the disease was conveyed in the milk from the infected dairy to the patient's house, but up to the present it is not clear as to how this milk became infected. Sir Charles Cameron, analyst to the township, reports that he has analysed the samples of milk sent to him, and finds them superior in quality to the average supply. He points out that it is only when the disease appears that the milk is examined, and then the terms are no longer present.'

30th August

The Dublin Penny Journal reported in awed tones on 30 August 1834 on the new Dublin to Kingstown railway: 'Hurried by the invisible, but stupendous agency of steam, the astonished passengers will now glide, like Asmodeus [a Biblical baddie], over the summits of the houses and streets of a great city – presently be transported through green-fields and tufts of trees – then skim across the surface of the sea, and taking shelter under the cliffs, coast among the marine villas, and through the rocky excavations, until he finds himself in the centre of a vast port, which unites in pleasing confusion the bustle of a commercial town with the amusements of a fashionable watering place.

Six locomotive engines have been built. The greatest mechanical perfection has been attained in these machines. The railways coaches of the first and second class may be almost called elegant; the third class carriages are superior to those in use on the English railways, and all are covered. the fares will be on a very low scale. and when the works are completed, passengers may step from the railway coaches to the steamers, again, on arriving will, with the mail bags, be conveyed in a quarter of an hour from the Royal harbour of George the Fourth to the centre of the Irish metropolis.'

31st August

An elderly and bearded man in a long coat left his carriage and entered the Imperial Hotel, O'Connell Street. It was Sunday, 31 August 1913, and over 300 Dublin Metropolitan Police, along with RIC members, lined the street – they were there to prevent 'Big' Jim Larkin from fulfilling his promise to address the crowds of strikers who had gathered.

At 1.25pm the elderly gent appeared on a balcony, removed the coat and beard – it was Larkin – and began to address the strikers while burning a copy of the official ban against his speaking.

He was quickly arrested. Stones were thrown and the police baton-charged the crowd. It was the police who were out of control – they'd taken enough from the strikers over previous days – and they handed out savage beatings to anyone unfortunate to be in their path – among them the congregation from Mass in the pro-Cathedral. It only took two minutes but by then 400 people had been injured as well as 50 policemen. The official enquiry would find that the DMP had acted properly and with great courage. In truth the DMP, were a discredited force – they would be amalgamated into the Garda Siochana.

Chapter Nine

September

1ST SEPTEMBER

Captain Richard Dawkins of *HMS Vanguard* (6,000 tonnes) probably wasn't think-ing much about small sailing vessels as he sailed out of Kingstown (Dun Laoghaire) Harbour on 1 September 1875.

The *Vanguard*, which had been based in Kingstown for four years, was travelling in dense fog in convoy with three other ironclads, *Warrior*, *Hector* and *Iron Duke* (a sister ship). The *Iron Duke* was sailing slightly off course and was in the process of returning to her proper station – a problem with steam meant that her foghorn was not being used to alert the other vessels of her position.

At about 12.50pm *Vanguard's* look-out warned that a sailing ship had been spot-ted directly ahead. As the Vanguard turned to avoid it the *Iron Duke* appeared out of the fog on her port side less than 40 yards away.

Collision was inevitable and to make matters worse the *Iron Duke* had an under-water ram which tore into the side of the *Vanguard* near the engines and boilers. The *Iron Duke* freed herself after a few minutes and sustained minor damage, the *Vanguard*, however, was mortally wounded.

Water was flooding in at the rate of 50 tons a minute while the pumps could move only 1.5 tons in the same time. And the pumps were powered by the engines which shut down 10 minutes after the collision. In just 70 minutes the Vanguard slid beneath the waves to the seabed 50 metres below, the tips of her masts still poking up through the swell.

2ND SEPTEMBER

On Tuesday, 2 September 1913, two tenement houses, 66-67 Church Street, col-lapsed without warning at around 8.45pm. The four-storey buildings had shops on the ground floor. Seven people died and many more were injured.

Mrs. Magee, one of the occupants, described what happened: 'I was standing in the hallway of the house, looking at the children playing in the streets. Other women were sitting on the kerb-stone so as to be in the air. Suddenly I heard a terrific crash and shrieking. I ran, not knowing why, but hearing as I did a frightful noise of falling bricks. When I looked back I saw that two houses had tumbled down. There was a

heap of bricks and stuff piled up on the street, where a moment or two before children were playing and women sitting, watching them.'

Demands for a Royal Commission to investigate the tragedy were turned down
but the Local Government enquiry was highly critical of both landlords and Dublin
Corporation.

Of the 400,000 people living in the city, 87,305 lived in the centre of the city in
tenement housing. 'We have visited one house that we found to be occupied by 98
people, another by 74 and a third by 73,' the enquiry noted.

3RD SEPTEMBER

In 1559 orders were given to remove all images and Popish relics from churches, and
to conduct services in English. It wasn't a popular move and, on Sunday, 3 September
it inspired what must have been the talk of the town for days afterward.

'There was in that Cathedral [Christchurch] an image of Christ in marble, standing with a reed in his hand, and the crown of thorns on his head. And while service
was saying blood was seen to run through the crevices of the crown of thorns, trick-
ling down the face of the crucifix. Vast numbers flocked to the sight; and one present
told the people the cause: 'that he could not but choose to sweat blood whilst heresy
was then come into the Church, the people fell upon their knees, thumping their
breasts particularly one of the aldermen and mayor of the city, whose name was
Sedgrave, and who had been at the English service, drew forth his beads, and prayed
with the rest before the image.' The Archbishop soon discovered the truth – a blood-
soaked sponge hidden in the crown of thorns. The four deemed responsible, one of
them a priest, Father Leigh, were imprisoned and 'banished the realm.'

As for the bleeding statue – it was destroyed on the Archbishop's order a week later.

4TH SEPTEMBER

The resurrectionists or 'sack 'em ups' added to the terror of death in olden Dublin
– their aim was to grab the body, either before or shortly after burial, and sell them
to surgeons for dissection. Sometimes the surgeons cut out the middleman, as was
reported in the *Dublin Gazette* of 4 September 1750: 'Last Friday evening some
young surgeons went in a coach to Donnybrook to take up the corpse of a child who
had been buried in that Churchyard the night before. While they were digging open
the grave the father of the child got information of it and assembling some of his
neighbours came to the place by the time they had got the body up; when they fell
on them, took the corpse back again and severely chastised the young gentlemen for
their pains.'

Here's another, undated, occasion when things went wrong for the 'sack 'em ups':
'It was in 'Bully's Acre' that an untoward calamity had befallen Peter Harkan, a well-
known Dublin surgeon, and hitherto a very successful resurrectionist. A party of
watchers having suddenly rushed forward, he succeeded in getting his assistants
over the cemetery wall, but when crossing himself, his legs were seized by the
watchmen, while his pupils pulled against their opponents with such effect that he
eventually died from the effects.'

5TH SEPTEMBER

Robbing a wig-maker, no problem … Unless it was the dashing Mr. Wallace who carried his curling tongs concealed about his person: 'Between eleven and twelve at night, as Mr. Wallace of Essex-street, peruke-maker, was passing through Pill-lane, he was accosted opposite the Fishmarket-gate by a lusty fellow, who asked him for charity, when he gave a penny, upon which the villain immediately collared him, drew out a long knife, and with the most dreadful imprecations demanded his money; but Mr Wallace tripped up his heels, and got the knife from him, when two of his associates coming to his assistance, Wallace pulled out his curling irons, and assured them if they came nearer he would blow their brains out, which irons the rogues imagining to be a pistol, took to their heels, and made off. He then conducted the first villain to St Mary's watch-house, but as the attempt was made in St Michan's parish, he was obliged to take him to the watch-house on Inns-quay, where he gave him in charge to the constable of the night, and while the wig-maker was writing his name and where he lived in order to be found to prosecute, the villain was suffered to escape.' [*Freeman's Journal*, 2-5 September 1769.]

6TH SEPTEMBER

On 10am on Monday, 6 September 1852, husband and wife William Burke Kirwan and Sarah Maria Louisa Kirwan took a boat out to Ireland's Eye. William, a professional painter, took his sketch book, Maria, a strong and daring swimmer, had her bathing costume.

Around 6pm a number of people in Howth heard repeated female cries coming from the island but nothing was done. When the boatmen returned for the couple they found only William, his wife, he told them, had left him a few hours earlier. After a search Maria's body was found on a rock at the water's edge. An inquest the following day returned a verdict of death by drowning.

And there the matter would have rested except for William Kirwan's secret life – he had kept a mistress, Mary Kenny, in Sandymount for many years and had had seven children with her. William was arrested and charged with the murder of his wife. There was nothing to prove his guilt but his 'scandalous' behaviour was deemed to make him capable of any foul deed.

He was found guilty and Judge Crampton, in sentencing him to be hanged, said: 'The wife whom you vowed to cherish you destroyed while you spared the courtesan.' The sentence was later commuted to life imprisonment. He spent a total of 27 years in prison before being released.

7TH SEPTEMBER

As Mr. Manders rode his horse towards his father's house at Brackenstown on Sunday, 7 September 1800, he had to stop briefly to adjust his saddle. No sooner had he alighted than two muggers, one of whom had a pistol, took his pocket-book and cash. They scarpered across the fields at the noise of an approaching carriage. But sometimes there is a satisfactory ending. Three days later Mr. Manders was in Thomas Street with his brother when he saw a familiar figure standing at the top of a cellar: 'Mr. M. looking close, recognised the ruffian to be the fellow who had robbed him ... The villain Farrell, apprised of his situation, put his hand in his breast to pull out a pistol – but before he had time to make any use of it, Mr. Alexander Manders struck him with a pistol across the face, which knocked Farrell down, and then secured him and the other, named Usher. There were found upon Farrell, besides pistols, two gold watches, and other articles, and a duplicate of another gold watch, which afterwards appeared to be Mr. Foyle's, of which he had been robbed a few days before, walking on the banks of the Canal. Both the offenders were lodged in gaol.' [*The Times*]

8TH SEPTEMBER

About 9pm on 8 September 1770 Barnaby Sherwin, his wife, Elinor, and son, Patrick, were murdered in the home in the townland of Turvey, near Donabate. A grandson, aged 19, was seriously injured.

Three men were arrested by Dublin High Sheriff, Sir Anthony King – John Ryan, John Farrell and Joseph Daw – and brought to the Newgate Prison. Daw made a full and graphic confession telling how he called his victims one by one to the back of their dwelling, stabbed each with a pitchfork and afterwards cut their throats; the old woman he strangled in her bed.

The trial was a formality and, in mid-October, Daw was brought back to Turvey and hung. Afterwards the body was hung in chains as a reminder to all those who might consider that crime could pay.

In May 1771, the body was taken down (a criminal offence in itself) and hurriedly buried.

And there the story would usually end except that Daw made a surprise re-appearance 168 years later when a 'man in armour' was discovered buried about 20 metres from Daw's Bridge, Turvey. The 'armour' was, in fact, body fetters, sometimes used for displaying the bodies of criminals.

9TH SEPTEMBER

From the early 1890s until the Dublin Metropolitan Police were disbanded they were a force to be reckoned with as a tug-o-war team. Their finest hour came on 9 September 1893 at a Military Tournament in Ballsbridge when they roundly defeated the Glasgow Police team – described as 'a solid wall of flesh and bone – impregnable and impassable.' The Scots weighed in at 163 stones 10 pounds, nearly a stone and a half heavier per man than the DMP team.

The crowd were in good form and were only with difficulty cleared from the arena before the event. The DMP proceeded to win both pulls whereupon they (despite their great weight), and their trainer, Inspector Booth, were carried shoulder high around the grounds.

The losing team took a less favourable view and promptly lodged complaints that spectators had helped the DMP pull and that the rope was too small.

A reporter from the *Sport* newspaper strongly refuted the claims, writing: 'As regards the allegation that the Metropolitans were assisted by spectators, it is manifestly false seeing that the last man in the team had the rope twisted round his waist, leaving no room for spectators to get a grip.'

10TH SEPTEMBER

The Protestant Archbishop of Dublin, Narcissus Marsh, was not a happy man when he wrote the following in his diary on 10 September 1695: 'This evening betwixt 8 & 9 of the clock at night my niece Grace Marsh (not having the fear of God before her eyes) stole privately out of my house at St. Sepulchre's and (as is reported) was that night married to Chas. Proby vicar of Castleknock in a Tavern and was bedded there with him – Lord consider my affliction.'

Narcissus had arranged for young Grace to be his housekeeper in the Palace of St. Sepulchre (part of it survives in the walls of Kevin Street Garda Station).
To lose a niece was bad enough, but for a confirmed bachelor the loss of a house-keeper must have been a much greater blow.

The elopement gave rise to a ghost story in which the Archbishop each night searches through the books in Marsh's Library (properly called St. Sepulchre's Library) looking for a letter which Grace had left expressing her sorrow at leaving him. Grace lived a very long life for the time, dying at the advanced age of 85. In death she was re-united with Archbishop in his tomb in St. Patrick's Churchyard.

11TH SEPTEMBER

'There is in Dublin a firm known as Williams and Woods, manufacturers of pre-serves, pickles, sauce and confectionery. This firm employs a large number of girls and women. Their industry is scheduled under the Trade Boards Act as a Sweated Industry. Under the provisions of this Act there is established what is known as a Minimum Wage Board, which has the power to fix the minimum rate of wages [The Board fixed wages at]:– 10/10 for Female Workers of 18 years and upwards, and 22/9 for Male Workers of 22 years and upwards. For younger workers the rates begin for Girls at 5/- per week, and for Boys at 6/-, proceeding by yearly increases to the amount stated for workers at 18 years. But small as they, are Messrs Williams and Woods refuse to pay them. And in order to evade the law and to continue sweat-ing their women workers, despite the law, this firm of loyal, God-fearing, Christian philanthropists have Served Notice of Dismissal upon 150 Women and Girls over 18 years of age, and are making ready to take in a number of young persons to fill the places of the people they are discharging. What an evil name Dublin is getting because of its greedy, soulless, unscrupulous employers!' [James Connolly, *Workers' Republic*, 11 September 1915]

12TH SEPTEMBER

General Richard Mulcahy, Commander-in-Chief of the Irish Army told Dáil Éireann on 12 September 1922 of trouble in south Dublin: 'For some weeks back a small band of Irregulars created a state of terror in Foxrock district. Their activities were not alone confined to outrages against the Government, but were also directed against private property. Robbery under arms and the plundering of private houses were rampant in Foxrock district up to last week. This gang attacked the late Commander-in-Chief's car from the very cottage in which last week two of them were killed and two captured. They fired on the troops that went to arrest them, and two of them were killed in the subsequent firing, on whom a jury yesterday returned the verdict, "*Killed by troops in the execution of their duty*". On the 14th of August a National soldier, who was on leave from the Curragh, was visiting his home in Dean's Grange. He was held up in Kill Lane by men in a motor car. They asked him was he armed, and he replied that he was not. Then one of this gang fired a shot, seriously wounding the soldier. While this soldier was in a critical condition in a hospital in Dun Laoghaire, he signed a statement, saying that the men who shot him were "Locals", Order has been restored in Foxrock district for the past week, and we have established a post there.'

13TH SEPTEMBER

It's always the officers who get the cushy treatment 'On Thursday last [13 September 1798] eight French Officers taken at Ballinamuck, were brought into Dublin under a very strong escort. Their names are Humbert, Sarazin and Fontaine, Generals; Heutte, Silbermann and Toussaint, Chefs de Brigade; Borrelly, Capitaine; and Foucaud, Sous Lieutenant. They are attended by seven servants, and were lodged at the Mail Coach Hotel, in Dawson Street. In the course of yesterday they were visited by many persons of distinction. The remainder of the French prisoners are not to pass through the metropolis on their way to England, but are to proceed by the Canal into the basin at Ringsend, where the transports will be ready to receive them on board.' [*The Times*] Three days later the French officers were reunited with their 845 men – a number of whom were Irish pretending to be French – and placed on board transport ships bound for Portsmouth and, eventually, France.

14TH SEPTEMBER

The Irish Catholic Chronicle of Saturday, 14 September 1867, reported: 'The parish of Kilternan, county Dublin, has lately witnessed as atrocious a piece of ruffianism as any that have been recorded for some time. An English family residing here, who are held in the highest respect and esteem by all who know them, recently sustained a most trying bereavement in the early death of a dearly loved young daughter. They laid the remains of the child in the parish burial ground, and over them, placed an "in memoriam" slab, with a simple cross carved on it. Hereupon, some of the Protestants found that their consciences were aggrieved by their religion endangered by such downright Popery. They called upon the deservedly popular and respected rector to have the offensive slab removed, and, on his declining to do any such thing, they positively went with hammer and chisel secretly, smashed out the cross, and flung the fragments into the garden of the sorrowing parent! It is only just to add that the sacrilegious outrage has provoked the sternest indignation amongst all well-minded people in the district. In the same locality, it will be remembered, the same "religious" sentiment lately smashed Lady Monk's stained glass memorial windows in Lord Powerscourt's church.'

15TH SEPTEMBER

The Freeman's Journal of 15 September 1871 reported on the condition of houses in Marrowbone Lane: 'two tenement houses at the junction of Cork Street. The first is miserable, tumble-down and wretched. I draw special attention to the second. It is a large house, three storeys high. A few miserable planks serve as an apology for a door. Half the roof has been blown or has fallen off the house and in this ruin there are human beings residing. The houses look back on a yard, ankle-deep in filth and garbage, with foul sewer, manure heap and every conceivable abomination. An open watercourse skirted one corner of the square. In this neighbourhood the Poddle is an open drain. It contains water which is little more than sewage, stagnant, sluggish, offensive in smell and appearance. A woman took a canful of water from this putrid stream as we watched. Neal's Court which is a square rather than a court is occupied by wretched tenements. No where in our journey did we see the evil of overcrowding more strikingly manifest. The square is ankle-deep in filth of every kind. In the centre is a reeking ash pit which seemed not to have been emptied for months. Goats, pigs and hens swarm about.

16TH SEPTEMBER

Cometh the hour, cometh the man – and, in 1803, that man was sure to be Major Sirr. 'Yesterday evening [16 September 1803] between six and seven, Major Sirr, attended by Hanlon, the Keeper of the Tower in the Castle, surprised an offender, against whom there was information as an insurgent, in a carpenter's shop in John-street, in the Liberty, where this fellow was at work. The Major, on entering the place where two other were also employed, promised that if any would offer resistance, he would fire; this did not deter; for the ruffian whom they wanted, finding himself nearly secured, sought for a pistol he had on doing which Major Sirr snapped at him, which missed fire. Hanlon immediately went to seize the fellow, but before he could, the latter fired, as did Hanlon at the same time, but he was unfortunately killed, and the desperado only shot in the left hand, where a ball lodged. The offender with the other two persons, were seized and lodged in the Castle guard-house last night; the defendant is a young man aged between 20 and 30 years of age.' [*The Times*]

17TH SEPTEMBER

The Dun Laoghaire Borough Gazette brought up the subject of grouses and grumbles in its second edition [17 September 1948] and decided to investigate problems at Traders' Wharf by interviewing an anonymous fisherman: 'At one time our harbour was one of the principal centres for the fishing fleets on the East Coast, but they don't come here – only a few – any more. Do you know that on a dark night coming in from sea, we have to feel our way alongside and then crawl ashore, risking our lives in the darkness. It is a wonder that no one has drowned in the process. I expect it is because we have come to know every inch of the wharf. The only light there is an oil lamp swung on the jetty, which serves only as a warning. Having made the jetty, we have to pick our way along, guided by the lights on the public road. Along the road that runs from the station, between the railway line and the harbour edge up to the Purty Kitchen almost, there is not a light. My opinion is that if the jetty and this road way were better lighted the fishing boats would make for Dun Laoghaire in greater numbers.'

18TH SEPTEMBER

Francis Higgins (*The Sham Squire*) recorded in his diary of 18 September 1800 the death of Lieutenant Edward Hepenstall of the 68th Regiment: 'a gentle man whose spirit during the (1798) Rebellion rendered much general good, and himself highly obnoxious to traitors.'

Obnoxious is hardly the word and many would have breathed a sigh of relief that 'the walking gibbet' had met his end.

Hepenstall, described as 'a Goliath in stature, and a Nero in feeling' was well known for brutality, a character trait which found full expression in 1798. 'If Hepenstall met a peasant who could not satisfactorily account for himself, he knocked him down with a blow from his fist, which was quite as effectual as a sledge-hammer, and then adjusting a noose round the prisoner's neck, drew the rope over his own shoulders, and trotted about the victim's legs dangling in the air, and his tongue protruding, until death at last put an end to the torture.'

It seems amazing but Hepenstall actually described his actions during one trial – Lord Norbury, the sadistic 'hanging judge', described the Lieutenant as having done no act which was not natural to a zealous, loyal, and efficient officer.

At least Hepenstall didn't die easy, according to Cox he became afflicted with morbus pedicularis; his body was literally devoured by vermin, and, after 21 days' suffering, he died in great agony. One suggestion for his headstone was the memorable:

> *Here lie the bones of Hepenstall,*
> *Judge, jury, gallows, rope, and all.'*

19TH SEPTEMBER

A report from *The Irish Catholic Chronicle And People's News of the Week*: Mr. Allen, police magistrate, attended at Mercer's Hospital on Tuesday evening, to take the depositions of Laurence Sherry, who is lying in a very precarious state from the effects of a blow inflicted on him on the 19th [September 1867] by James Wall, a fellow-workman, in a forge in South Anne-street. Sherry deposed as follows: 'Wall and I were quarrelling; I hit him a slap on the face with my open hand; he then stooped down and took up a piece of iron; another man and I took hold of him and shook the iron out of his hand. Some time after he began calling me names; I went over towards him, and whether I struck him with my hands or elbow I don't know; he then took up a sledge and struck me on the left side.' Prisoner then stooped down, opened the eyes of the dying man, and addressing him appealingly, said: 'Will you forgive me?' Sherry replied, 'It is not the first time you raised a weapon to me.' Mr. Allen then signed a committal, and the prisoner was sent to Richmond bridewell.

20TH SEPTEMBER

The Privy Council met on 20 September 1672 to consider the recent expulsion from Dublin Corporation of eight Alderman and Mr Davys, who was both the City Recorder and Clerk of the Tholsel. The expulsions followed a series of riotous Council meetings and the introduction of 'Lord Berkeley's Rules'. These rules more or less ordered everyone to behave themselves, limited items for debate to items previously submitted and, crucially, insisted that all members take the Oath of Supremacy, and the Oath of Non-resistance which declared abhorrence upon any pretence of taking arms against the King or those commissioned by him. Crucially, the eight expelled members were charged with crimes and misdemeanours but were not summoned to defend themselves. It was also believed that the key figure was Davys – that the whole expulsion had been engineered to strip him of his lucrative jobs.

After a meeting from nine to six (the third to discuss the case over a nine-day period) the Privy Council declared the expulsions illegal, ordered their reinstatement, made the City Treasurer pay costs, dismissed the Lord Mayor, Tottie, and those who had replaced the 'Evicted Eight'. The Council also ordered that all acts passed by the Corporation during the interregnum should be expunged from the records. Two parchments, covering 12 months, were taken out, leaving a permanent gap in the records of the city.'

21ST SEPTEMBER

By 21 September 1170 Strongbow with his army had come across the Dublin mountains and was camped at Donnybrook. King Rory O'Connor and his Irish army were camped outside Dublin. Inside the town a truce was in the air and Laurence O'Toole, the Archbishop, was the man chosen.

While O'Toole was attempting to prevent the sacking of Dublin, two of Strongbow's knights, Milo de Cogan and Raymond le Gros, gathered together some like-minded hooligans and attacked the city at Dame Gate and Christchurch. O'Connor, deciding that whichever side lost would be severely weakened, withdrew.

And so, Dublin went up in flames as the wooden houses were set ablaze. Merchants and traders were slain, their wives and children drowned.

Laurence O'Toole rushed backed to the city where he, unsuccessfully, tried to stop the destruction but, at least, survived. When the dust had settled O'Connor laid siege to Dublin for two months until he, too, was surprised by Strongbow and soundly defeated at a running battle on the site of the Phoenix Park.

22ND SEPTEMBER

During the four weeks ending on 22 September 1917, 10,359 people visited the Royal Victoria Baths, Dun Laoghaire – 3,410 using the Inside Baths and 6,949 chose to bathe in the Open Sea. 'The details are: Warm Salt Water Baths – Ladies, 1,564, Gentlemen, 1,552, Sea Weed, 70; Cold Salt Water Baths – Ladies, 123, Girls, 10, Gentlemen 91; Open Sea Baths – Ladies, 2,234, Children, 2.032, Gentlemen, 1,951, Boys 732. 456 dresses and caps and 767 costumes were hired. 154 persons paid for admission.'

A school ticket for Montague Roby's Famous Midget Minstrels, 1893.

The Attendants on the bathing platforms were changed during the period because it had been found that they were failing to prevent the nefarious practice of bathers passing on their costumes, thus depriving the baths of income. In the first week just 30 bathing costumes were hired out (one in 40 of bathers), by the end of the month the figure had risen to 154 (one in four).

During the same period 1,266 people used the Baths and Wash House – 345 used the Baths and 920 the Wash-House: Hot Baths – Men, 173, Women, 44, Children, 119, Steam Bath, 10; Wash-house, One-hour Tickets, 780, Two-hour tickets, 140.

23RD SEPTEMBER

Catherine M'Canna was executed near St. Stephens Green on Wednesday 23 September 1730. If her last words are to be believed, she had it coming. 'I drew my first Breath in this City, and descended of very honest parents, but I wicked wretch about ten Years ago committed a Robbery, and the said Robbery being found with me, I Swore it was my poor Mother gave it me, upon the same she was hanged, tho' innocent of the fact Oh my God! what shall become of me, who have spent my time in Whoring and Thieving since I came to the Knowledge of committing either.' She tells how, a short while previous, she had been spared hanging at Kilmainham. 'I no sooner got my Liberty, but (Dog like return'd to his Vomit), I followed my old Trade again about the beginning of August last, I went to the *Pyde Bull* in St. Thomas Street, and stole there out the value of five Pounds in Linnen but I was soon taken and committed to Newgate, but when I was Try'd and lawfully convicted for the same, I began to plead my Belly [pregnancy], thinking to save my life but all was in vain, for my jury of Mattrons would not foreswear them selves for me, so I must Dye this Day.'

24TH SEPTEMBER

Unfair taxation is not just a contemporary problem – but at least in the case of protests over window tax in Dublin no-one was claiming that it was a stealth tax. *The Dublin Post* in a report also carried by *The Times* dated 24 September 1814 noted: 'The parishes of St. Bridget, St. Mark, and St. Werburgh, have resolved to petition against the tax. Their respective resolutions are firm and constitutional; but it must be acknowledged that those of the parish of St. Werburgh are pre-eminent for the soundness of judgement with which the grievance is examined, and efficacy of the remedy which is recommended for the cure of this national evil.'

The Werburghers noted that if the tax was abolished, it would only result in the imposition of a new tax to replace the lost revenue. However, they noted a different solution: 'They advert to the multiplication of offices, the unnecessary increases of officers, and to the enormous amount of the sinecures. They pray for a modification of the one species of grievance, and for the abolition of the other.' The window tax continued until 1851, when it was replaced with a council tax.

25TH SEPTEMBER

The eleven-day inquest into the death of Thomas Ashe in Mountjoy on 25 September 1917 reported: 'We find Thomas Ashe died of heart failure and congestion of the lungs and that it was caused by the punishment of taking away from his cell the bed, bedding, boots, and left to lie on the cold floor for 50 hours, and then subjected to forcible feeding in his weak condition, after a hunger strike of five or six days. We censure the Castle authorities for not acting more promptly, especially when the grave condition of the deceased and other prisoners was brought under their notice by the Lord Mayor. That the assistant doctor called in, having no previous practice in such operations, administered unskilfully forcible feeding. That the taking away of the deceased's bed, bedding and boots was an unfeeling and barbarous act, and we censure the Deputy Governor for violating the prisoner rule, but we infer that he was acting under instructions from the Prisons Board of the Castle, which refused to give evidence and documents asked for.'

Ashe, a national school teacher, had been convicted of sedition after addressing a meeting. He was serving a two-year sentence.

26TH SEPTEMBER

Dubliner John Nicholson led a life straight out of an adventure novel after joining the British Army at the age of 16 in 1837. He took part in the Afghan War (1842), was captured and spent several months in captivity. During the Sikh War (1848) he distinguished himself at Attock, the Margulla Pass, Chillianwallah and Guzerat (and, no, I don't have a clue where they are either). In 1850 he left for home on leave – on his way engaging in an unsuccessful plot to liberate Kossuth [a Hungarian politician] from captivity in a Turkish fortress. On his return to India, the now Colonel Nicholson, was on hand in Peshawar when the Indian Mutiny broke out. He removed a large treasure to a place of safety, dismissed some native regiments, and at Murdan helped to put to rout a force of the mutineers. On this occasion he was fully twenty hours in the saddle, travelled seventy miles, and cut down many fugitives with his own hand. Taking command of a column for the relief of Delhi he annihilated a large force of the enemy at Trimmoo, fought the battle of Nujufgurh, in which between 3,000 and 4,000 of the mutineers were slain. Already he had been created Brigadier-General. While heading an attack on a Sepoy position, he was mortally wounded; and died on the 23 September 1857, aged 35.

27TH SEPTEMBER

In the wake of Parnell's death, passions were running high and *The Freeman's Journal*, among other newspapers, was campaigning against the political influence of Catholic priests. Then, fearing financial difficulties, the *Freeman* changed side, enraging the Parnellites.

On Saturday, 27 September 1891, the Parnellites posters set up and handbills distributed throughout the city containing the following announcement:

'Funeral Procession Of *The Freeman's Journal*, The Nationalists of Dublin are invited to assist at the interment of the late lamented freeman's journal, Which departed this Life on Monday last from an acute attack of clerical intimidation, softening of the backbone, And other painful disorders.

The melancholy cortege will start from the Gray statue on Sunday next, at 3.30 o'clock sharp, for the family burial vault of The Sham Squire, Kilbarrack Churchyard, where funeral orations will be cheerfully delivered by well-known Dublin speakers. The remains will be suitably cremated, and committed to the vile dust from whence they sprung, Unwept, unhonoured, and unsung. Bands will attend. All are welcome.'

Several thousand turned up, along with a large number of police, and four bands. At the graveyard a coffin, painted black was produced and 'copies of *The Freeman's Journal* and *The Evening Telegraph* having been placed in it burned amid the cheers of the spectators.'

28TH SEPTEMBER

Ask elderly people about their memories of exotic fruit and the chances are they'll remember the first shipments of oranges and bananas after the reason for the 'The Emergency' ended. But there are earlier tales, like this one, from the Freeman's Journal, of a gardening adventure on 28 September 1763: 'Wednesday last, John Hall, was committed to Newgate by Wm. Chamberlain, Esq.; for stealing a large quantity of pineapples out of the hot-house of Mr. John Phelan, gardener, at Harold's Cross, in the county of Dublin, and for stabbing and cutting with a cast knife, John Austin and Edmond Bolan, who were placed as watchmen near said hot-house. It is not doubted but this dangerous fellow and his accomplices are the villains who have robbed so many gardens lately near the city, and that said Austin and Bolan, on conviction, will receive the reward so timely, and so generously promised by the worthy high sheriff of said county, as they fairly hazarded their lives in apprehending the above offender. Public spirited rewards in this way will be the most effectual means to rid the Kingdom of such Vagabonds.'

29TH SEPTEMBER

'Constable Hayes (140C) while on his beat the previous evening [29 September 1899] happened upon a number of boys engaged in the pastime of tossing half-pence. The appearance of the constable created consternation amongst the juvenile gamblers, who fled in all directions. Daniel M'Cluskey, aged 16, of Upper Dominick street, was unlucky enough to suffer capture, and to be ordered by Mr. Wall to pay a fine of five shilling or in default to got to prison for a week.'

'Thomas Roche, aged 51, described as having no fixed residence and no business, was found by Constable Heron begging in Marlborough street. He had already been convicted three times this year, and was now sentenced to a month's imprisonment with hard labour.' [*Evening Telegraph*]

30TH SEPTEMBER

The Irish Catholic Chronicle reported in 1867: 'At the Head Office on Monday [30 September], three men named John Molloy (labourer), John Carey (labourer) and James Carey (sawyer), were charged by Acting Inspector Dagg, with having caused a disturbance in Thomas-street on Saturday night. It appears that the prisoners had been drinking in Mrs. Andrew's public-house, where a disturbance ensued, which caused the police to interfere. The prisoners having been brought outside, a large crowd collected, and stones were thrown repeatedly at police. Inspector Flowers and four horse police then arrived and were also assaulted by the crowd, who vigorously fired stones at them. One of the policemen named Byrne, was struck with a stone, and so seriously injured, that it was necessary to remove him to hospital. One of the horses was also injured. Some of the police drew their revolvers and formed square, and thus kept off the crowd, while others brought the prisoners to Newmarket station. Some of the principal disturbers escaped and were not since arrested. The prisoners were fined one pound each, and one pound costs.'

Chapter Ten

October

1ST OCTOBER

Victorian enthusiasm for mail saw technology quickly adapted to ensure quicker deliveries as this account of new arrangements for postal acceleration demonstrates: 'At 6.15am a special train was despatched from Westland-row, which arrived at the Carlisle Pier, Kingstown, at 6.30am. The bags containing the mails have been lowered into the Post-office on board the *Leinster*, she at once prepared to start, and left her moorings at 7am, sharp, and in less than five minutes was well out of the harbour. The voyage was accomplished with comparative ease in three hours and twenty-two minutes. The *Leinster* left 2.20pm, with the morning mails from London, and arrived again at Kingstown at 5.20pm. As this vessel arrived about forty-five minutes before the time anticipated, there was consequently no train to meet her, and the mail bags were for more than a quarter of an hour lying on the pier before the special train to Dublin arrived. Messrs. Smith and Sons, news agents of Sackville-street, were enabled to leave the London daily journals at the various newspaper offices in Dublin at a few minutes after six o'clock, which, under the old system, were seldom delivered before eleven o'clock at night.' [*Irish Times* and *Daily Advertiser*, 1 October 1860]

2ND OCTOBER

'Edward Strahan, a labourer of Charlemont street, was charged [2 October 1899] with a series of offences. He met Sergeant Rous, of the 4th Battalion Rifle Brigade, who was out for a walk with his wife and child. With the observation, 'You are no man to fight the Boers,' he struck the sergeant a blow on the neck with the butt-end of a whip. Prisoner then kicked him as he lay on the ground, then turned round and kicked the perambulator in which the sergeant's child, aged two years, was sitting, over into the gutter. The child was violently thrown out, but happily sustained little or no injury. In the struggle to save his child the sergeant's uniform, trousers, cap, cane, and gloves were damaged.' [*Evening Telegraph*] Strathan got two months hard labour for the assault, one month for upsetting the child and a fine of £5 or an additional month.

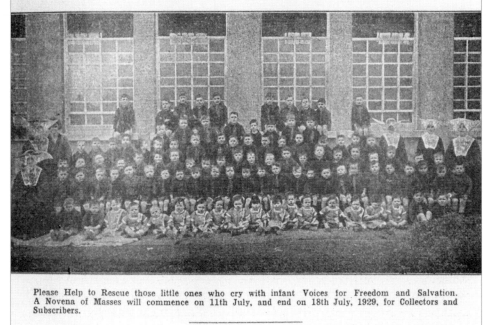

An ad for St Therese's Home for Catholic Children from 1929.

3RD OCTOBER

As far back as 1730 the Foundling Hospital in James' Street was coming up with new ways to ensure that abandoned children were safely, and anonymously, delivered to it. The Minute Book of the Court of Governors of 3 October of that year states: 'Hu (Boulter) Armach, Primate of All-Ireland, being in the chair, ordered that a turning-wheel, or conveniency for taking in children, be provided near the gate of the workhouse; that at any time, by day or by night, a child may be layd in it, to be taken in by the officers of the said house.'

In five years – 1791 to 1796 – no less than 5,216 infants were sent to the Infirmary. A solitary one recovered. A House of Commons Committee reported on the Infirmary, noting that the children were 'stripped' when sent up to the Infirmary (to die), and had the old clothing that they came into the House in put on them. That they were then laid, five and six huddled and crushed together, in the receptacles called cradles, 'swarming with vermin,' and they were then covered over with filthy and dirty blankets, which had been 'cast' as unfit for use. Then they were given 'The Bottle' – containing a strong sleeping draught – and left to die.

4TH OCTOBER

In times gone by when a servant went missing, with or without some of the family possessions, it was not unusual for advertisements to be taken in the Dublin newspapers to advertise the fact. Saturday 4 October 1760. 'This is to give notice that Sarah Savage serves as Cook, is a very bad woman, she is a Thief and notorious in other respects. Lest she should impose on any other families she is not known to, I take this public method of advertising her. She is a tall thin woman, dark Hair, small hollow eyes, a wide Mouth and takes a vast quantity of Snuff. Her age is about forty. John Olpherts.'

And another example: 'Ran away from the service of Captain William Stewart of Caple Street, Dublin John Smith, above 5 four high, well set, full round face, fresh complexion has blewish eyes and thick black bushy hair, aged about 26, at going off wore an old blew coat, a pair of new blew breeches lined with shammy, and had yellow puffs and a new hat edged with broadsilver lace. Whoever secures him so as to be had by the same Captain Steward shall have a pistole [a Spanish gold coin] reward.' [*Whalley's Newsletter*, March 1722]

5TH OCTOBER

Just because you were a member of one of Dublin's Guilds didn't necessarily mean that you were entitled to engage in all aspects of their work – which, considering the qualification of Daniel Rowle, was probably a very good thing. 'I Daniel Rowle of the City of Dublin Barber and Perukemaker [wigs] doe hereby oblige myselfe my heiress Executors & Administrators in the penall sum of one hundred pounds sterl. to be paid unto the Master & Wardens of the Corporation of Barbers & Chirurgeons [physicians or surgeons trained through apprenticeship] Appothocaries [pharmacist] & Perukemakers Dublin that I will not at any time hereafter intrude upon the said Corporation by practising Pharmacy or any part of Chirurgery, Phlebotomy &

A steam train on the Dublin lines.

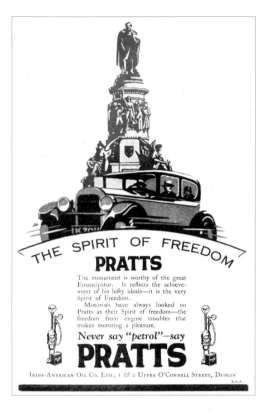

THE SPIRIT OF FREEDOM

PRATTS

The monument is worthy of the great Emancipator. It reflects the achievement of his lofty ideals—it is the very Spirit of Freedom.

Motorists have always looked on Pratts as their Spirit of freedom—the freedom from engine troubles that makes motoring a pleasure.

Never say "petrol"—say

PRATTS

IRISH-AMERICAN OIL CO. LTD., 1 & 2 UPPER O'CONNELL STREET, DUBLIN

Just one of the many ads for the burgeoning Irish motorcar trade.

tooth drawing only excepted, with the County of the Citty or five miles distance of the said Citty. I will not imply any person to practice the same for me neither will I teach or instruct any person to trim or make Peruks unless the same be bound an apprentice to me for the tearme of seaven years. Witnesse my hands & Seale the 5th day of October 1694.'

6TH OCTOBER

The numbers of cars on Irish roads was small in 1904, but that didn't prevent motorists from feeling that they were being hounded by the police. On 6 October a special meeting of members of the Irish Automobile Club was held in Dublin to consider the heavy fines for speeding which had been imposed on motor-cars and motor bicycles. Horace Plunkett presided and admitted that he had often overshot the national speed limit of 12mph.

'The chairman thought they should admit that the action of a great many of their motoring friends had not been wise, and that the mistake most of them had made ... was not unnatural and easily explained. He thought they forgot that the ordinary passenger in the street was not aware that a machine which travelled at such an apparently dangerous speed could at any moment be rapidly diverted from its course or brought to a dead stop in once of twice its own length.' [*The Times*]

After a discussion a motion expressing readiness to co-operate with the police, and hoping that pedestrians would do the same, was passed.

[During the Gordon Bennett Rally the previous year the competing cars had to keep to the 12mph limit while passing through towns and villages – the average speed of the winning car was 49.2mph.]

7TH OCTOBER

Conquer Hill, Clontarf, was scheduled to be the scene of Daniel O'Connell's great mass meeting – up to a million people were expected to hear him call for the repeal of the Union with Britain, by force if necessary. It was the culmination of a series of monster meetings which aimed to make the British to back down and accede to Irish demands.

The great event was scheduled for Sunday. Two days earlier there were rumours in the city that the monster meeting would be banned – and it was, at 3.30pm on Saturday, 7 October 1843.

On the following morning regiments of infantry and cavalry occupied Conquer Hill, a brigade of artillery was sited nearby, three warships were anchored close by and the guns of the Pigeon House were trained on Clontarf.

Not surprisingly, O'Connell had backed down on the Saturday evening. It was a move which greatly weakened his influence with the British, proving that while he was willing to threaten resistance; he was not prepared to rebel. Likewise, it cost him the support of younger men – they would go on to form the Young Ireland movement. O'Connell's great success was Catholic Emancipation 14 years earlier; his proposed Repeal of the Union was not to be.

8TH OCTOBER

The Dublin Penny Journal gave an interesting account of the first trials of the Dublin to Kingstown Railway: 'On Saturday, the 8th [October 1834] instant, the first trial of the steam engine *Vauxhall* with a small train of carriages filled with ladies and gentlemen, was made on the line of railway from Dublin to the Martello tower at Williamstown. The experiment is said to have given great satisfaction, not only as to the rapidity of motion, ease of conveyance and facility of stopping, but the celerity and quickness with which the train passed, by means of the crossings from one line of road to another. The distance was about two miles and a half which was performed four times each way at the rate of about thirty-one miles an hour. The control over the machinery was complete, the stopping and reversing the motion was effected without a moment's delay.'

'Having joined in one of these trips we were delighted with the perfect ease and safety with which it was performed; there is so little motion perceptible even when going at the quickest rate, that we could read or write without the slightest inconvenience.'

9TH OCTOBER

If you look closely at old maps of Dublin Bay you will see many changes – including the disappearance of Clontarf Island.

The coastline in the early nineteenth century, before the reclamation of the North Strand, ran from Ballybough Bridge to Amiens Street, Beresford Place to Grattan Bridge. Clontarf Island was then well away from the shore.

A Beaver Street publican, Christopher Cromwell, had built a wooden house on the island and used it as his summer residence, sometimes staying for a week at a time. On 9 October 1944 Christopher and his nine-year-old son, William, were on the Island during a tremendous storm, one of the greatest recorded in Dublin Port. A policeman on his beat – he'd had to move inland as his beat was under water – saw the light in the house go out at 10pm.

The following morning the bodies of the Christopher and William, weighed down by their heavy fishing boots, were found on the shore of the island, the house had disappeared.

The boats which could have saved them had been blown by the storm as far as Annesley Bridge.

10TH OCTOBER

On 10 October 1918 the *RMS Leinster* left Dun Laoghaire, bound for Holyhead. About 16 miles out the ship was torpedo and sunk by the German submarine *UB-123*. 501 of the 771 people on board were lost.

The ships crew was largely drawn from the towns of Holyhead and Dun Laoghaire. The ship carried mail between Dun Laoghaire and Holyhead. (The RMS in the ship's name stood for Royal Mail Steamer). The ship had an onboard post office staffed by members of Dublin's Post Office. There were 22 sorters on duty that day.

The ship had 180 civilian passengers on board – among then Fanny Saunders from York Road, Dun Laoghaire, was on her way to see her daughter Janet, who was dying in Liverpool. Twenty-three years earlier Fanny's husband Frank had been lost on Christmas Eve 1895, when the crew of Dun Laoghaire Lifeboat lost their lives attempting to save the crew of a sinking ship. Fanny lost her life in the same sea that had taken her husband. Their daughter Janet died in hospital two days later. 115 of the 180 civilian passengers on the ship were lost. Among the ships which raced to the rescue was the *Helga* – two years earlier she had been used to shell central Dublin during the Easter Rising.

11TH OCTOBER

This story dates from 11 October 1814, but it does have a timeless quality, it would have been strange in any century. 'Edward Quin, one of the combinators in the coach making business, who had been guilty of a gross and cruel assault, with intent to murder, received the second part of his sentence; he was whipped from the Royal Exchange. On the last day it appeared that the common executioner had by no means done his duty, and for this occasion another person was procured; his figure was highly grotesque – he appeared to be a strong able man, in a grey coat, with an immense wig; but his face was the most singular part of his appearance, – it was fully covered over with yellow ochre, strongly tattooed over with deep lines of black; he, however, fully answered the purpose for which he was employed; cutting the unfortunate and misguided criminal's back at every stroke, which he bore with a firmness and sternness worthy a better cause; he chewed a bullet between his teeth the whole of the way, not suffering even a groan to escape him; and when arrived at the Exchange, smiled at the crowd with the air of a martyr.'

12TH OCTOBER

'Shaving and Trimming the Dean' – By a deed dated 12 October 1564, a barber and his wife (being the grantees) 'undertake to diligently perform by themselves, or a substitute, the office of barber in shaving and trimming the Dean [Robert Mossom DD], chapters, and vicars choral, when required, to come once a week for the pur-pose of shaving, and should some of the brethren be absent on the shaving day to come when sent for, and also to poll and round the six choristers, receiving the like payment as Thomas Grace, the late barber. Covenant for voiding grant after 2 or 3 admonitions for negligence, and covenant for distress by grantees.'

13TH OCTOBER

The Guild of Barber-Surgeons was always on the lookout for anyone who might be selling unlicensed 'wiggs' in Dublin. On 13 October 1718 their Minute Book records: 'Whereas many great frauds and abuses are daily committed and practiced in and about the City of Dublin by divers persons who sell hairs therein by mixing of hairs cutt off of several heads together tho of different colours, mixing bleached hairs horse hairs and live hairs together and by giving false colours to hairs by dipping and dyeing the same and by other irregular and unfair management and do also lett down the same by falsely and unfairly tying the same all which and the like knav-ish and unfair doings of the said persons sellers of hairs tend to the great loss and abuse of the Brethren of this corporation in particular and to the wearer of wiggs in general.' Continuing on the document warned that all such persons should be persecuted with the utmost severity of the law. The practice must have continued because 'unmerchantable wiggs' were still on the streets in 1757. The same Guild, in 1760, was published advertisements 'against shaving and dressing wigs or hair on the Lord's Day.'

14TH OCTOBER

John Philpot Curran, politician and legal defender of many of the United Irishmen (though not to the extent of letting his daughter, Sarah, marry a rebel, i.e. Robert Emmett), lived in various Dublin locations – first on Redmond's Hill, then in Fade-street, and afterwards on Hog Hill (St. Andrew-street), Ely Place, 80 Stephen's Green.

He was known for his quick wit, and it was demonstrated under pressure when he fought a duel with a fellow lawyer, John 'Bully' Egan. Egan was a large man while Curran was small – a fact which Egan was unhappy with, complaining that

John Philpot Curran, politician,
defender of the United Irishmen,
and quickwitted under fire.

'the disparity between his immense girth and height and Curran's few feet gave his antagonist a great advantage. 'I might as well fire at a razor's edge as at Curran,' said Egan, 'and he may well hit me as easily as a turf stack.' 'I'll tell you what, Egan,' replied Curran; 'I wish to take no advantage upon you whatever. Let my size be chalked upon your front, and I am quite content that every shot which hits outside that mark shall not count.'

When Curran died, 14 October 1817, aged 67, he was buried at Paddington, London. In 1834 he was re-interred in Glasnevin cemetery – two years after it opened the cemetery was looking for a star guest to encourage burials there.

15TH OCTOBER

The Freeman's Journal reported on trouble in the city on 15 October 1763: 'At Noon-day, a most licentious and inhuman Set of People, called a Mob, proceeded outrageously through several Parts of the City, and violently entered a Shop in Dame-street, and another in Francis-street, and took a Quantity of Broad Cloth from each Shop, and searched a Gentleman's House at Harold's-Cross. This Madness of the Mob is, at length grown epidemical, and rages like a Plague among the lower People. Our present Magistrates, who know their Duty, and are earnest to discharge it, cannot be prepared at a Minutes Warning, nor present in so many Places at once. While these Wretches, like flying Parties of Hussars, advance and retreat, fall on and disappear, almost in an Instant; according as they see the Object of their Fury defenceless, for fear the approach of Danger to themselves. What then is to be done? Are we to have no Government, or what may be worse than no Government, Soldiers billeted upon us and stationed in every Street. These, indeed, are the dreadful Extremities, to which our madding and deluded Countrymen would drive us. We therefore invite all considerate Lovers of Ireland to give their best Advice, towards our avoiding the two Extremes of an ABSOLUTE ANARCHY, or a MILITARY REGENCY.'

16TH OCTOBER

There was rioting in Dublin on October 16 1881 after the arrest of John Dillon, MP, and other Land Leaguers. *The Freeman's Journal* reported: 'Charging headlong into the people, the constables struck right and left, and men and women fell under their blows. No quarter was given. From the Ballast Office to the Bridge, and from the Bridge to Sackville Street, the charge was continued with fury. All was confusion, and nought could be seen but the police mercilessly batoning the people. Some few of the people threw stones, of which fact the broken gas-lamps bear testimony; but, with this exception, no resistance was offered. Gentlemen and respectable working men, returning homewards from theatres and houses of friends, fell victims to the attack, and as an incident of the conduct of the police it may be mentioned that, besides numerous others, more than a dozen students of Trinity College and a militia officer – unoffending passers-by – were knock down and kicked, and two postal telegraph messengers, engaged in carrying telegrams, were barbarously assaulted.' Mr. David Gray, MP, witnessed the event: 'I saw them beating children and acting the most wanton and shameful way.' The Chief Secretary replied: 'It cannot be altogether a milk-and-water business clearing streets.'

17TH OCTOBER

'The proprietor of a local omnibus appeared to-day before Mr. Barton, at the Kingstown Police-court, at the instance of Acting-Inspector Toohey, for allowing the rain, on a recent occasion, to enter the interior of the vehicle, to the discomfort of the passengers. The defence was that the vehicle had been fully repaired a short time before, but the drought of the past months had opened some of the seams of the roof, which was now mended. The magistrate said that in no city within his experience was there such a bad omnibus and cab accommodation as in Dublin. From the complaints recently coming before him in Dublin, he found that the drivers were, to a great extent, insolent, extortionate, and untidy; and he was determined to give the public full advantage of the law in counteracting such a state of things. Therefore, in cases of this kind, he invariably inflicted a fine of 5s, which he did on the present occasion.' [*Kingstown Gazette*, 17 October 1868]

18TH OCTOBER

Martin Mackanally, 25, was executed for the crime of Ravishment (rape) on 18 October 1727 at Kilmainham. As was customary, his last words were recorded (or made up) and published as quickly as possible to ensure the greatest possible profit. 'I drew my first unfortunate Breath in St. James Street of honest Parents who tenderly nourished me untill I came able to shift for my self, then I thought I was no ways obliged to them but alas! I was like a great many when I got any Pence, I would go and drink till I would get my self Drunk, then go and Quarrel with Friend or Foe, which folly often put me to abundance of trouble. Last St. Lawrence's Day I went to the Fair of Palmerstown along with some other young Lads, thinking of no harm, where we continued untill it was prity duskish, and coming home we met with one Neal and his Wife a going home ... also my Companions told him they would take away his Wife I knock'd him down, the rest was about the Wife, but I declare that one of them had not the time to have carnel knowledge of her (let alone three).'

19TH OCTOBER

'Friday night [19 October 1798] Mr. Alderman Truelock, who has laboured for several months past under a state of mental derangement, put and end to his existence with a pistol, at his house at Symond's Court, near Ball's Bridge. This unfortunate Gentleman's prevalent symptom of insanity was a persuasion that his family and servants were leagued in a plot to poison him. On the night of that fatal day, when sitting alone with his Lady, he suddenly seized a pistol which hung over the chimney-piece for the protection of his house and fired at her, and the ball passed through the back of her neck. Mrs. Truelock, with much fortitude and presence of mind, ran out of the room in order to send one of her servants for a Surgeon; and the instant she quitted the room, the Alderman bolted it on the inside, and with a second pistol dispatched himself. The servants, alarmed by the report, broke open the door, and found that the unfortunate Gentleman had effected his fatal purpose by placing the muzzle of the pistol in his mouth, as the ball passed diagonally through the occiput.'
[*The Times*]

20TH OCTOBER

As the 1913 Lockout progressed it was clear that many families could no longer afford to feed themselves. A plan was put together to send the children of the striking families to England where they would be looked after by sympathisers.

William J. Walsh, Archbishop of Dublin, was having none of it. In a letter to the newspapers on 20 October, he wrote: 'The Dublin women now subjected to this cruel temptation to part with their helpless offspring are, in the majority of cases, Catholics. Have they abandoned their Faith? Surely not. I can only put it to them that they can be no longer held worthy of the name of Catholic mothers if they so far forget that duty as to send their little children in a strange land, without security of any kind that those to whom the children are to be handed over are Catholics, or indeed are persons of any faith at all.'

James Connolly replied: 'Nobody wants to send the children away; the IGTWU least of all desires such a sacrifice. But neither do we wish the children to starve.'

There were violent scenes as parents brought their children to the docks. Priests and Catholic parents blocked entry to the ships. The plan was dropped.

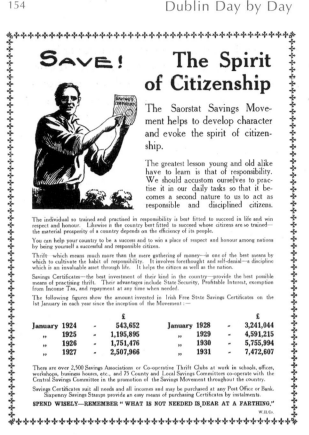

The Early Free State encourages Thrift and saving amongst its citizens.

21ST OCTOBER

The Archbishop of Dublin denounced Jim Larkin's plans to send hungry children of locked-out workers to England on October 21 1913.

In October starvation was becoming very real and it was proposed that some of the children of the strikers would be sent to England. Larkin backed the idea, but it was strongly opposed by the Archbishop of Dublin, William J. Walsh.

In a letter to the newspapers he wrote: 'I can only put it to them that they can no longer be worthy of the name of Catholic mothers if they so far forget that duty as to send away their little children to be cared for in a strange land, without security of any kind that those to whom the children are to be handed over are Catholics, or indeed are persons of any faith at all.

There were scuffles at the docks as parents brought their children and Larkin, faced with public hostility to the plan, had to back down.

22ND OCTOBER

The Lord Mayor of Dublin, Fergus Farrell, wanted to celebrate the safe return of Irish soldiers who had fought in the Crimean War (1845-55). The committee set up decided that a Banquet was the best idea and the venue was Stack A in the Custom

House Docks which had the space needed for the 4,000 guests – 1,000 civilians were admitted at a cost of ten shillings for each gentleman and five shillings per lady.

The banquet was held on 22 October 1856 and the food consumed on the day was prodigious: '250 hams, 230 legs of mutton, 250 pieces of beef, 500 meat pies, 100 venison pasties, 100 rice puddings, 250 plum puddings weighing one ton and a half, 200 turkeys and 200 geese, 2,000 rolls, 3,500lbs of bread, 3 tons of potatoes, 8,500 quart bottles and 3,500 pint bottles of port.' A Dublin merchant, Henry Brennan, also provided a pint of port or sherry for each of the guests.

There were many speeches, Lord Gough declared the Banquet 'the happiest moment in a long life of military vicissitude', Isaac Butt MP offered 'a thousand welcomes to those who fought for us in far off lands, Lord Talbot de Malahide remembered 'the memory of the fallen.'

And then, at 4.15pm, it was all over – the sated troops were marched to the railway to return to barracks.

23RD OCTOBER

It may seem ridiculous today, but for several centuries it was widely believed that the date of the creation of the world was Sunday, 23 October 4,004BC (it is often quoted as happening at 9am – but not even the finder, James Ussher claimed to be that accurate). He had worked the date out through his own bewildered interpretation of Scripture.

Ussher calculated the dates of other biblical events, concluding, for example, that Adam and Eve were driven from Paradise on Monday, 10 November 4004, BC, and that the ark touched down on Mt Ararat on 5 May 2348 BC – a Wednesday'.

Usher, 13, a Dubliner, was one of the first entrants into Trinity College. He graduated in 1600 – was Professor of Theology there in 1607 and was appointed Archbishop of Armagh in 1625.

He wasn't a man to mince his words about Catholics: 'The religion of the papists is superstitious and idolatrous; their faith and doctrine erroneous and heretical; their church apostatical; to give them therefore a toleration, or to consent that they may freely exercise their religion is a grievous sin.'

He fled Ireland during the Rebellion of 1641, never to return. He died at age 75 in 1656 and was given a state funeral in Westminster Abbey.

24TH OCTOBER

The blind Lord of Howth who died on 24 October 1589 certainly had a way of dealing with trouble – extreme violence! Estranged from his wife since 1578 – he was ordered to pay her eight pounds a month – he was convicted in the Castle Chamber in July 1579 of beating her with great barbarity because she had protested against 'his dissolute life.' He was also convicted of beating his daughter so severely that she later died. A servant who had befriended his wife was given a severe thrashing. Fines of £1,000 were imposed, and their non-payment led to his imprisonment for more than six months.

The sole member of his family named in his will was his eldest son, and it was his wish that no one except his said son should 'intermeddle with his goods and chattels.'

Besides his son, he mentioned his servant, Richard Hanlon, to whom he left a farm and some live stock; his page, Lawrence, to whom he left his grey horse and his cape, which was of the same colour; and one Belle White, to whom he left a house for her life.

25TH OCTOBER

The Endowed Schools Commissioners opened an inquiry into the Swords Borough School on 25 October 1855, and in due course reported: 'Charges of excessive severity were preferred against the master. It was also alleged that in the girls' school some of the pupils were often employed until a late hour at needlework for the schoolmistress, and that the loss of apprenticeship fees was threatened in case of refusal. Both the principal schoolmaster and the schoolmistress, his daughter, were examined with reference to such of these charges as related to their departments. The evidence given by each was at variance with that of the pupils whom we examined on the same subjects, and appeared to us to be undeserving of credit. We visited this school and found the attendance small, and the state of instruction in the boys school very unsatisfactory. Since the time we visited the school, and received evidence respecting it, the principal master has been dismissed but his son-in-law, the former assistant master, has been appointed to succeed him; his daughter, the principal mistress, retains her place; and the dismissed master himself is allowed to reside in the schoolhouse. It is not likely that such inadequate measures of reform will secure public confidence in the management of the establishment, and render the school generally available for the inhabitants of Swords.' Simmering underneath the inquiry was a dispute over religious teaching; Catholic children had been withdrawn by their parents.

26TH OCTOBER

You're having a quiet drink with your mates and suddenly all hell breaks loose: 'Yesterday [Sunday, 26 October 1823] about half-past one o'clock, the Lord Mayor and Sheriff Perrin entered a public-house in North King-street, where they surprised upwards of one hundred and twenty men, about seventy of whom made their escape; fifty-one were found secreted in various parts of the house, and seven on the roof. Great resistance was made before they could be secured, which was not affected until the military guard stationed at Newgate, came to his Lordship's assistance. It is not yet ascertained what the object of so numerous an assemblage could have been in one house; the persons committed are principally from the neighbourhood of Glasnevin, Finglassbridge, and St. Margaret's.' [*Dublin Freeman's Journal.*]

27TH OCTOBER

Dublin Corporation Waterworks Committee, which had met daily for the previous three weeks, issued their report on 27 October 1893 on providing extra water to the city: 'In consequence of the long-continued drought, the supply of Vartry water is exhausted ... further expenditure should be made in order to secure a continuous supply of water. The Committee arranged with the Board of the Grand Canal Company for a supply from that same source, taken from the fifth and eighth locks, which has been sufficient for the south side of the city, and a district of the north side to which the water could be brought. But the contingency of a still longer drought has to be provided against, to meet which the Committee arranged with the Board of the Midland Railway Company to take a supply of water from the eighth lock, or other higher level of the Royal Canal, to carry it in pipes along the canal back, and empty it direct into the city mains. It was necessary to take the water from this level in order to avoid the contamination of the canal nearer the city, and secure a higher a pressure. The Board of the Midland Railway Co. have agreed to supply the water at a charge of one halfpenny per thousand gallons.'

28TH OCTOBER

The Dublin Chronicle of 28 October 1788 had the sort of news to send a shiver of fear through the population particularly when they came into the proximity of very small dogs!

'Thursday morning an accident happened at the Blackrock, which has been attended with most melancholy consequences: A fine boy, about fourteen years old, passing by a gentleman's house, the lady's lap-dog ran out and bit him; in about two hours the youth was seized with convulsive fits, and shortly after with the hydro-phobia; and, not withstanding every assistance that night, his friends were on Friday obliged to smother him between two beds.' (*Dublin Chronicle*)

The paper returned to the story in the next issue as the anonymous youth had by then passed on to his eternal reward! 'The improbability of such a murder being committed within three miles of the metropolis, and near so many polished and well-informed people as reside at the Blackrock, is much greater than if it had been asserted to be in a very remote part of the country, far distant from any faculty of medicine.'

It does beg the question – can you be murdered by a dog?

29TH OCTOBER

J. Byrne Power, Medical Officer, presenting a report on the state of health in the Kingstown Commissioners area, for the four-week period ending 29 October 1898 noted: 'I recently inspected some of the common lodging-houses in the township, and found them in a wretched condition. In fact, no one but those members of the Sanitary Authority who accompanied me to those places on former occasions could form an idea of their filthy, squalid condition. From a return furnished to me by the Sub-Sanitary Officers, I find that in the six houses in Patrick-street which I inspected there is a total of 21 rooms, in which 107 lodgers are supposed to rest at night. The total breathing space in these 21 rooms is only 18,400 cubic feet, which gives an average of only 172 c.f. per head. This is little more than half the recognised minimum (300 c.f.) which is now universally considered to be far too low. I find that even this allowance is only reached in 7 of the 21 rooms, that in 10 rooms the space is less than 200 c.f., while in two rooms in one of the houses there are 18 lodgers in 1.260, or only 70 c.f. per head. This is a deplorable state of affairs, and must favour the spread of disease, especially tuberculosis.'

30TH OCTOBER

The Lord Lieutenant put on major show at Dublin Castle on 30 October 1745 to celebrate the king's birthday. George Falkiner, publisher, was on hand to record the events: 'The Square of the Castle being finely painted new on each window of the Castle were the Letters GR with a Crown above them and 38 Lamps burning to each. The Supper Room was all decorated in the most beautiful manner with fine Paintings, Illuminations and Statues, the Entrance into it having a Temple of Minerva. Within the Temple there rose a large and beautiful Obelisk which seemed all one Blaze of Light from the Number of wax Tapers which illuminated it; and over the Side-board which surrounded the inside of the Temple at a proper Height were several Statues which poured a perpetual Flow of the choicest Wines of all sorts into Basins properly placed to receive them, from whence the Liquor was conveyed into the lower Castle Yard, where it played off in several Fountains of Wine during the Whole of the Entertainment to give the Populace and Opportunity to drink his Majesty's Health and long Life, and Confusion to his Enemies.'

31ST OCTOBER

Even a century ago commuters expected their trams to be on time, and didn't appreciate anyone messing about with the route. The Clontarf Commissioners, at their meeting of 31 October 1899, meditated on the problem: 'The strong opinion which exists in Clontarf and Dollymount against the change of place of starting from Nelson's Pillar to Abbey street found expression at the Clontarf Commissioners to-day. The Public have now to wait be times in slush and rain for the trams from Palmerstown Park, and then there is often a stampede for the cars at Abbey street. Mr. Tickell complained of the unpunctuality with which the tram service had been carried on for some days past. Sometimes they would have a tram every two minutes then not one for 15 or 20 minutes. At present nearly 300 trams passed the O'Connell Monument every day, and he did not know what the Corporation were doing in allowing the Tramway Company to make a railway through O'Connell Street. He thought the board should ask the company to stop the running of the trams from Palmerstown Park to Dollymount and to run the cars to the Pillar as before. A member suggested that it was the traffic in O'Connell street and other thoroughfares in the city that prevented the trams keeping good time.' (*The Evening Telegraph*)

Chapter Eleven

November

1ST NOVEMBER

Kevin Barry, 18, IRA member and first-year medical student at UCD, was hanged at 8am on 1 November 1920 for the murder of a British soldier, Private Matthew Whitehead, during an attack on a small group of soldiers collecting bread for Collinstown Camp from Patrick Monk's Bakery on Upper Church Street.

When ordered to lay down their weapons the soldiers began shooting – the IRA retired quickly but Barry, whose gun had jammed, failed to notice in time and was captured hiding under a lorry. Private Whiteside died while undergoing surgery for a stomach wound caused by a .45 calibre bullet – Barry had been armed with a .38 Parabellum.

It was afterward claimed that Barry had been tortured while in custody but it seems to have amounted to no more than a badly twisted arm. Tried by court-martial, Barry refused to recognise the court and was sentenced to death.

British Ministers, refusing to reprieve Barry, noted that he was only slightly younger than the dead soldier and 'that it was precisely young and irresponsible men of this type who were the main cause of the present disturbance in Ireland.'

2ND NOVEMBER

The extraordinary life of Dubliner Thomas 'Buck' Whalley, 34, came to an end on 2 November 1800 in the 'George Inn' at Knutsford, Cheshire. Rheumatic fever was the official cause. Another version has it that he was stabbed to death by one of two sisters (possibly Sarah or Sally Jenkinson) he was romancing at the time – neither being previously aware of his attachment to the other. Yet another legend would have it that he was stabbed by a mistress he had picked up on his travels.

He was buried in Knutsford churchyard. His stone read: 'Underneath is interred the body of Thomas Whalley, Esquire, of the City of Dublin, who died November 2nd, 1800. Aged 34 years.'

According to local lore Buck didn't go quietly: 'A strange circumstance, took place just before his funeral,' notes Green's *Knutsford*. 'The body had been placed in a leaden coffin and brought into the old assembly room, and the workmen had just made up the coffin, when Mr. Robinson, an Irishman, who also was a dancing-master of that day, stepping upon the coffin, danced a hornpipe over the body.'

In his last years, Buck had written his memoirs as a warning to others, but his executors suppressed them and they were not published until 1906.

3RD NOVEMBER

Colonel Henry Luttrell, 63, of Luttrellstown led a charmed life until 3 November 1717. He had been shot by an unknown assassin the previous day as he proceeded in his sedan chair from Lucas' Coffee House (where City Hall stands today) to his town residence in Stafford Street.

Educated in France, he returned to Ireland to serve James II and commanded a troop of horse. But as it became clear that he was backing a loser, Luttrell backed out of the battle of Aughrim and, later, during the siege of Limerick, narrowly escaped being shot after he was discovered to be corresponding with the enemy. When Limerick fell he openly joined King William.

Shortly after his death a particularly bitter ditty appeared:

> *If HEAV'N be pleased when mortals cease to sin,*
> *And HELL be pleased when villains enter in,*
> *If EARTH be pleas'd when it entombs a knave,*
> *ALL must be pleased – now Luttrell's in his grave.*

Towards the end of the century it is said that Henry Luttrell's tomb was broken open at night by some of the peasantry of the neighbourhood, and his skull taken out and smashed with a pickaxe by a labourer named Carty.

4TH NOVEMBER

The equestrian statue of King William III was a source of pride to some and detested by many – including the students of Trinity College who, it was said, disliked the fact that the horse's backside faced their front entrance.

It was usual for a large civic procession and festivities to be held at the statue on November 4 (William's birthday) but in 1805 the events were postponed for a day because it was a Sunday.

On the Saturday night the watchman was approached by a man, seemingly a painter, who stated that he had been sent by the city authorities to decorate the statue for the approaching festivities; adding that it was best to have the work done by night to prevent any attempt to stop the work. The unsuspecting watchman assisted the painter in mounting the statue, and the latter plied his brush most industriously for some time. Descending, he coolly requested the watchman to keep an eye to his painting utensils, while he went to his master's house for some more colours, necessary to complete the work. The night, however, passed away without the return of the painter, and at daybreak, on Sunday morning, the statue was found to be completely covered with a sticky mix of grease and tar; while the bucket that had contained the mixture was suspended by a halter fixed round the insulted monarch's neck.

The adventurous artist was never discovered.

Waiting for Pope John Paul II on Cathal Brugha Street. Photo by Andrew McGlynn

5TH NOVEMBER

The Dublin Newsletter of 5-8 November 1748 reported on a regulation which had been introduced to organise traffic in Dublin: 'The new Regulations of the carriages which pass over Essex Bridge has been attended with such good effects that the Lord Mayor [Robert Ross] intends to make the Regulation more extensive, and for that purpose will speedily issue his orders for all drivers of public carriages to keep the gutters, or the middle of the streets through which they pass, on their left hand; and if they are obliged by the stopping of carriages, or any other accidents, to change their side, they are as soon as possible to return to it again. As His Lordship and the Governors of the Workhouse are determined to enforce the observance of this Order, so it is not doubted but that Ladies and Gentlemen will oblige their coachmen to attend to this Regulation, which is designed to make the passing, even through the narrowest street, more expeditious and safe than it is at present.'

Driving on the left side of the road was made compulsory in Britain and Ireland in 1853.

6TH NOVEMBER

Frederick E. Jones was a busy man on 6 November 1806 – he was expecting guests that evening! He'd even gone to the trouble of bringing in a detachment of the Tipperary Militia – the 'guests' he was expecting were thieves.

Around 7pm Captain Jones answered a knock on the front door: 'the robbers rushed in, two of them following O'Reilly into the parlour, in which were Lieutenant

Hamerton and Dr. Kearn, tutor to Jones's son. Here a desperate struggle ensued; seven soldiers fired through the closed door of the room in which the combatants were engaged, [hitting] Hamerton ... with which one of the robbers, striking at him, nearly took off his ear, and then dealt Captain O'Reilly two blows on the head, also wounding Dr. Kearn. The robbers then retreated, and one of them, rushing to the hall-door, received a ball in his thigh and another through his body, from which he died in the course of the night. Jones had taken with him three soldiers to the top of the stairs, where the principal attack was expected; and on their coming in one of the gang rushed thither, shouting 'Up-stairs, boys, for the money and plate!' upon which a soldier, fired, crying – 'Down-stairs, boys, for the powder and ball!' and shot the burglar through the heart. The remainder of the gang were made prisoners.'

7TH NOVEMBER

Chemist John W. Mallet is a Dubliner better remembered outside of Ireland for his work on the atomic weights of lithium, aluminium, and gold. Graduating from Trinity at the age of 21 he travelled to America to help his father's earthquake research. He would spend the rest of his life there but never took American citizenship. When the Civil War began in 1861, he immediately enlisted in the Confederate Army as a private, but was quickly recruited by officers who recognized his value to the South as a scientist. He was appointed Superintendent of the Confederate Ordnance Laboratories, and made major contributions to the development of munitions and explosives for the rest of the war.

After the war, Mallet taught at Tulane University, then in 1868 was appointed professor of chemistry and later chair of chemistry at the University of Virginia. There he designed the first course on industrial chemistry offered in the U.S. In 1880 he was elected a fellow of the Royal Society of London. In 1882 he was elected President of the American Chemical Society, which he had helped to found just a few years earlier. He died at the age of 80 on 7 November 1912.

8TH NOVEMBER

'Julia Smith, Daisy Henderson, and Mary M'Cann, women of the unfortunate class, were charged by Michael Brosnan with having robbed him that morning between one and two o'clock of £50. Yesterday he drew £50 in ten £5 notes from the Bank of Ireland. He passed the early part of the night at the Empire Theatre of Varietes. Then he went to Montgomery street, where he spent the rest of the night. He put his coat, in the pocket of which was his money, on a stool in a room. He saw the prisoner Smith standing near his coat, and soon afterwards he missed his coat. He identified the three prisoners in whose company he had been. Constable 174C deposed that he arrested Smith and M'Cann. In answer to the charge they said they never saw the complainant. When the complainant made the charge between one and two o'clock that morning he was quite sober. Constable 103C, who arrested Henderson, deposed that she stated she knew nothing about the matter. The prisoners were remanded until Monday, Henderson and M'Cann being admitted to bail. [5 November 1899, *The Evening Telegraph*]'

9TH NOVEMBER

'There was some excitement in the Masterpiece Cinema in Talbot-street, Dublin, today [9 November 1925] when the war film *Ypres* was to have been exhibited for the first time. A large audience had gathered to see the picture, which portrays many famous actions in which Irish soldiers took part, and the demand for seats was so great that the management could not cope with it. Just as the performance was about to begin, however, a number of armed men arrived in the cinema and having held up the staff at the point of the revolver, seized the eight reels of the film with which they decamped. As they were leaving they were attacked by some of the attendants who managed to capture one of them and handed him over to the police. The other escaped in a waiting motor-car.

... The whole city has been looking forward to the *Ypres* picture. The matter has a serious aspect in view of the fact that it has occurred during Armistice week, and it is impossible to avoid the suspicion that the outrage was intended to create bad blood among the ex-Service men, whose susceptibilities has been touched by the Government's refusal to allow the Armistice Day demonstration to be held in College Green.' [*The Times*]

10TH NOVEMBER

When Terence Bellow McManus, a Young Irelander of 1848 died in Los Angeles in 1861, it was decided by the Irish Republican Brotherhood that he would be buried in Ireland. The body was conveyed across America with pomp and ceremony, brought by boat to Cork, and thence to Dublin for his burial on Sunday, 10 November 1861.

The Archbishop of Dublin, Cullen, refused to allow the body to lie in state in any of the churches of the diocese so it was brought directly from Kingsbridge Station to Glasnevin. Up to 150,000 people followed the coffin: 'the procession solemnly paused with uncovered heads, at every spot sacred to the memory of those who had fought and died in the good fight against English tyranny; in Thomas Street, at the house where Lord Edward Fitzgerald met his death, and the church where lie his remains; at the house in High Street where the remains of Wolfe Tone had been laid before removal for final interment; especially opposite the spot where Robert Emmet was executed. 'In passing the Castle,' says a chronicler of the period, 'the procession slackened its pace to the utmost, and lingered on its way in silent but stern defiance.'

11TH NOVEMBER

Sentenced to be hung as a traitor the following day Wolfe Tone cut his throat with a penknife as the gallows was being erected in the yard outside his cell in the Provost Prison (now St. Bricin's Military Hospital) on the night of 11 November 1798.

Tone, knowing the death sentence was a formality – he had, after all, brought a French invasion fleet to Ireland – had requested that he be shot by a platoon of grenadiers, arguing that he was a serving soldier in the French army – an argument which had fallen upon deaf ears.

At four o'clock next morning a surgeon came and closed the wound. As the carotid artery was not cut, he said that Tone might recover. 'I am sorry,' said Tone, 'that I have been so bad an anatomist.'

The Blue Light, 1987. Photo by Andrew McGlynn

On the morning of 19 November the surgeon whispered to an attendant that if he attempted to move or speak he would die instantly. Tone overheard him, and making a slight movement said: 'I can yet find words to thank you, sir. It is the most welcome news you can give me. What should I wish to live for?'

12TH NOVEMBER

No news is too small to print, particularly on a quiet week. 'A Man was thrown down in Dame-street [12 November 1764], by a Coach driving by far too quick for him to get out of the Way, but providentially received no other injury than a severe Fright, a few small Contusions, and a dirty jacket. A Woman who had left her Habitation in Search of her Husband, and, as it is supposed, refreshed her Spirits too freely at the different Houses of Call, coming home too heavily laden, stumbled, and unfortunately fell with her Side against a large Stone, at the Corner of Chequer-lane, in George's-lane, and expired on the Spot. – This Misfortunate is inserted as a Caution to all Wives, who practise this ungenteel Custom. John Gallaspy, formerly of Bristol, who has been greatly afflicted for several Years past with the Gravel and Stone, has been lately cut at Mercer's Hospital, by Mr. Morris, Surgeon. The Stone extracted from him proved to be a great Size, but the Patient is thought to be past all Danger, and in a fair Way of Recovery. The Man who robbed the Hackney Chaiseman on the Road between Donnybrook and Dublin, a few Days ago, was taken and sent to Newgate.' [*The Public Register*, or *Freeman's Journal*]

13TH NOVEMBER

Samuel Little, Clerk to the Midland Great Western Railway Company of Ireland, decided to work late in his office at Broadstone on 13 November 1856. The following morning he was found dead – his throat had been cut. £334 was missing but a large sum of money remained in open view in the office. A month later some of the missing money was found – in an attic store at Broadstone.

Progress in the case ground to a halt until the middle of 1857 when a Mrs. Spollin dropped her husband right in it. James Spollin, she told police at Frederick Lane station, was the guilty party. And Spollin did fit the part – he was a painter and carpenter with ease of access to most of Broadstone, crucially, including the office where Little was found.

After Spollin's arrest another £200 of the money was recovered – though probably without his assistance. At his trial at Green Street Courthouse the two main witness against Spollin were his own children, Joseph, 16, and Lucy, 11. After a brief trial James Spollin was found 'not guilty'.

14TH NOVEMBER

When Alderman John Carleton resigned his position as City Treasurer in 1814 he said it was because he needed to concentrate on his own business. Within a few months, however, it was becoming clear that Carleton had taken more than the odd envelope from the Corpo – auditors reckoned he'd lifted £31,177 12s 10½d from the city coffers. An extraordinary letter from Carleton, thanking the Lord Mayor and councillors for 'expressing their opinion of my integrity', must have been greeted with hollow laughter in City Hall. As with many fraudsters Carleton sought to cast a veil of fog over the entire proceedings. 'It has come my most serious determination to insist on the commission of bankruptcy being proceeded against me, hoping therefore to convince the world and those friends that had advocated my case, that the insinuations which have been made, that under a commission I shall be obliged to answer and account at the peril of my life, has no terror for a man, who though miserable and unfortunate, will at that peril prove to the world that he has not been fraudulent,' he wrote to the Lord Mayor on 14 November 1814. As a measure of their belief in his integrity, he was thrown off the Council in February 1815.

15TH NOVEMBER

English embargoes in the 1770s had closed most of Ireland's overseas markets and Dublin businessmen were less than happy. In October 1779 the Lord Lieutenant had been petitioned to lift the embargoes – to drive the point home the petitioners, the Speaker and House of Commons members, passed through streets lined with armed Irish Volunteers.

On 15 November, writes Gilbert: 'about 8,000 working manufactures, mostly armed with swords and pistols, assembled before the Parliament House on College Green, and in the adjacent streets crying 'A free trade! The rights of Ireland. They stopped several members going to the House, and administered oaths to such as they suspected. Mischief being apprehended, a troop of horse was ordered to patrol the streets, and a party of Highlanders came to disperse the mob, but the latter remained resolutely determined to keep their ground. The Lord Mayor perceiving that any forcible attempts to disperse them might be attended with fatal consequences, dismissed the military, and, mildly addressing the populace enjoined them to depart peaceably.'

They did so. The Lord Lieutenant, at the request of Parliament, offered five hundred pounds for the discovery of the rioters. A boycott of English goods finally did the trick, and freedom of trade was granted.

16TH NOVEMBER

One of the early works of the Ballast Office (or Corporation for Preserving and Improving the Port of Dublin) was the provision of a lightship at the north-end of the Kish Bank, about 10 miles from Dublin.

It was marked by buoys at either end but at night vessels often had to anchor until morning brought better visibility – to continue was to risk grounding the ship. The Dutch-built ship, about 140 tons, and manned by 14 sailors, was placed in position on 16 November 1811. It had three large lanterns, one on each mast with the middle one four to six feet higher than the others. Ships coming from Holyhead could expect to see the lights about two to three hours after leaving port.

It was moored by a mushroom anchor – 'from its exact resemblance to a mushroom,' noted *The History of Dublin* (1818) 'the chain to which it is attached is fastened to the stalk. The advantage derived from this type of anchor is that the vessel can freely swing; making her, as the sea term is, ride easy, by accommodating the length of the cable to the height and strength of the waves and the swell of the sea.'

17TH NOVEMBER

Charles Manners, 4th Duke of Rutland, Viceroy of Ireland, died at the Phoenix Lodge [Áras An Uachtaráin] towards the end of October, 1787.

Nearly three weeks later his body coffin went on display in the Irish Parliament [Bank of Ireland], College Green. John Gilbert wrote: 'The entrance to the chamber was through a suite of rooms, lighted with wax, and hung with superfine black cloth. The floors were covered with black cloth the state-room was similarly decorated, the coffin being laid under a grand canopy, ornamented with large plumes of black feathers. The embalmed body was deposited in a cedar coffin, lined with satin, enclosed in one of lead, over which was a coffin of mahogany, richly inlaid, enclosed in the state coffin. On each side stood six mutes [sic], dressed in long black gowns and caps supporting branches of wax tapers. Every respectable person was admitted, a number of the Battle-axe Guards attending to preserve regularity; and strict decorum and silence were observed. On 17 November, at 11am, the coffin, preceded by the choirs of the two Protestant cathedrals, chanting a dirge, was conveyed to the funeral chariot, at the great portico, and thence brought in grand procession to the waterside.'

18TH NOVEMBER

The equestrian statue of King William ('of glorious memory' etc.) in Dame Street was regularly interfered with, notably on the night of Sunday, 25 June 1710 when the King's face was plastered with mud, and his Majesty deprived of his sword and truncheon.

The official response was predictable outrage with the House of Lords, the following day, resolving 'that all persons concerned in that barbarous fact are guilty of the greatest insolence, baseness, and ingratitude, and desire his Excellency the Lord Lieutenant to discover the authors of this villany (sic), with a reward to the discoverer, that they may be prosecuted and punished accordingly.'

The Lord Lieutenant was not found wanting and promptly offered a large reward. It was afterwards found that three young men, students of Trinity College, were the perpetrators and that it was done for the hell of it. The consequences were serious. The students were expelled from the University, sentenced on 18 November 1710, to six months' imprisonment and a fine of £100 each, which was however, later reduced to five shillings.

19TH NOVEMBER

The Prince of Wales packet ship and the military transport Rochdale, both having sailed from Dublin the previous day, sank during a violent storm in Dublin Bay on 19 November 1807, killing 385 people. *The Prince of Wales* ran onto rocks off Blackrock – the Captain, crew, two soldiers, and the steward's wife and child took to the only lifeboat, abandoning the troops onboard. The weather was so atrocious that they rowed the lifeboat parallel to the shore for quite some time until one of the sailors fell overboard and found he was in shallow water. They then walked into Blackrock and made no effort to have a rescue organised. The 120 people left on onboard perished during the night.

The Rochdale, suffered a similar fate near the Martello Tower in Seapoint, just 12 feet from the shore. In atrocious weather conditions it was impossible for would-be rescuers to help and at the time the ship struck the night was so dark and the snowstorm so dense that those on board probably did not know just how close they were to land. Over 260 perished – fewer than half of the bodies were recovered.

20TH NOVEMBER

The foreword to a proposal for the improvement of Dublin Bay harbours, recalled the tragedy of the loss of the *Prince of Wales* and *Rochdale* ships during a storm in the Bay. 'Sun-rise in Dublin Bay, on 20 November 1807, exhibited a shore, whose boundary was marked by a terrific line of parted limbs and shattered bodies – The storm of the preceding day and night was dreadful: A Trader and two crowded Transports were driven by the Tempest into the Bay – fourteen men were saved

Winetavern Street, 1975. Photo by Andrew McGlynn

– four hundred men, women and children were lost!!!

'The general view appalled the most callous heart; but the Rigging and Hold of the Rochdale were scenes of elaborate horror. Over the Tafrail a Woman's corpse hung by a broken leg, whilst her inverted garments covered her mangled face, and her hair floated on the surge: in the main chains part of a brave Soldier's body remained suspended by the neck: Casks and Men were intermingled in the Hold but the mutilations must not be detailed.

'The broken fragments of trunks, wearing apparel, arms, provisions, naval wreck &c. &c. which accompany them, form altogether, perhaps as dreadful a scene as ever has been-contemplated by human nature.'

21st NOVEMBER

Sunday, 21 November 1920 was a busy day in Dublin. Michael Collins' 'Apostles' killed 14 members of the 'Cairo Gang' – British Intelligence agents operating undercover in Dublin. Among the assassins was Sean Lemass (Taoiseach, 1959-1966). Later in the day British troops opened fire on the teams and the spectators in Croke Park for a match between Dublin and Tipperary – 14 were killed and over 60 injured. Among the dead was player Michael Hogan (a stand at the ground is now named after him).

In the wake of the murders Dublin Castle issued an extraordinary statement: 'A number of men came to Dublin on Saturday under the guise of asking to attend a football match between Tipperary and Dublin. But their real intention was to take part in the series of murderous outrages which took place in Dublin that morning. Learning on Saturday that a number of these gunmen were present in Croke Park, the crown forces went to raid the field. It was the original intention that an officer would go to the centre of the field and speaking from a megaphone, invite the assassins to come forward. But on their approach, armed pickets gave warning. Shots were fired to warn the wanted men, who caused a stampede and escaped in the confusion.'

The Times, commented: 'an army already perilously indisciplined and a police force avowedly beyond control have defiled by heinous acts the reputation of England.'

22ND NOVEMBER

After a failed conspiracy in 1607 to take Dublin Castle most of the planners wisely chose to flee to Europe. One of those not quick enough off the mark was Lord Delvin who was committed to Dublin Castle for 'divers most wicked and atrocious acts of treason, committed against our lord the king, his crown and dignities, by him, Richard Nugent, lord Delvin.' After a few days it was clear that Delvin, who was being remarkably well cared for, was planning an escape and the authorities ordered that he be made secure by Tristram Ecclesten, constable of the castle. 'But Ecclesten, in contempt of the deputy, not only suffered the lord Delvin to abide in his upper apartment, without placing any guards over him, but also permitted his lordship's servant John Evers to come to him, and bring to his gentleman, Alexander Aylmer, who attended him in his confinement, certain cords, by the help whereof, his lordship on 22 November 1607, descended by the wall of the castle and escaped.'

Lord Delvin was one of the lucky ones – he made good his escape and, in 1608, voluntarily submitted himself to the King and was pardoned.

23RD NOVEMBER

'On Wednesday evening [23 November 1808] at the early hour of five o'clock, Mr. Ennis was stopped at Santry, by two armed footpads; one of the ruffians was furnished with a dragoon's sword, and the other with a pistol. On being asked for his money, Mr. Ennis denied he had any. 'We shall see', said one of the villains, pointing his sword in the act of stabbing Mr. Ennis, while the other fellow seized his horse. That Gentleman was obliged to dismount. On his dismounting, however, he rushed upon the ruffian with the pistol, and knocked him down, and would have succeed in wrestling the deadly weapon from his gripe [sic] had not the other miscreant wounded him in the arm with the sword: he turned round, and in parrying another thrust, the weapon passed through his hand, and cut him desperately. While thus employed the robber with the pistol arose, and with the stock gave him a desperate blow on the temple. Mr. Ennis fell, and while he was down, the ruffian with the sword made a lunge at him, which would have passed through his body, had he not happened most providentially to have a pocket-book in his side pocket, which saved his life. They then proceeded to rifle his person, and cut off both his breeches pockets. [*The Times*]

24TH NOVEMBER

John Lonergan, a Trinity graduate and tutor to Thomas O'Flaherty, Kilkenny was tried and convicted in 1781 of petit treason (i.e. the murder of one's lawful supe-rior) after O'Flaherty died of poisoning. Lonergan had been having an affair with the deceased's wife, admitted buying arsenic, but denied the murder.

Lonergan was executed at the City Gallows, Baggot-street, on 24 November, pro-testing his innocence to the last. After 20 minutes his body was cut down and given to his friend, the Rev. Eugene M'Kenna, Raheny, at whose house legend has it he was brought back to life. Whether it was true or not many of his friends said that they had seen him in Dublin after his execution.

The public generally believed, unlikely as it may seem, that in some cases it was possible to restore life by opening a vein within a short time of hanging. The idea was so prevalent that most convicts facing the gallows at that time tried to make arrangements to have their body cut – just in case it worked! The practice is men-tioned in an old and almost unintelligible ballad ('Luke Caffrey's Kilmainham Minit'):

> We tipped him a snig, as he said,
> In de juggler, oh dere where de mark is,
> Bud when dat we found him quite ded,
> In de dust-case we bundled his carcase,
> For a Protestant lease of the sod.

25TH NOVEMBER

Most of the IRB leaders were in prison and the authorities were in possession of copious documents the trials would be a formality and Ireland would be at peace for a while. The 'most wanted' James Stephens was safely lodged in Richmond Prison or was he! On November 25 1865 the news flashed round the city – Stephen's had escaped. Two of the prison officers, Breslin (hospital superintendent) and Byrne (night-watchman) were members of the IRB and had smuggled him out during the night. Posters promising a reward of £1,000 were prominently displayed around the city, cavalry scoured the country and police raided suspect houses. Gunboats put to sea and overhauled and searched fishing-smacks and coasters. Stephen's spent the next three months in the house of a Mrs. Butler in Summer Hill. 'One Sunday evenings a handsome open carriage-and-four drove through the streets of the Irish metropolis, two stalwart footmen seated in the dickey behind. Two gentlemen reclined lazily on the cushioned seat. They proceeded northwards through Malahide and towards Balbriggan. Near the latter place, close by the sea, the carriage stopped. One of the occupants got out, walked down to the shore, where a boat was waiting. He entered, and was pulled off to a lugger in the offing.' James Stephens, the 'Central Organiser of the Irish Republic,' was on his way to France.

Delete present caption and insert: 'Cumberland Street 1984. Children find rich pickings after an early morning street sale. Photo by Andrew McGlynn.

26TH NOVEMBER

The Victoria Cross was originally only awarded to those who had survived after performing outstanding acts of valour in the face of the enemy. During WWII over half were awarded posthumously.

The sole Dubliner to receive the VC during WWII was Royal Northumberland Fusilier Capt. James Joseph Bernard Jackman, 25, from Glenageary. In November 1941 Jackman took part in operation 'Crusader' in which Allied troops broke out of Tobruk which was under siege by the Afrika Corps. He led a motorised machine-gun platoon through heavy shell-fire to successfully attack an enemy strong-hold which had just fought off a full battalion and a tank squadron. This was the action for which the VC was awarded.

On the afternoon of the 26 November two tank regiments being escorted by Jackman's company came under exceptionally heavy artillery fire. Jackman ordered an advance to the top of a ridge to return fire. Fusilier R. J. Dishman later wrote: 'Capt. Jackman came and lay down on the gun line, and began to observe through his binoculars. He then gave us the orders to fire at a truck and a motor cyclist. 'Give them a burst,' he said, and just as those words were said a mortar bomb dropped in front of our left-hand gun, wounding three and killing Capt. Jackman and Corporal Gare instantly.' He is buried in Tobruk War Cemetery, Libya.

27TH NOVEMBER

'The occasion of the funeral service for Queen Alexandra at Westminster Abbey was marked by many signs of respect and mourning in Dublin [27 November 1925]. The Free State flag was flown at half-mast from the Government buildings and from public offices. The same flag and the Union Jack floated together from the Bank of Ireland in College Green, and Trinity College flew the college flag above its stately portico.

'Memorial services for Queen Alexandra were held simultaneously with the Abbey service at St. Patrick's Cathedral and at Christ Church Cathedral. Both buildings were filled to the doors and the services were deeply impressive. The Governor-General of the Free State was represented in Christ Church Cathedral by Senator SL Brown, KC, who occupied the Royal pew. This pew, the choir stalls, and the lectern, were draped in purple. The attendance included representative of Alexandra College, Dublin, and of the Grad Lodge of Freemasons in Ireland.' [The *Times*]

The Horse Fair, Smithfield. Photo by Andrew McGlynn

28TH NOVEMBER

'An extraordinary elopement, which has recently occurred in Dublin, was made known today [28 November 1895]. The parties are foreign Jews in humble life, and the male lover, a boy of 12 years, was named Goldberg, while the female, named Bessie Schleinder, is aged 25, and is said to be attractive. Goldberg's relatives are bakers, and Miss Schleinder's father owns a toy-shop in the city. Some time ago the couple applied to be married at a registry office, and the registrar, amazed at the youthfulness of the intending bride-groom, refused to marry them. The minister of their congregation and their relatives were also made aware of the circumstances. The result was that the intended marriage was stopped and they were each kept under surveillance by their relatives and friends. Young Goldberg, however, left home about a week ago, stating that he would be back in an hour, but he did not return, and his relatives, becoming suspicious, made inquiries, and it was then found that Miss Schleinder had also disappeared. The boy was known to have £15 in his possession, and the parties are believed to have left Dublin together, and to be now in Sheffield, where one of them has relatives.' [*The Times*]

29TH NOVEMBER

The Dublin Gazette in October 1740 reported: 'Mr. Edward Sewell, a degraded cler-gyman, who lived for some time past at the World's End, and followed the business of coupling beggars together, was tried and convicted of marrying the son of an eminent citizen to a Roman Catholic young woman, and is to be executed for the same Saturday night.'

In fact, Mr. Sewell got a reprieve until Saturday, 29 November 1740. Not one, but two versions of his final words were quickly circulated – in both he is peni-tent, but each differs significantly. In one Sewell traces his misfortune to his having been seduced: 'Having received Orders, I officiated in the Curacy of Carlingford, St. Michan's, Christ Church, Dublin, and several other Places, where I behav'd as a Gentleman until most unfortunately a vile Woman prostituted herself, and seduced me to her dire Embraces; upon which she Reported that I Married myself to her, which is utterly false ... I never was Married or Contracted to any Woman under Heaven, but to the Woman now my unhappy Wife, by whom I have two innocent but unfortunate Babes.' To the end he claimed that, while he had performed many illicit marriages for cash, he didn't know that by marrying Richard Wilson, a Protestant, to Margaret Talbot, a Catholic, he was committing a capital crime.

30TH NOVEMBER 2005

Oscar (Fingal Wills O'Flaherty) Wilde, 46, Dublin wit and writer, died in exile in the small and shabby Hôtel d'Alsace, Paris, where he was living under the pseudo-nym Sebastian Melmoth (his great uncle, Charles Maturin, had written the Gothic novel *Melmoth the Wanderer*), on 30 November 1900. He had lived in Paris since his release from prison in 1897 after two years hard labour in Pentonville, Wandsworth, Reading and Holloway prisons.

His wife, Constance, had abandoned the Wilde name and reverted to an old fam-ily name, Holland, to save herself and their sons from further notoriety. The cause of death was given as 'cerebral meningitis', most likely caused by a failed ear operation earlier in the month. There are two options for his dying words, either 'I am dying as I lived – beyond my means' or 'Either this wallpaper goes, or I do'.

He was given a pauper's burial in a 'sixth class' grave outside the walls of Paris. Nine years later his friend, Robert Ross, had the body re-buried in Père-Lachaise cemetery under a tomb designed by Jacob Epstein. The inscription, taken from *The Ballad of Reading Gaol* reads:

> *And alien tears will fill for him*
> *Pity's long broken urn*
> *For his mourners will be outcast men*
> *And outcasts always mourn.*

Chapter Twelve

December

1ST DECEMBER

The first trip of an electric tram, by the Dublin Southern District Tramways Company, was made from Haddington Road, Ballsbridge, to Dun Laoghaire on 1 December 1895. Michael JF McCarthy was impressed: 'New cars were put on the line and the result was that all Dublin and every country visitor to Dublin were rushing to ride [them]. Never was such a revolution in locomotion seen in Ireland; a pleasant drive at eight miles an hour or more, through nine miles of lovely inland and bay scenery for four pence! The unlucky Dublin, Wicklow, and Wexford Railway Co.'s business between Dublin and Dalkey seemed ruined by the blow. Stuffy railway carriages against open air and comfortable seats and a pleasant roadway; all first-class, against first, second, and third class.'

So successful was the electrification that the Dublin United Tramways Company, purchased the DSDTC for over a quarter of a million pounds, and immediately set about total electrification of the system. Within four years the work, covering 66 miles around the city, had been completed and the last of the horse-drawn trams ran on the Bath Avenue line in January 1901.

2ND DECEMBER

The Lord Lieutenant had banned the newspapers from reporting on the meetings of banned organisations. Timothy Daniel Sullivan, editor of *The Nation* and Lord Mayor of Dublin, had absolutely no intention of complying and made several appearances in court (one of which involved Sullivan in full Mayoral dress, Councillors ditto, and the City regalia being paraded).

On 2 December 1887, the dance came to an end and Sullivan was sentenced to two months in prison for a 'first class misdemeanour'. 'I thought I had got off lightly,' he later wrote. His first place of confinement, Richmond Prison, was familiar to him as he was a 'Visiting Justice'.

He was later moved to Tullamore jail where he learnt that: 'The Corporation of Dublin paid me the compliment of voting me the Honorary Freedom of the City. As I could not attend at the City Hall to sign the roll of honorary burgesses, they passed a resolution that the Corporation, in full State, should proceed to Tullamore

Jail, bringing the Roll for my signature. But, for their admission within the gates the assent of the Prisons Board was necessary, and as it could not be obtained the project was abandoned.'

3RD DECEMBER

In 1758 rumour swept the city that there was to be a union with Britain – not, by any means, a popular desire. On 3 December crowds surrounded the Parliament House (now Bank of Ireland, Dame Street). All those attempting to enter were made to swear 'fidelity to Ireland, and that they should vote against the Union.' All wisely chose to swear but Lord Inchiquin who had a stammer, was lucky to escape without injury.

Lord Chancellor Bowes took the oath twice, the second time in front of Lord Chief Justice Caulfield – the crowd having some vague notion that that made it official and binding. The mob burst into the House of Lords and showed their contempt for the institution by placing an elderly and feeble lady on the throne – where she sat contentedly smoking a pipe!

Dublin Castle asked the Lord Mayor, John Tew, to sort it out, a request he turned down. Eventually the Commander-in-Chief, General Leslie, put the cavalry on the street with order to use their sabres only and not to fire. The troops did an excellent job, killing 16 people in short order.

On the first tasks undertaken by the elected members after the disturbances was to pass a resolution making it 'a high crime' to 'assault, insult, or menace' any Member on his way to or from the Parliament.

4TH DECEMBER

'Whereas the frequent Loss of Ships on the Coast, near the Entrance of the Bay of Dublin, has been considered as chiefly owing to the want of proper Charts; and the Committee of Merchants of the City of Dublin having approved of the Proposals of Mess. Scale and Richard, for making a Survey and publishing a Chart of the Coast from Wicklow Head to Skerries, Notice is hereby given that the same will speedily be carried into Execution in the best Manner, under the Sanction and Encouragement of said Committee, and Subscriptions are taken in for this useful and necessary Work by Sir Edward Newenham, Tho. Blair, Esq.; in Fleet-street, Theoph Thompson, Esq.; and Mess. Williams and Thomas Bancroft on the Batchelor's-Walk, Mess. Rob. and Alex Jeffrey in Eustace-street, and by Mr. Chr. Deey, Secretary to said Committee, who will be answerable for the Subscription-money which shall be paid them, or for the Delivery of the Charts in due Times to the Subscribers. [4 December 1764, *The Public Register*, or *Freeman's Journal*]

5TH DECEMBER

Someone wanted Edward Johnson dead and on Wednesday, 5 December 1804 he or she got their wish. Around 8am a man in his mid-20s, knocked at the door of Simpson's Hospital and asked to see Mr. Johnson. He was brought to Johnson's room, sat down, and said he was from Johnson's area of County Donegal. Johnson, who was totally blind, didn't recognise the voice, but the stranger told him the visit was merely one of friendship, undertaken for Johnson's wife and family, with whom he was acquainted. After a while he invited Johnson to go with him for a drink. When this was declined, he took a small cake from his pocket and, giving it to him, took his leave, saying that a female friend of Johnson's would call on him later that day. Johnson divided the cake with Thomas Mallow (or possibly Morley), who was also blind. As the day wore on both men became very sick and Johnson, 46, died. Mallow, 24, followed the next morning. An immediate inquest was held – it found that both men had been wilfully murdered, by poisons, by person or persons unknown. And there the story ends, no-one was every charged with the crime.

6TH DECEMBER

In 1663 Colonel Thomas Blood (later to be found stealing the Crown Jewels in the Tower of London) was involved in an abortive attempt to storm Dublin Castle, take the Duke of Ormond, James Butler, captive, and start an insurrection. Ormond had many of the plotters executed and Blood fled to Holland. Seven years later, on 6 December 1670, Blood, who still bore a grudge against Ormonde, waylaid his coach as it passed through St. James's Street when returning to Clarendon House in London. Blood, and his son-in-law, Thomas Hunt, took the Duke from his coach intending to take him to the 'common gibbet' at Tyburn to revenge the death of those of Blood's companions hanged earlier in Ireland. However, the Duke, after having been fired at, ridden over, and struck with swords and pistols was rescued after Blood rode ahead to arrange the rope on the gallows. It was believed by some that George Villiers, second Duke of Buckingham, had engaged Blood to perpetrate this crime, and Ormonde's son, Lord Ossory, uttered the threat, in presence of King Charles II., that should his father 'come to an untimely or violent death … I shall pistol you though you stood behind the King.' When Blood died in 1680 his body was dug up after a few days – to make sure that it was really him!

7TH DECEMBER

'On Tuesday last, at 7 minutes, 4 seconds past 3, Post Meridian descended to the Antipodes or Nadir (the Lower Regions?) at his lodgings, under the sign Leo in Taurus, or Bull Alley, Dublin (corner of Patrick Street) the Umbra or Penumbra of Mr. Isaac Butler, Ptolmean Philomath, Judicial Astrologer, Discoverer of Losses, Botanist, and Calculator of Nativities, having passed the meridian of life and his grand climacteric, in the 66th year of his age.' Or to put it another way, Isaac Butler, 66, almanac publisher, botanist, etc. died on 7 December 1755. Cause of death? He 'hastened his end by laudanum taken in brandy, which he prescribed for himself, in order to die like Socrates and other antient sages.'

Butler and another almanac publisher, La Boissiere, didn't see eye to eye on the 'science' of predicting. Butler's Almanac *A Voice from the Stars, for 1727*, predicted a series of evils and misfortunes for his rivals and even predicted the date of his death. La Boissiere, however, lived and, to make matters worse, Butler's father, was killed in the same week.

'Why,' said La Boissiere, 'why did he not set himself to read his own father's horo-scope, and, from a foreknowledge of the impending fate that awaited him, have kept him at home on that unlucky day, March 5th.'

8TH DECEMBER

One of the most remarkable funerals ever seen in Dublin took place on 8 December 1867. An estimated 150,000 people lined the three-mile route on a cold and gloomy day. 60,000 people marched with the coffins to Glasnevin cemetery. The difference between this and other funerals was that the coffins were empty – as was the case with another thirty 'funerals' being held at the same time around Ireland.

The reason was the execution some days previously of Allen, Larkin and O'Brien who had been convicted of the murder of Sgt. Brett during the freeing of Fenian leaders Colonel Kelly and Captain Timothy Deasy as they were being transported in a prison van back to a Manchester prison.

The executions were only part of the problem, the sentence may have been harsh but the men were undoubtedly guilty. What really inflamed and united Irish opinion was the fact that the three had been buried in quicklime in unconsecrated graves inside Salford prison. The mock funeral procession took a circuitous route, recalling that of the Fenian Terence Bellew McManus six years earlier. To no-one's surprise, four days later a proclamation was issued declaring mock funerals to be illegal.

9TH DECEMBER

On the 9 December 1641, the Irish army of the Pale assembled at Swords under the leadership of many of the Roman Catholic gentry of the county. A contingent, which had been at first assembled at Santry, under Luke Netterville, joined them. 'The Lords Justices issued a proclamation calling upon this army of insurgents to disperse, and ordering that nine of the chief leaders should come before the Council the next morning, to explain their conduct. This proclamation having been disregarded, Sir Charles Coote was sent against the rebels. He was a good but stern soldier; he made short work of the insurgents. He burned the village of Santry, and slew some rioters there; and finding Swords fortified, he stormed it, put its defenders to flight, and killed about two hundred of them. At Kilsallaghan the Earl of Fingal, with some of the Barnewalls, Seagraves, and others, assembled a force about the castle. It is stated that their position was made very strong by the woods surrounding the castle, and by defences which they raised. It was not strong enough, however, to resist the Earl of Ormond, who attacked and carried it, driving the enemy out of the castle, which he left a ruin.'

10TH DECEMBER

Other soldiers got a Victoria Cross, but Dubliner John Dunne, 15, received a bugle from Queen Victoria for his heroism on the field of battle on 10 December 1899. 'Bugler' Dunne, as he came to be known, was with the 1st Battalion of the Dublin Fusiliers during the battle of Colenso in the Boer War.

The Fusiliers were pinned down at the Tugela river, partly due to inaccurate artillery fire from their own side. Young Dunne, whose father had told him the Fusiliers never retreated, took it upon himself to sound the advance 'whereupon a number of his comrades fixed bayonets and tried to cross the ten feet deep river, and were shot down. Dunne was wounded himself.'

In fact his company lost 37 men killed and wounded out of a full strength of 84. As he was being carried from the field his rescuers threw his bugle into the river. Queen Victoria later presented him with a bugle to take its place: 'Presented to Bugler John Francis Dunne, 1st Battalion Royal Dublin Fusiliers, by Queen Victoria, to replace the bugle lost by him on the field of battle at Colenso, on the 10th December, 1899 when he was wounded.'

11TH DECEMBER

Charles Edward Jennings was born in 1751 at Saul's Court, Dublin, moving to France at the age of 12. An exceptional soldier, he rose quickly through the ranks – he was made a colonel on the battle field of Jemappes and become known across France as 'le brave Kilmaine' (after Kilmaine in Mayo where his father came from). He was appointed Commander-in Chief of the Army of the North at the age of 42. Immediately afterwards he was entrenched with his troops in a position known as Caesar's Camp near Valenciennes. The enemy in much superior numbers was threatening it on all sides, and only 40 leagues lay between it and Paris, so that, if any defeat befell Kilmaine, there would be a clear road for the enemy to the capital. The Irish officer accordingly carried out a masterly retreat, which was described as 'the most glorious exploit in his career.' In Paris, however, there was consternation at the news. As a result he was deprived of his command and dismissed from the army. Back in the army, in 1798, Kilmaine was appointed Commander-in-Chief of the Armée d'Angleterre destined for the invasion of Britain and Ireland.

On 11th December of that year he died at Paris. A superb tactician, a dashing cavalry officer, he was described by Captain Landrieux, his aide-de-camp, as 'the only officer in whom Napoleon ever placed complete confidence.'

12TH DECEMBER

Hell hath no fury as Dr. William Wilde discovered. He had become infatuated with one of his patients, 19-year-old Mary Josephine Travers, and for several years all went well. But when Dr. Wilde tired of Mary Josephine she plotted her revenge.

Her method was a novel one, she wrote a pamphlet *Florence Boyle Price: or a Warning in which the young and innocent Florence is seduced by a Doctor Quilp in his consulting room while she was under the effects of chloroform*. Oddly, she signed it *Speranza*, the pen name of Lady Wilde.

The pamphlet was distributed whenever Dr. Wilde appeared in public, Mary Josephine hired boys to sell it for her. Mrs. Wilde was charged with theft when she seized one of the pamphlets and refused to pay for it.

Mrs. Wilde had had enough. She wrote an inflammatory letter to Mary Josephine's father, demanding that he exercise some control over his offspring. When the letter was found by Mary Josephine she sued Lady Wilde for libel.

The case opened on 12 December 1864. Isaac Butt defended Mary Josephine, describing her as a deluded and naive young woman betrayed by a famous doctor. The judge wasn't fooled and the jury evidently shared his feeling that there was a pair of them in it. They found that Mary Josephine had been libelled but only awarded her one farthing!

13TH DECEMBER

Which one of us, at some stage in our lives, has not wanted to burn down some great public building? 'Mr. Justice Keogh this day [13 December 1862] passed sentence upon two paupers, Anne Duffy and Ellen Carey, who pleaded 'Guilty' to the charge of setting fire to the South Dublin Union Workhouse. His Lordship said that the prisoners had been found guilty of a great offence, but as they gloried in their crime it would be a waste of time to address any observations to them in the way of remonstrance. He would therefore sentence them to four years' penal servitude. The prisoners were delighted, and immediately said, 'Thanks your Lordship; – we have got out of hell, at all events.'

Seventeen male paupers were then brought up and were sentenced to the same punishment. Several of them cried out 'Thank you, my Lord and gentlemen of the jury, – we have got out of a house of persecution.' They seem to have learnt from some of their associates in the workhouse, who had personal experience of prison life, that convicts are much better treated than paupers; and it was for the express purpose of getting themselves transferred from the workhouse to the prison that they attempted to burn down the building.' [*The Times*]

14TH DECEMBER

Willie 'The Bird' Flanagan, who died, aged 58, in Walkinstown House on Monday, 14 December 1925, was a well-known Dublin gent of independent means who delighted in practical jokes.

He got his nickname after arriving at Earlsfort Terrace roller skating rink in March 1909, dressed as the Holy Ghost, after laying an 'egg' – a rugby football painted white, he was chased out of the rink by outraged skaters.

In 1907 he rode his horse into the Gresham Hotel and asked for a drink. On being told by a porter that it was after hours, he replied, 'It's not for me, you fool, it's for the horse!' During WWI he attended a performance at the Olympia Theatre – in the middle of the show he stood up, removed his overcoat, and revealed himself as the spitting image of the Kaiser.

On another occasion he visited a public house in the Dublin mountains, ordered a glass of whiskey and proceeded to pour it into a bottle which he then pocketed. The publican, panicking, tried to get the sample back, explaining that it had accidentally been poured from a bottle kept for sick animals. 'The Bird', claiming to be an excise inspector, refused, relenting only on payment of a 'fiver" and free drinks.

15TH DECEMBER

On 15 December 1813 a committee was formed to work out ways of raising funds for the Royal Hospital, Donnybrook. As there were only two people on it – Dr. Guinness, Provost of Trinity College, and the Rev. Mr. McGuire, the committee report was ready within a few days. It read: 'Your committee are of the opinion that the best mode of proceeding would be by an address to the Publick stating the object of the Institution, the advantages it has produced, its means of support and its want. But some difficulties have occurred in considering the topic which prevent your committee from being able to present a draft of such a statement. The Publick will naturally expect from the very name of the Hospital that its object is to remove from view patients whose diseases render them offensive and the importance of doing this suggests itself as the first topic to be employed. But as the regulations of the hospital permit patients to go abroad and as some of them do not strictly belong to the class now described, your committee find it very difficult to give strength to this part of the statement ... were a proper walk provided at the hospital for the patients there would no longer exist any necessity for permitting them to go abroad.'

16TH DECEMBER

'The melodrama of the *Forest of Bondy, or Dog of Montargis*, was exhibited at Crow-street [Theatre], the principal incident of which turns upon a dog discovering a murder. There was found in Dublin an extraordinary animal belonging to a rope-maker in Francis-street, who volunteered his services for the occasion, and delighted the audience several nights by his untutored sagacity. On Friday, 16 December 1814, [during a performance before the Lord Lieutenant] the entertainment was altered and the Dog did not appear. It was rumoured that the Dog had received no compensation for his services, or return for the extraordinary profits of the managers. The audience took his part; the manager was called for, and when he would not appear, they became outrageous, and proceeded to demolish the lustres [lights] and the rioters groped their way out of the house.' (*The History of the City of Dublin*, 1818).

There was trouble each following night but the manager would not appear. Eventually he published an advertisement stating that as 'it was proposed to him to appear personally and apologise, or quit the management, he preferred the latter.' The further theatrical career, if any, of the Dog, is not recorded.

17TH DECEMBER

After the Invincibles [See 6 May] had been disposed of, the Government had Invincible turned informer James Carey on their hands, and the question was what to do with him? They decided to ship him off secretly to their Colony at Natal in South-East Africa.

On July 4th, 1883, at Dartmouth, he embarked on the *Kilfauns Castle* under the name of James Power. A fellow-passenger was one Patrick O'Donnell. They had no previous knowledge of each other, but on the voyage became acquainted and occasionally had refreshments at the bar.

A monk clears the path on the Quays. Photo by Andrew McGlynn

At Cape Town, O'Donnell was shown a portrait of James Carey the informer – he recognised it at once as that of his acquaintance' Mr. Power.' Carey sailed in the *Melrose* for Port Elizabeth, and shared a cabin with O'Donnell. While the two men were in the refreshment saloon together, O'Donnell drew a revolver and fired three shots into Carey's body killing him almost instantly. O'Donnell was taken into custody and brought back to London where he was put on trial for murder. The trial lasted just one day – he was convicted and sentenced to death. He was executed in Newgate on 17 December 1883.

18TH DECEMBER
'This afternoon [18 December 1899] a batch of Trinity Boys, who were apparently determined to cheer Mr. Chamberlain with news of a victory, attacked the Mansion House, removed the city flag, tore it to shreds, beat the caretakers, and knocked down a lady. Their numbers are estimated at 150. They chose as the time of attack when only four person were in the Mansion House, namely, the house steward and three workmen. The students came up Dawson Street in a body and scaled the wall

of the Mansion House garden. Some of them climbed the pole and tore down the city flag. Others threw stones at the Mansion House, and smashed the glass of the portico. [The police were rung but no police arrived] They cheered for Chamberlain and repeatedly shouted 'Down with the Boers' and indulged in a good deal of shouting and jeering. [Two workmen were then assaulted] The men on the flag staff cut the string and lowered the flag it was torn to ribbons, all the students dragging at it. [The students moved back into Dawson Street.] The caretaker of the house next to the Mansion House, was passing. The students attacked her, struck her, knocked her down, and dragged her along the gravel. The students bore three Union Jacks in the attack.' [*Evening Telegraph*]

19TH DECEMBER

Mrs. Delany of Delville, Glasnevin, was one of the great hostesses of her day – Dean Swift was a frequent guest and is said to have written the *Drapier Letters* there. In her letter to her sister dated 19 December 1752 she wrote: 'My companion, Miss Bushe, made me go with her to Drumcondra, half a mile away, to see a new manufactuary that has been set up there, of printed linen done by copper plates; they are excessive pretty, but I will not describe them as I hope to bring you a small sample next summer.' The editor of the letters noted: 'I have seen part of a curtain done there, which has a beautiful design of boys on the branch of an oak tree looking into a bird's nest. It is a very fine chintz printed in brilliant colours on a white ground and the shades appear like an etching through the colours: the design was by a celebrated artist.'

A large building, described as 'The Drumcondra Manufactory', is shown on the Tolka river about half-way between Glasnevin and Drumcondra on Rocque's 1756 map.

20TH DECEMBER

In the wake of the Irish Rebellion of 1640 Commissioners were appointed on 20 December, to determine the losses suffered by citizens. Randall Dymock [alias Dymorke], a Dutchman, Rector of Clontarf, made the following deposition to Commissioners John Sterne and Henry Brereton: 'At Clontarffe where I am my household did live before these grievous and woeful troubles began. I flitting to Dublin so savt my life with my sonnes. The town of Clontarffe was burned and pillaged by the soldiers of Dublin, my house [although my household was there] lost all we had to the value of thirty pounds sterling. My sonne in the afternoone not knowing any thing before of the enterprise went down to knowe what was doone found the house pillaged, thinking to bring my people to Dublin, two rebell horsemen with 12 footmen besett him took him prisoner to Swords, whereby he lost his horse the price 12 pounds sterling. Being threatened to be hanged, a gallows being set up to hange him with another Dutchman, yet they both escaped by god's providence.'

All in all Rev. Dymock reckoned that he had lost a total of 164 pounds 3 shillings 4 pence.

21st December

Thomas Sheridan was Manager of the Smock-Alley Theatre, a job which encompassed far more than might at first be thought. As traffic at that time passed on whichever side of the street it chose – and many of the streets were very narrow – there was much confusion generated as the crowds came to see successful plays. To stop the confusion Sheridan introduced one of the earlier one-way systems in the city.

'As there have been several Complaints made of the Difficulty of passing and repassing to and from the Theatre, on Account of the meeting of Coaches in so narrow a Place, it is hoped that all Ladies and Gentlemen will order their Coachmen to drive to the Theatre by the Passage from Essex-street and the Blind-quay, and in going from the Play to enter the Passage from Fishamble-street, which is the only Method to obviate such Inconvenience. And that this Rule may be punctually observed, Guards shall be placed at each of the above Entrances to prevent any Coaches from passing but according as to the above Order.' [*Dublin Journal*, 21 December 1745]

The system worked so well that the Music-Hall in Fishamble Street soon followed suit.

22nd December

The Dublin Intelligence reported in 1711 on causes of death in the city for the quarter year ending on 22 December 1710. The terms within the square brackets have been added in an attempt to make some sense of the more obscure terms: 'Aged 61, Bloody-Flux [Dysentery] 5, Burnt by Accident 1, Consumption 44, Convulsion 19, Chincough [Whooping cough] 3, Collick [Stomach or intestinal spasm] 3, Childbed 2, Drowned 5, Dropsie [Abnormal swelling of the body or part of the body due to the build-up of clear watery fluid] 12, Despair 1, Died suddenly 1, Died in the Street 1, Evil 1, Fever 128, Fits 49, Frite 1, Falling Sickness [Epilepsy] 2, Gripes [Influenza] 6, Gripes and [illegible], Gout 4, Gravel [Sandlike concretions formed in the passages of the biliary and urinary tracts] 3, Hanged 4, Head-Ach 1, Impostum [nasty swelling, cyst or abscess] 3, Impotent 1, Infants 7, Liver-grown 1, Loosness 4, Measles 8, Overgrowth of the Lites 1, Plurisie 2, Rickets 2, Shortness of Breath 1, Shot 3, Smallpox 3, Sore Mouth 1, Teeth 6, Tempany 2, Worms 2, Yellow-Jaundice 1.'

23rd December

Knock, knock! 'Who's There?' 'The Irish Republican Army come to collect one million rounds of ammunition!' 'Fair enough.'

The IRA raid on the Magazine Fort, the Irish Army's main ammunition depot, on 23 December 1939 didn't happen as described above it was even easier. The sentry at the gate was overpowered, the garrison captured, and all without a shot being fired. Four lorries arrived and the 50-strong IRA group quickly filled them. A park ranger was discovered examining cut telephone wires outside the fort, when he resisted he was knocked senseless.

The lorries and most of the men had left when an Army lorry arrived. Shooting broke out but the IRA made a successful retreat. So far, so good. Unfortunately the

IRA had failed to think ahead and had completely underestimated the sheer volume of ammunition seized. Most of the prepared 'dumps' were far too small.

By the following morning the country was in uproar – spotter planes were in the skies, roadblocks were everywhere, IRA suspects were being arrested en masse, and Gardai and the Army turned the countryside upside down. In the event most of the ammunition stolen was quickly recovered, as were other IRA munitions.

24TH DECEMBER

The clipper ship *Palme*, seven days out of Liverpool, was battling heavy seas on 24 December 1895 when the captain, Axel Emanuel Wirren, decided to make for Kingstown Harbour (Dun Laoghaire). The ship missed the harbour entrance, but found shelter outside the end of the West Pier. One of the two anchors broke in the gale and the ship, sending up distress signals, by 11am, was grounded on Razor Bank. The events were watched by a crowd which had gathered at the end of the pier – ideally placed to watch a tragedy unfold.

Two lifeboats, the *Hannah Pickard* and *Civil Service No. 1* were launched. As the *Civil Service No. 1* reached the *Palme* it overturned, and although designed to right herself she failed to do so. The 15 crew, some of whom managed to clamber onto the hull were, one by one, swept off.

The *Palme* attempted to launch a boat but it was immediately dashed to pieces. By morning the scale of the disaster was clear, the lifeboat and some bodies were found at Merrion strand – that evening the death toll had risen to 13 (the bodies of two crew members, William Dunphy and Alexander Williams, were not found until some days later) – the greatest single disaster ever to befall the RNLI. The crew of the *Palme* had no option but to sit out the gale – they were finally rescued on Stephen's Day when the weather improved.

25TH DECEMBER

Friar John Clyn, author of *The Annals of Ireland*, noted that, in the six months ending 25 December 1348, 14,000 people had died from the plague in Dublin: 'That pestilence deprived of human inhabitant villages and cities, and castles and towns, so that there was scarcely found a man to dwell therein; the pestilence was so contagious that whosoever touched the sick or the dead was immediately infected and died; and the penitent and the confessor were carried together to the grave; through fear and dread men scarcely dared to perform the offices of piety and pity in visiting the sick and in burying the dead; many died of boils and abscesses, and pustules on their shins or under their armpits; others died frantic with the pain in their head, and others spitting blood; that year was beyond measure wonderful, unusual, and in many things prodigious so have I reduced these things to writing; and lest the writing, should perish with the writer, and the work fail together with the workman, I leave parchment for continuing the work, if haply any man survive, and any of the race of Adam escape this pestilence and continue the work which I have commenced.' Only one further entry was made by Clyn.

26TH DECEMBER

It was the scandal which rocked Dublin at the close of the nineteenth century. A family which had, over a period of 150 years, build up a reputation for honesty and integrity was destroyed by a man who singularly failed to live up to the family motto of 'Sans Tache' (Without Stain).

That man was Frank DuBédat who, by 1889 was head of the family and of the successful Dublin stockbrokers and bankers, William George DuBédat and Sons of Foster Place. In October 1890 he became President of the Dublin Stock Exchange. He was an imposing figure, five feet nine or ten and weighing in at over 20 stone. He was influential, charming and respected but he was also a rogue.

He had fraudulently taken money from clients and, through extravagant living and failed investments, had lost it all. On 24 December 1890 he wrote letters to his wife, Rosie, from London and promptly disappeared. Within days the family firm had collapsed with debts of over £100,000 and he was struck off the list of members of the Dublin Stock Exchange. Six months later he was arrested in Capetown, South Africa, and sent back to Dublin where, after a one-day trial he was sentenced to 12 months hard labour and seven years penal servitude.

27TH DECEMBER

'The remains of the late Edward Barrett, Esq, having been interred in Glasnevin churchyard [27 December 1829] persons were appointed to remain all night to protect the corpse from the "Sack-'em-Up gentlemen ... " on Saturday night last, some of the gentry made their appearance, but soon decamped on finding they were to be opposed. They returned on Tuesday morning with augmented forces, and well armed. About ten minutes after two o'clock, three or four of them were observed standing on the wall of the churchyard, while several others were endeavouring to get on it also. The party in the churchyard warned them off, and were replied to by a discharge from firearms. This brought on a general engagement ... upwards of 58 to 60 shots were fired, one of the body snatchers was seen to fall; his body was carried off by his companions. Some of them are supposed to have been severely wounded, as a great quantity of blood was observed outside the churchyard wall. During the firing, which continued for upwards of a quarter of an hour, the church bell was rung by one of the watchmen, collected several of the towns people and the police to the spot but the assailants were by this time defeated and effected their retreat.' [*Freeman's Newsletter*]

28TH DECEMBER

William Hutchinson, first Harbour Master at Kingstown and one of Dun Laoghaire's great lifeboatmen wrote of the attempts to save the crew of the brig [a sailing vessel with two masts rigged with square sails] *Ellen* which had gone ashore in foul weather near Sandycove on 28 December 1821: 'with a volunteer crew of 14 men, I embarked and with much difficulty reached the stern of the vessel. At this time the vessel was lying nearly head to the sea which broke completely over her and while the crew were in the act of getting into the lifeboat she filled – while we were baling out water with our hats a sea of which I shall never forget aspect overwhelmed the

[life] boat and washed six of us out of her. Two, fortunately, caught hold of the rope three then unfortunately perished. I, with difficulty, regained the lifeboat and with the remainder of the crew were drove among the breakers without oars.' Leaving the lifeboat to get to shore another lifeboatman was lost. [The four who died were Hugh Byrne, Thomas Fitzsimons, John Archbold and Thomas Grimes.] Eventually the *Ellen* was driven onto the shore and all aboard her were safely taken off.

29TH DECEMBER
Dubliner Denis Valencie was Chief Officer on the *MV Kerlogue* when, on 29 December 1943, 168 German sailors were rescued from the Bay of Biscay. They were survivors of an engagement between an outgunned German flotilla of ten ships and the British Cruisers *HMS Enterprise* and *Glasgow*. The Kerlogue was guided to the sailors by a German plane which dropped flares. On arrival upwards of 300 men were in the water and the crew of the Kerlogue battled in a heavy sea for ten hours until, with no available space left onboard, they had to leave the remaining sailors to their fate. The Kerlogue was carrying a cargo of oranges so, while the diet may have been boring, they had sufficient food for the journey back to Ireland. Three of the rescued died during the three days it took to get to Cobh – the German sailors were transferred to the Curragh Internment Camp. The German Ambassador in Ireland delivered a letter to the Government, later passed on the to *Kerlogue's* Captain, Thomas Donohue, in which he wrote: 'To you and your crew my profound gratitude as well as my high appreciation of unhesitating valiant spirit which has prompted you to perform this exemplary deed, worthy of the great tradition of Irish gallantry and humanity.'

30TH DECEMBER
Mother Mary Aikenhead of the Sisters of Charity, Sandymount, wrote on 30 December 1833 to the Royal Commission looking into poverty in Ireland. Part of her report dealt with Ringsend and Irishtown: 'The fishermen and poor sailors ... reduced to sickness by cold and want, are objects of great compassion. Excessive poverty produces a want of cleanliness which aggravates this misery. The lanes and streets are filled with filth in Ringsend and Irishtown; there are no sewers; no attention is paid to the ventilation of the houses, and the poor are obliged to buy even the water which they drink; it is of the worst description, and tends to promote disease as much by its scarcity as by its quality. The poor have no bed clothes; we have often seen them expire on dirty straw, and are frequently obliged to furnish them with covering before we can approach them to administer to their wants. Their sufferings from want of fuel, want of water, and of covering, can only be credited to indulge in liquor; they often resort to it in despair to drown the recollection of their sufferings. The small sum which will procure spirits is insufficient to provide a meal.'

31ST DECEMBER
There has been a brewery at St. James' Gate for at least 300 years. The first record is for the year 1670 when one Giles Mee, a brewer, obtained from the Corporation

Street politics - Cumberland Street, 1972. Photo by Andrew McGlynn

a lease of certain water-rights described as the 'Ground called the Pipes in the parish of St. James.' Those right later came into the possession of Sir Mark Rainsford, brewer, of St. James's Gate.

Documents preserved in the Public Registry of Deeds, Dublin, record that in the year 1693 Alderman Sir Mark Rainsford had a brewhouse at St. James's Gate. He went out of business in 1715 and leased the premises for 99 years to Paul Espinasse.

The Espinasse family carried on the brewing business for some 45 years, when for some unknown reason the lease fell out, and on the 31st December, 1759, the premises were demised by Mark Rainsford, Esq., of Portarlington (Sir Mark Rainsford's son) to Arthur Guinness, of the City of Dublin, Merchant, for 9,000 years, to be held 'in as ample and beneficial a manner as the same were formerly held by Paul Espinasse or John Espinasse' at a rent of £45 per annum.

Bibliography

"The Crowning of a King at Dublin, 24th May 1487," by F. X. Martin. Published by the Friends of Christ Church Cathedral.

"Harold's Cross," by Joe Curtis. First Return Press. 2004.

"Death and Design in Victorian Glasnevin." Dublin Cemeteries Committee. 2000.

"Dublin Burial Grounds and Graveyards," by Vivien Igoe.Wolfhound Press.2001.

"The Shelbourne and its People," Michael O'Sullivan and Bernardine O'Neill. Blackwater Press. 1999.

"Dublin Historical Record." Vols. 1-58. The Old Dublin Society.

"Blackrock Society Proceedings." Vols. 1-13.

"The Sea Hound – the story of an Irish Ship," Daire Brunicardi.

"The Spy in the Castle," by David Neligan. Prendeville Publishing Limited. 1999.

"An Historical Guide to the City of Dublin," By G. N. Wright, A. M. London: Printed for Baldwin, Cradock, and Joy. 1825. Second Edition.

"Annals, Anecdotes, Traits and Traditions of the Irish Parliaments, 1171 to 1800." By J. Roderick O'Flanagan, B.L. M. H. Gill and Son. 1895.

"Dublin: A Historical and Topographical Account of the City," by Samuel A. Ossory Fitzpatrick. Illustrated by W. Curtis Greene. First published 1907.

"The History and Antiquities of the City of Dublin, From the earliest accounts," by the late Walter Harris. Printed for Laurence Flinn, in Castle -street; and James Williams, in Skinner-row. 1766.

"History of the Dublin Catholic Cemeteries," by William J. Fitzpatrick, LL.D. Continued and Edited by his Son, under the direction of a Sub-Committee of the Board. Dublin. Published at the Offices, 4 Rutland Square. 1900.

"Life In Old Dublin," by James Collins. James Duffy and Co. Ltd., 38 Westmoreland Street. 1913.

"The Neighbourhood of Dublin," by Weston St. John Joyce. 1912.

"The New Neighbourhood of Dublin," by Joseph Hone, Maurice Craig and Michael Fewer. A. & A. Farmar. 2002.

"The Lives of the Lord Chancellors and Keepers of the Great Seal of Ireland – from the earliest times to the reign of Queen Victoria," by J. Roderick O'Flanagan. 1870.

"Lucania: Topographical, Biographical, Historical," by Rev. William S. Donegan, C.C. Browne & Nolan Limited, 24 & 25 Nassau Street. 1902.

"Picturesque Dublin Old and New," by Frances Gerard. Hutchinson and Company, London. 1898.

"Irish Wit and Worthies," by W. J. Fitzpatrick. 187⅔.

"Hoggers, Lords and Railwaymen." Custom House Docks Heritage Project. 1996

"Seventy Years of Irish Life," by W. R. Le Fanu. Edward Arnold. 1896.

"Dublin's Little Jerusalem," by Nick Harris. A. & A. Farmar. 2002.

"An Affair of Honour – Irish Duels and Duelists," by Michael Barry. Eigse Books, Fermoy. 1981.

"An Irish Almanac – notable events in Ireland from 1014 to the present," by Aidan H. Crealey. Mercier Press. 1993.

"A Peculiar Place – the Adelaide Hospital, Dublin, 1839-1989," by David Mitchell. Blackwater.

"Irish Voices from the Great War," by Myles Dungan. Irish Academic Press. 1995.

"Ireland Before The Union," by William J. Fitzpatrick, J.P. W. B. Kelly. 1867.

"Dublin – Baile Átha Cliath," by D. F. Moore. Three Candles Ltd., Dublin. 1965.

"Through Street Broad and Narrow – a history of Dublin Trams," by Michael Corcoran. Midland Publishing. 2000.

"The Vicinity of the International Exhibition, Dublin – an historical sketch of the Pembroke Township," by Francis Elrington Ball. Carraig Books Reprints. 1983. Originally published 1907.

"A History of the County of Dublin," by Francis Elrington Ball. Vol. 1-6. 1902-1920.

"A view from the DART, by Vincent Caprani. MO Books. March 1988.

"A Candle in the Window – a history of the Barony of Castleknock," by Jim Lacey. Marino. 1999.

"A Book of Dublin." Published by the Corporation of Dublin. 1920.

"St. John's Monkstown – the story of an Irish church," by Ralph William Harden, B.A. Hodges, Figgis & Co., Ltd. 1911.

"Tom Corkery's Dublin." Anvil Books. 1980.

"Memorable Dublin House," by Wilmot Harrison. W. Leckie & Co., 59 Bolton Street. 1890.

"North Dublin," by Dillon Cosgrave. Four Courts Press. 1977. Originally published 1909.

"Mountjoy – the story of a prison," by Tim Carey. The Collins Press. 2000.

"Life by the Liffey – a Kaleidoscope of Dubliners," by John O'Donovan. Gill and Macmillan. 1986.

"On the Borders of the Pale – a history of the Kilgobbin, Stepaside and Sandyford area," by Rob Goodbody. Pale Publishing. 1993.

"Dublin – a study in Environment," by John Harvey. B. T. Batsford. 1949.

"Dublin Street Names, Dated and Explained," by C. T. M'Cready. Carraig Books Ltd. 1987. Original published 1892.

"Dublin Castle and the 1916 Rising," by Leon Ó Broin. Helicon Limited. Second Printing April 1966.

"By Swerve of Shore – exploring Dublin's Coast," by Michael Fewer. Gill & Macmillan. 1998.

"Those Days are Gone Away," by Michael Taaffe. Hutchinson of London. 1959.

"The Real Donnybrook – Ramblings and Memories of 'The Brook'," by Richard Lattimore. Kamac Publications. 1997.

"The Very Heart of the City – the story of Denis Guiney and Clerys," by Peter Costello & Tony Farmar. Clery & Co. (1941) Ltd. 1992.

"The Story of a Famous Tavern – The Bailey, Dublin" by Ulick O'Connor. The Bailey Ltd.

"Black's Guide to Dublin and the East of Ireland." Adam and Charles Black, London. 1912. 27th Edition.

"New Ireland: Political Sketches and Personal Reminiscences of 30 years of Irish Public Life," by A. M. Sullivan. 7th Edition. Cameron & Ferguson, 88 West Nile Street.

"For the Life of Me," by Robert Briscoe (with Alden Hatch). Little, Brown & Co. 1958.

"The Roads to Sandymount, Irishtown, Ringsend – a history of the Road and Street Names of our area." Published by Sandymount Community Services. 1996.

"The Meadow of the Bull – a history of Clontarf," by Dennis McIntyre. Second Edition 1995. The Shara Press.

"Historic Merrion." Researched and written by Colin Conroy. Published by Maidenswell Research. March 1996.

"Christ Church Cathedral Dublin – a sketch of its history and a description of the building," by Herbert W. Kennedy, BD. 1926.

"Dalkey – Society and Economy in a Small Medieval Irish Town," by Charles V. Smith. Irish Academic Press. 1996.

"Eccentric Archbishop – Richard Whately of Redesdale," by Bryan MacMahon. Published by Kilmacud-Stillorgan Local History Society. 2005.

"The Last Post – Glasnevin Cemetery. Being a record of Ireland's Heroic dead in Dublin city and county, also places of historic interest. Published by National Graves Association (teo), 74 Dame Street, D.2. First published 1932. Reprinted 1994.

"Stillorgan Again but different ...," by Bonnie Flanagan. Genprint Ltd. 1996.

"Lifeboats in Dublin Bay – a review of the service from 1802-1997," by John de Courcy
    Ireland. Published by the Dun Laoghaire branch of the RNLI.
"A History of Cabra and Phibsborough," by Bernard Neary. Lenhar Publications. 1983.
"A Maritime History of Ringsend." Published by Sandymount Community Services. 2000.
"The Second City – portrait of Dublin 1700-1760," by Patrick Fagan. Leinster Leader Ltd. 1986.
"Lewis' Dublin – a Topographical Dictionary of the Parishes, Towns and Villages of Dublin
    City and County," compiled by Christopher Ryan. The Collins Press. 2001. First
    published 1837.
"St. Patrick's Blue & Saffron – a miscellany of UCD sport since 1895," by Patrick N. Meenan.
    Quill Print & Design. 1997.
"Arctic Ireland – the extraordinary story of the Great Frost and Forgotten Famine of 1740-
    41," by David Dickson. White Row Press Ltd. 1997.
"The Irish Body Snatchers," by Dr. John Fleetwood. Tomar Publishing. 1988.
"The Great Dying – the Black Death in Dublin," by Maria Kelly. Tempus Publishing
    Limited. 2003.
"In Dublin's Fair City," by G. Ivan Morris, London: Home & Van Thal, Ltd. 1947.
"Christ Church Cathedral Dublin," by William Butler. London: Elliot Stock, 62 Paternoster
    Row, 1901.
"Medieval Dublin – an illustrated guide (with maps) to the Town within the Walls," Drawings
    by Liam C. Martin. Text by Violet Martin. Xpress Publishing Limited. Undated.
"Ghosts of Kilmainham." Published by the Kilmainham Jail Restoration Society.
"Short Histories of Dublin Parishes," by Most Rev. N. Donnelly, D.D. Parts 1-18. Carraig
    Chapbook facsimile reprints.
"A Directory of Dublin for the Year 1738 – compiled from the most authentic sources."
    Dublin Corporation Public Libraries. 2000.
"The Heartland: Heritage – North of the Liffey," by Mícheál Ó Cróinín. Published and
    Printed by Ray Fay, 76 Malahide Road, D. 3. Undated
"Hill's Guide to Blackrock with a Description of the Neighbourhood," first published c.
    1892. Carraig Chapbooks No. 2 facsimile edition, 1976.
"Ireland 120 Years Ago," by John Edward Walsh. M.H. Gill & Son Ltd, undated but c.1907.
"Recollections of an Irish National Journalist," by Richard Pigott. First published 1882.
    Facsimile reprint by Tower Books of Cork, 1979.
"Historical Reminiscences of Dublin Castle from 849 to 1895," by F.E.R. Sealy, Bryers and
    Walker, 94, 95 & 96 Middle Abbey Street. 1900. Fourth Edition.
"Brief Sketch of the Parishes of Booterstown and Donnybrook," by Rev. Blacker. George
    Herbert, 117 Grafton Street, Dublin, 1874.
"History of the Royal College of Surgeons in Ireland," by Sir C. A. Cameron. Fannin & Co.,
    41 Grafton Street. 1886.
"Reminiscences of Sir Charles Cameron, CB," Dublin; Hodges, Figgis & Co., Ltd. 1913.
"The Story of Dublin," by D. A. Chart, M.A. Illustrated by Henry J. Howard. J. M. Dent &
    Co., London. 1907.
"The Sham Squire and The Informers of 1798," by William J. Fitzpatrick. Third Edition.
    Dublin: W. B. Kelly, 8 Grafton Street. 1866.
"The History and Antiquities of Tallaght In The County of Dublin," by William Domville
    Handcock, M.A. Second Edition. Revised and Enlarged. Dublin, 1899.
"Gallows Speeches from Eighteenth-Century Ireland," by James Kelly. Four Courts Press.
    2001.
"The Phoenix Park Speed Trials 1905," by Bob Montgomery. Droeilín Publications Ltd. 1999.
"Fingal and its Churches," by Robert Walsh, M.A. William McGee, 18 Nassau Street. 1888.
A Frenchman's Walk Through Ireland, 1796-7. (Promenade d'un Francais dans l'Irlande)
    Translated from the French of De Latocnaye by John Stevenson, Belfast, 1917.
"Dublin 1660-1860," by Maurice Craig. Allen Figgis Ltd. 1980.
"In the Mind's Eye – Memories of Dún Laoghaire." Dun Laoghaire Borough Heritage
    Society. 1991.
"Secret Dublin," by Pat Liddy. New Holland Publishers (UK) Ltd. 2001.

"A Walk Around Dublin," by Vincent Caprani. Appletree Press. 1992.

"Dublin," by Desmond Clarke. B. T. Batsford Ltd. 1977.

"The Guilds of Dublin," by John J. Webb. Kennikat Scholarly Reprints.

"The Royal Hospital Donnybrook, a Heritage of Caring 1743-1993," by Helen Burke. 1993.

"Kilmainham – the history of a settlement older than Dublin," by Colum Kenny. Four
     Courts Press. 1995.

"Mud Island – a History of Ballybough," The Allen Library FAS Project (Ed. Noelle Dowling
     and Aran O'Reilly.)

"Glasnevin Cemetery – an Historic Walk." Dublin Cemeteries Committee. 1997.

"The Candle Factory – 500 Years of Rathbone's, Master Chandlers," by Bernard Neary. The
     Lilliput Press. 1998

"Around the banks of Pimlico," by Máirín Johnston. Attic Press. 1985.

"Dublin's Meath Hospital – 1753-1996," by Peter Gatenby. Town House, Dublin. 1996

"Inchicore Kilmainham and District," by Seosamh O'Broin. Cois Camóige Publications. 1999.

"History of Dublin," by Sir John T. Gilbert. Joseph Dollard, Wellington Quay. 1903.

"The Book of Blackrock," by Liam Mac Cóil. Published for The Blackrock Council of
     Community Servies by Carraig Books. 1977.

"The Old Toughs – from Milton to Mons and the Western Front, 1911-1918 – a brief history
     of the Royal Dublin Fusiliers, 2nd Battalion," by Patrick Hogarty. 2001.

"County Dublin in '98 – some Little-known Incidents of the Insurrection of 1798."
     Published by Maurice O'Connor. (1948).

"Prince of Dublin Printers – The Letters of George Faulkner," by Robert E. Ward. The
     University Press of Kentucky. 1972.

"Ireland 100 Years Ago – The dream of old Ireland," by Richard Lovett. Bracken Books 1995
     (First pub. 1888 by The Religious Tract Society)

"In the Shadow of St. Patrick's – a Paper read before the Irish National Literary Society,
     April 27, 1893," by P. J. McCall. Facsimile edition published 1976 by Carraig Books,
     Blackrock.

"History and Description of Santry and Cloghran Parishes, County Dublin," by Benjamin
     William Adams, D.D. Mitchell and Hughes, 140 Wardour Street, W., London. 1883.

"Dublin's Famous People and where they lived," by John Cowell. The O'Brien Press. 1996.

"Thomas Sheridan of Smock-Alley," by Esther K. Sheldon. Princeton University Press. 1967.

Dun Laoghaire Journal. 1991-2005. Dun Laoghaire Borough Historical Society.

"The Story of the Pavilion, Kingstown/Dun Laoghaire," by Michael McGovern and Tony
     McGuirk. Dun Laoghaire Borough Historical Society. 2003.

"The Dublin Metropolitan Police: A Short History and Genealogical Guide," by Jim Herlihy.
     Four Courts Press. 2001.

"With the IRA in the Fight for Freedom (1919 to the Truce) – The Red Path of Glory." The
     Kerryman Limited, Tralee.

"The Forty Foot – A Monument to Sea Bathing," by Frank Power and Peter Pearson.
     Environment Publications.

"Forty Foot Gentlemen Only," by Mervyn Wall. Allen Figgis. 1962.

"Kevin Barry, the incident at Monk's Bakery and the making of an Irish Republican legend"
     by Joe Ainsworth. Published in History: The Journal of the Historical Association.

"The Changing Face of Dundrum," by Jim Nolan. 1993. Elo Press Ltd.

"Four Roads to Dublin – a History of Rathmines, Ranelagh and Leeson Street" by Deirdre
     Kelly

"The Civil War in Ireland," by Eoin Neeson. Mercier Paperback. 1969.

"The Town of the Road – the story of Booterstown," by Hazel P. Smyth. Pale Publishing 1994.

Web

www.newspaperabstracts.com

www.irelandoldnews.com